DEWEY AND EDUCATION IN THE 21ST CENTURY: FIGHTING BACK

DEWEY AND EDUCATION IN THE 21ST CENTURY: FIGHTING BACK

EDITED BY

RUTH HEILBRONN
UCL Institute of Education

CHRISTINE DODDINGTON
Homerton College, University of Cambridge

RUPERT HIGHAM
UCL Institute of Education

United Kingdom – North America – Japan – India – Malaysia – China

Emerald Publishing Limited
Howard House, Wagon Lane, Bingley BD16 1WA, UK

First edition 2018

Copyright © 2018 Emerald Publishing Limited

Reprints and permissions service
Contact: permissions@emeraldinsight.com

No part of this book may be reproduced, stored in a retrieval system, transmitted in any form or by any means electronic, mechanical, photocopying, recording or otherwise without either the prior written permission of the publisher or a licence permitting restricted copying issued in the UK by The Copyright Licensing Agency and in the USA by The Copyright Clearance Center. Any opinions expressed in the chapters are those of the authors. Whilst Emerald makes every effort to ensure the quality and accuracy of its content, Emerald makes no representation implied or otherwise, as to the chapters' suitability and application and disclaims any warranties, express or implied, to their use.

British Library Cataloguing in Publication Data
A catalogue record for this book is available from the British Library

ISBN: 978-1-78743-626-8 (Print)
ISBN: 978-1-78743-625-1 (Online)
ISBN: 978-1-78743-960-3 (Epub)
ISBN: 978-1-78754-340-9 (Paperback)

INVESTOR IN PEOPLE

Contents

Editor Biographies — vii

Contributor Biographies — ix

Acknowledgements — xv

List of Tables — xvii

List of Figures — xix

Editors' Introduction: The Book, the Conference and Fighting Back
Ruth Heilbronn, Christine Doddington and Rupert Higham — 1

PART 1
DEWEY, EXPERIENCE AND TECHNOLOGY

Chapter 1   Preserving Rich Experience in the Digital Age
Bob Coulter — 21

Chapter 2   The Emergence of Makerspaces, Hackerspaces and Fab Labs: Dewey's Democratic Communities of the Twenty-first Century?
Sally Eaves and Stephen Harwood — 37

Chapter 3   Constructing Creative Democracy at School by Reading the Classics: A Dialogue between Martha Nussbaum and John Dewey
Gonzalo Jover, Rosario González Martín and Juan Luis Fuentes — 61

PART 2
DEWEY, EXPERIENCE AND BODIES

Chapter 4 Dewey and the Alexander Technique: Lessons in Mind–Body Learning
Charlotte Woods, Malcolm Williamson and Jenny Fox Eades   *83*

Chapter 5 Black Bodies in Schools: Dewey's Democratic Provision for Participation Confronts the Challenges of 'Fundamental Plunder'
Sue Ellen Henry and Kathleen Knight Abowitz   *101*

Chapter 6 Education in the Open: The Somaesthetic Value of Being Outside
Christine Doddington   *119*

PART 3
DEWEY, EXPERIENCE, DEMOCRACY AND EDUCATION

Chapter 7 Dewey and the Democratic Curriculum
Neil Hopkins   *141*

Chapter 8 Dewey Anticipates Habermas's Paradigm of Communication: The Critique of Individualism and the Basis for Moral Authority in *Democracy and Education*
Brian Dotts   *161*

Chapter 9 The Role of the Educators' Disposition and Mental Processes in a Student's Experience of Democracy
Victoria Door and Clare Wilkinson   *183*

Chapter 10 Dewey's Notion of Interest: Antithetic to or Sympathetic with Educational Development?
Valentine Ngalim   *201*

Epilogue: The Persistence of Dewey's Pragmatism: On Possibilities and Risks
Gert Biesta   *217*

Index   *221*

Editor Biographies

Christine Doddington is Emerita Fellow of Homerton College, Cambridge, and was formerly a Senior Lecturer in Education at the Faculty of Education, University of Cambridge. She writes mainly in the field of Philosophy of Education with a particular interest in the arts and the work of John Dewey. Publications include chapters in *The Routledge International Handbook of the Arts and Education* (2015) and *Wellbeing, Education and Contemporary Schooling* (2017). She most recently co-authored a chapter entitled 'Dewey, Aesthetic Experience and Education for Humanity', with Andrea English in *The Oxford Handbook on Dewey* (OUP, forthcoming), and has a chapter in *Philosophy as Interplay and Dialogue* (LIT Verlag, forthcoming). She is an Elected Executive Member of the Philosophy of Education Society of Great Britain (PESGB) and of the International Editorial Board for *Education 3-13: International Journal of Primary, Elementary and Early Years Education*.

Ruth Heilbronn gained her PhD in Philosophy of Education at the UCL Institute of Education and has led teams in teacher education and secondary schools. Publications include research on the induction of newly qualified teachers for the Department for Education (Research Report 338, 2002) and articles and book chapters on ethical teacher education, values education, reflective practice and ethical deliberation. Relevant publications include *Teacher Education and the Development of Practical Judgement* (Continuum, 2008) and co-edited books: *Research-Based Best Practice for Schools* (Routledge, 2002); *Critical Practice in Teacher Education*, with John Yandell (IoE Press, 2010); *Philosophical Perspectives on Teacher Education*, with Lorraine Foreman-Peck (Wiley Blackwell, 2015); and *Dewey in Our Time*, with Peter Cunningham (UCL IoE Press, 2016). She is an Executive Member of the PESGB.

Rupert Higham is a Lecturer in Educational Leadership at the UCL Institute of Education and is Programme Leader for the Applied Educational Leadership and Management MA. His research seeks to enhance teacher and student agency through responsible leadership. Theoretically, he has explored Deweyan Pragmatism as a foundation for democratic agency. Empirically, he has worked with schools in several countries on values-led improvement through the *Index for Inclusion*, and more recently, with an international network of schools on deepening democratic culture. Rupert is also a Founding Member of Cambridge Educational Dialogue Research, a new research centre dedicated to improving the quality of educational dialogue.

Contributor Biographies

Kathleen Knight Abowitz is a Professor in the Department of Educational Leadership at Miami University in Oxford, Ohio. She is currently serving as Chair of the Department and has been on Faculty since 1995. Her scholarship uses political and moral philosophy to address questions of community, the public and democracy as these concepts relate to education and P-16 schools and institutions. Her books include *Publics for Public Schools: Legitimacy, Democracy and Leadership* (Paradigm Press, 2013), and *Engaging Youth in Leadership for Social and Political Change* (Jossey-Bass, 2015). She is Past President of the John Dewey Society and the Ohio Valley Philosophy of Education Society.

Gert Biesta is Professor of Education in the Department of Education of Brunel University London; Visiting Professor at NLA University College Bergen, Norway; and NIVOZ Professor for Education at the University for Humanistic Studies in the Netherlands. He jointly coordinates the Educational Theory SIG of EARLI (European Association for Research Learning and Instruction). From 1999 to 2014, he was Editor-in-Chief of the journal *Studies in Philosophy and Education*. He has written many books and journal articles. He is currently a Co-editor of the Routledge Book Series, *New Directions in the Philosophy of Education*, with Michael Peters, and of *Theorizing Education*, with Julie Allan and Richard Edwards.

Bob Coulter, EdD, is currently the Director of the Litzsinger Road Ecology Center, a field site managed by the Missouri Botanical Garden. Previously he was an award-winning Elementary Grade Teacher. He has published more than 100 articles and has chapters in more than a dozen edited volumes. He is also the author of two books: the Choice Award-winning *No More Robots: Building Kids' Character, Competence, and Sense of Place* (2014), and more recently *Building Kids' Citizenship through Community Engagement* (2018).

Victoria Door is the Director of CPD at the Professional Association of Alexander Teachers (PAAT). She first encountered Dewey through reading *Human Nature and Conduct* and *Experience and Nature* when training as a Teacher of the Alexander Technique. Dewey continued to provide inspiration for her as she went on to combine her experience as a Teacher of the Alexander Technique with her work as a Languages Teacher in the UK secondary school system. In 2002, she moved to Keele University where she led the MFL PGCE and completed a PhD (Bath) in language learning and attention. Her books include *Developing Creative and Critical Educational Practitioners* (2014) and *Save Our Teachers' Souls* (2016). Currently, she is researching and writing on Dewey's contribution to, and support of, Alexander's work. As part of this, Victoria is exploring how Dewey's and Alexander's ideas can be practically incorporated in teacher education, in conjunction with PAAT.

Brian Dotts is an Associate Professor of Educational Foundations at the University of Georgia where he teaches undergraduate and graduate courses in Educational Foundations related to politics, policy, constitutional law, history, historical inquiry and research methods, sociology, social and political theories, philosophy and multiculturalism. He has published widely on the history of American education, specifically focusing on education and political theories during the American Revolution and early national period, common school politics during the Antebellum Era, John Dewey and Social Reconstructionism during the early twentieth century, and Educational Foundations as an academic field. His primary theoretical lens is Critical Theory. He is co-editor of *The Elusive Thomas Jefferson: The Man behind the Myths* (McFarland Publishing, 2017).

Jenny Fox Eades has worked in education since 1987. She qualified as a Special Needs Teacher and has taught children from 4 to 18 across the ability range. For 15 years, she worked as a Freelance Education Adviser, in the United Kingdom, Australia and Denmark, running workshops and projects on well-being in schools and speaking at conferences. Her PhD is in well-being in education and explores a more contemplative approach to educational research. Jennifer is the author of several education books and school programmes, including *Celebrating Strengths: Building Strengths-Based Schools* (Capp Press, 2008) and *Strengths Gym* (PPRC, 2011) a Personal, Social and Health Education (PSHE) programme for high schools.

Sally Eaves combines a depth of experience as a Chief Technology Officer, Director of Education, Practising Professor of FinTech and

Global Strategic Advisor, consulting on the application of disruptive technologies for both business and societal benefits. She is an award-winning thought leader in innovation, digital transformation and emergent technology, notably blockchain, artificial intelligence, machine learning and robotics. A Member of the Forbes Technology Council, she is an accomplished author with regular contributions to leading business, technology and education publications, and a new book *Edge of Disruption* confirmed for 2018. She is an international keynote speaker and respected online influencer across multiple social media channels, particularly in the fields of blockchain, artificial intelligence, technology for good and leadership in innovation.

Juan Luis Fuentes is an Assistant Professor in the Department of Theory and History of Education at Complutense University of Madrid. He has been a Visiting Scholar at Eastern Washington University (US), Roehampton University (UK), Freie Universität (Germany) and University of Birmingham (UK) and is a Member of the 'Civic Culture and Educational Policies' research group at Complutense University of Madrid. His principal research interests include theory and philosophy of education, character education, intercultural education and the use of Information and Communication Technologies in the educational sphere. He is an Associate Editor of *Educación XX1* and has received the 'Antonio Millán Puelles Award' and the 'Young Researcher Award'.

Stephen Harwood is a Practitioner turned Academic, currently holding the post of Lecturer at the University of Edinburgh Business School. His interest in social complexity and the handling of complex social problems has led to research into how to teach management topics, as well as, specifically, how to deliver a research methods course. This shifts attention from the teaching of abstractions to how the real world of organizational practice can be embedded into the student's learning experience, for example, how research has relevance to the management world of practice. This has resulted in an interest in the work of John Dewey along with others such as Charles Peirce and Lev Vygotsky. Much of this research has been written up in the form of journal, conference and working papers.

Sue Ellen Henry is a Professor of Education and Director of the Teaching and Learning Center at Bucknell University. Her scholarship focuses on social class influences on children's experiences in schools, the influence of emotion in the classroom and multicultural education. She is the author of *Children's Bodies in Schools: Corporeal Performances of Social Class* (2014, Palgrave) and her work has been published in *Teachers College Record*, *Educational Theory*, *Educational Studies* and *Emotion, Space and Society*. Her current research focuses on the body hexis that elementary teachers associate with children of various social class backgrounds.

Neil Hopkins is currently a Senior Lecturer in Education at the University of Bedfordshire, teaching undergraduates, postgraduates and supervising doctoral students. He also teaches on the PGCE/Cert Ed for Post-Compulsory Education at the University. He is the author of *Citizenship and Democracy in Further and Adult Education* (Springer, 2014). He is Bedford branch Secretary for the PESGB and is responsible for research in the School of Teacher Education at the University of Bedfordshire. He is currently an External Examiner for PGCE/Cert Ed Post-Compulsory Education at the University of Essex.

Gonzalo Jover is Professor of Education at the Complutense University in Madrid, where he was Head of the Department of Educational Theory and History of Education from 2006 to 2009 and Adviser to the vice chancellor of Postgraduate Programs and Continuing Education from 2010 to 2012. He also served as Adviser for the Spanish Ministry of Education during the ninth Parliamentary Term. At present, he holds the position of Associate Dean for Research at the Faculty of Education. He has been Visiting Scholar at Boston University, Teachers College of Columbia University and Queen's University (Canada), as well as Visiting Professor at several European universities. He is President of the Spanish Pedagogical Association and Associate Editor of the *Revista Española de Pedagogía*. He has authored more than 100 publications.

Rosario González Martín holds a PhD in Education from Universidad Complutense de Madrid where she is an Associate Professor in the Department of Theory and History of Education. She has held Associate Professorships in Philosophy of Education at the Universidad Autónoma de Madrid and Universidad de Santiago de Chile. She is a Member of the research group 'Civic Culture and Educational Policies', of the 'Phenomenology, First Philosophy Association' and of the 'Spanish Association of Personalism'. She is currently engaged in the project 'The Value of Civic Commitment in the University: Design, Development and

Evaluation of a Service-Learning Programme'. She has organized and directed an international conference on 'Emotion, Ethics and Education' and is Member of the Colloquium on Violence and Religion of the International Association of Scholars of Mimetic Theory.

Valentine Ngalim is the Chair of the Philosophy Department and a Senior Lecturer in Higher Teacher Training College, Bambili, of the University of Bamenda, Cameroon. He gained his PhD in the Philosophy of Education from the UNESCO Chair of Central Africa, under the supervision of the University of Marien Ngouabi, Brazzaville, Congo. His research interest centres on critical issues in education, with particular emphasis on educational politics, curricular issues and subject didactics. He has published several articles and a book titled *Lack of Harmonisation in the Curricula of Cameroon Secondary Education: Causes in Centre and Northwest Regions* (2014, Saarbruecken, Scholars Press).

Clare Wilkinson is currently the Special Educational Needs Coordinator in a secondary academy in Hertfordshire, England. She has previously held posts of Deputy Head of Learning, Head of Year, SenCo and has served on the school's Senior Leadership Team. She has taught for over a decade in the state sector, teaching history, religious education and child development at a range of levels. She has an interest in the writings of Dewey, especially the relationship between teaching and pedagogy, and the extent to which Dewey's philosophy is vital for the current teaching profession as it goes through yet another period of financial constraints.

Malcolm Williamson, BA (Open), Associate of the Royal College of Music (ARCM), studied at the Royal College of Music and played with several orchestras, including the National Orchestra of Iceland and the Royal Scottish National Orchestra. He was introduced to the Alexander Technique as a student and subsequently was trained to teach the method with Alexander's assistant Walter Carrington. He was Chairman of the main professional body (Society of Teachers of the Alexander Technique) from 1994 to 1996 and a Teacher-Trainer from 2001 to 2017. He campaigns for the Alexander Technique as a foundation to music education and has taught at the Royal Northern College of Music, Manchester, for over 30 years. He gave the Annual F. M. Alexander Memorial Lecture in 2016, 'Beyond Words', an exploration of the influence of William James's *Principles of Psychology* on the evolution of Alexander's technique for greater Constructive Conscious Control and choice in an individual's reactions.

Charlotte Woods has almost four decades of international experience in education. Her early career was as a Language Teacher, Teacher Educator and Educational Manager, including 10 years with the British Council in Italy, Portugal and Morocco. This was followed by 20 years in academia, during which time she completed a doctorate investigating workplace emotion and well-being. In 2015, Charlotte retired from a Senior Lectureship in Education at the Manchester Institute of Education, University of Manchester. She trained for three years at the Manchester Alexander Technique Training School with Malcolm Williamson and qualified as a Teacher with the Society for Teachers of the Alexander Technique in July 2017.

Acknowledgements

We would like to thank the following:

Chapter 6: This chapter was originally published by Christine Doddington as 'Education in the open: The somaesthetic value of being outside', in *Other Education* 3(1), 2014, editor Helen E. Lees. We acknowledge full permission to reprint here. http://www.othereducation.com/index.php/OE/article/view/41

Chapter 8: This chapter originally appeared in Brian W. Dotts, 'Dewey anticipates Habermas's paradigm of communication: The critique of individualism and the basis for moral authority in democratic education', in *Education and Culture*, 32(1), pp. 111–129. This material appears courtesy of Purdue University Press. All rights reserved. http://docs.lib.purdue.edu/eandc/vol32/iss1/art9

List of Tables

Chapter 8

Table 8.1   Understanding the Cultural Requirements for
            Change and Reconstruction 164

List of Figures

Chapter 2

Figure 1	Education as Experienced Naturally in Contrast to the Traditional View.	40
Figure 2	Education as Experienced Naturally and Its Feed into a Formal Setting.	43
Figure 3	Conceptualizing Makerspaces (Based upon Analysis of NESTA, 2015).	49
Figure 4	Signage from Access Space Main Lab	51
Figure 5	A 20×20 Canvas Exhibition at Access Space	52
Figure 6	A Quiet Zone at Bristol Hackspace	54

Editors' Introduction: The Book, the Conference and Fighting Back

Ruth Heilbronn, Christine Doddington and Rupert Higham

Abstract

This chapter introduces the book through discussing the context in which it came about, namely a conference to mark the centenary of the publication of Dewey's *Democracy and Education*. The first section relates to the book's subtitle by describing and analysing the context in which speakers at the conference engaged in a 'fightback' against educational policies found to be narrowly based on economic aims, and to have lost sight of the humanistic aims of education, aims which Dewey analysed and championed. The book is structured around three key areas, all related to Dewey's philosophy of education − the first concerns technology, the second, embodiment and the third, democracy and development. A discussion on the significance of each of these areas for contemporary educational theory is followed by detail on the individual chapters within them. This chapter concludes with an introduction to the cautiously optimistic and forward-looking epilogue by Gert Biesta on the matters and issues raised in the book.

Keywords: Dewey; *Democracy and Education*; aims of education; humanistic education

Introduction

The year 2016 marked the centenary of the publication of Dewey's *Democracy and Education* with a plethora of books and centennial celebrations, including an international conference at Cambridge in October 2016[1]. The book sets out Dewey's philosophy of education in a succinct manner in 26 chapters, each with a chapter-ending summary. It may therefore act as an introduction to his vast body of work, on which we touch in the chapters of this book. Significantly in calling the conference, the planning group sent out 'a call to action' inviting interested people to consider the book's relevance within the current policy context that seems so at odds with Dewey's philosophy of education.

A major theme of this conference and all the celebrations of 2016 was this 'call to action', to fighting back against what is happening in several dimensions – political and social but also educational, in a globalized economic environment. Significantly in many education systems worldwide, we see the aims of education to be predominantly subsumed to economic ends, related to gaining skills, qualifications and employment in a global economy (Ball, 2001; Apple, 2004, 2005). In such systems, pupils are routinely audited to ensure that they achieve these skills, as are teachers to monitor their 'effectiveness' in curricular 'delivery'. Teachers are positioned as delivery technicians and students as deliverers of examination results.

Necessarily, assessment is based on audit and metrics: league tables and performance management are brought into play to control the 'delivery' of results. This has been defined as a performativity culture and there are many warnings about its effects in education (e.g. Davies, 2003; Ball, 2012; Murray, 2012). When assessment is put to the fore, this tends to drive curricula and pedagogy, and this can skew teaching and lead to the inducements of fear and bribery to motivate learning and an over-reliance on mechanical routines. As Ravitch warns,

> It behoves us to take seriously concerns that the current emphasis on testing and inspection distorts the purposes

---

[1] The conference was a collaboration between the Philosophy of Education Society of Great Britain (PESGB); the History of Education Society, UK; The Faculty of Education, University of Cambridge and Homerton College. It took place between 28 September and 1 October 2016. There were 150 papers from 25 countries.

of education. We no longer speak of education as a process of human development. (Ravitch, 2013, p. 265)

In focusing the conference and this book on the work of John Dewey in a twenty-first-century context we are fighting back against this interpretation of social and political life, and particularly of this view of the aims and purposes of education which Dewey termed 'technical rationalism' and has been later called 'technicism'.

The book represents a view of education for humanistic not economic aims. Qualifications are only part of the preparation for becoming an adult in any society. Technological changes are bringing about social change to the extent that we cannot predict what kind of employment and challenges young people will have to face as adults, nor the kinds of jobs that will exist when they are adults. It follows that education should be broadly based in order to enable people to be flexible, adapt what they know and also to enjoy what they are able to do, as preparation for life in uncertain times. This suggests that basing educational aims on purely economic terms is not satisfactory.

Taking humanistic aims for education means not starting from the idea of skills and preparation for employment, although these are important, but from a question about what should count as an educated young person today. This question requires thinking about which human qualities we wish to nurture and develop and how education may foster them. Michael Oakeshott's discussion is valuable here in arguing that education has no 'extrinsic' end or purpose (i.e. a qualification) outside the intrinsic end of becoming human (Oakeshott, 1972). Education should evidently develop the knowledge and understanding thought to be related to employability, but should aim more widely at educating people for managing life and relationships so that they may develop both practical capacity and the ability to make sensible and grounded decisions, given changing economic and social conditions. 'Moral seriousness' (Pring, 2012) is a quality that has been highlighted as important for the individual and for society. This would involve having a sense of responsibility for the community, which might include kindness and respect towards others. This takes us into thinking not only about the knowledge and the skills that schools should aim to inculcate but also about the qualities and dispositions we think pupils need to develop. Often, and perhaps increasingly, the language of 'skills' and knowledge eclipses these vital human qualities.

In resisting such a narrow and restricted view of education we draw on the work of John Dewey with particular reference to his own engagement in the political and educational causes of his day. Not only was he an advocate for the kind of pedagogy implied by the chapters in this book, but he also took an active part in public life, for example his assuming the chair of a controversial commission into charges made against Leon Trotsky in Moscow in the 1930s (Dewey, 1937) and his defence of Bertrand Russell in relation to Russell's being refused appointment of the chair of philosophy in the City College of New York on grounds of immorality (Dewey, 1940).

The conference keynote speakers also brought out the notion of 'fight-back'. We briefly summarize below their talks, in order to point to their body of work and their wider field of educational research, since all are engaged in making a considerable contribution to the critique of educational policies and practices and what they have to say on the theme of 'fight back' is significant.

First, Barbara Stengel (2016) mounted 'a spirited defence of the possibility inherent in public schools and the potential of the teachers who work there to enhance those possibilities'. She sought 'to discover grounds for agency and constructive identity in what most construe as a dispiriting educational age' (ibid.) and identified:

> [t]he central problematic of teaching today: a potentially crippling disjunct between teachers' self-understanding as educators and the systemic (political and institutional) orientation toward achievement construed so narrowly as to be anti-educational. (Ibid.)

Stengel deplores the fact that 'This disjunct locates educators in an emotional and action space that can be – and too often is – experienced as hopeless'. But she suggests, 'with the help of John Dewey, ... teachers may not be as "stuck" as it seems'.

Alison Peacock, chief executive of the Chartered College of Teaching, was also an advocate of the fight back against technicism. In her talk, she stated that 'too often the education system stops children doing amazing things by looking at children in terms of numbers and letters slapped onto their foreheads'.[2] She reported on the project *Learning without Limits*, in which nine teachers working in different schools ran

---

[2]The citations are taken from this keynote talk, available at https://www.youtube.com/watch?v=wfQB2RHuhLk

classrooms on core principles of inclusion, co-agency and trust (see also Peacock, 2016).

Rosa Bruno-Jofré's keynote speech showed how the connections between discourses and political situations are relevant to work in our current context, through her example of Dewey's reception in Chile in the 1920s and other Latin American contexts. She traced a search for a political ethic of social change with Dewey at the centre which is significant for our times. (This builds on her work of Deweyan interpretation; see Bruno-Jofré, 2010 and Bruno-Jofré and Schriewer, 2012.)

Gert Biesta's keynote talk asked whether, in seeking to make a connection between education and democracy, Dewey was actually concerned about the political project of democracy and its educational demands, or whether he remained caught in European conceptions of education-as-formation (Bildung). This question needs posing in the context of the book, in which we are claiming for Dewey a relevance to understanding and acting on our current issues in education. The third part of the book is particularly concerned with the idea of democracy in education. The focus is on how Deweyan ideas of democracy connected to the way in which people relate to each other; to the respect for individual voice; for consensual decision-making and for a Deweyan democratic culture, rather than democracy as a political project. Such a culture differs from the current educational policy culture of top-down imposition of strategies and policies. The book returns to challenging questions raised by Biesta in the Epilogue.

The current context became the focus of the conference panel session, posed as a question: *John Dewey – Too Toxic for Policy?* Richard Pring started this session with a background on the positioning of Dewey's ideas in England, citing an influential government report into primary education (known as the Plowden Report), which argued for a Deweyan type of curriculum, in reaction against traditional learning disconnected from children's experiences (HMSO, 1967). Pring reported how the Plowden Report drew virulent criticisms and the accusation of John Dewey as 'the proximate cause of all our educational decline'.

Arguments between the so-called traditionalists and progressives in education still run deep in education today and this was picked up by Melissa Benn who talked on the theme of the profound and hostile rejection of progressive ideas in our time, and argued that there has always been resistance to a return to an arid traditionalism. In her journalism and activism she represents and supports a growing number of parents and 'a new generation of educators and parents who say "No! Enough! We want something else"' (see e.g. Benn, 2012).

Lynda Stone described a complex current culture in the United States today. There is seemingly total acceptance of the regime of standardized testing and a great emphasis on knowledge and achievement, over an education based on experience and the social good. She claimed that education has lost focus on ethics and ethos. But there are what she calls 'small democracies' from which we can draw hope, such as teachers working consensually in professional learning communities on areas that they choose, that are not imposed on them from the top down (see also Stone, 2016).

All the keynote speakers in one way or the other were arguing for a kind of education we might broadly call 'Deweyan'. When we talk of 'fighting back' in the title of this volume, we have constantly in our minds the current context of not only the wider policy context we have called technicist, but the local choices that are made in consequence of high stakes assessment for the school curriculum, where the arts and the humanities are frequently sidelined to make time for Science, Technology, Engineering and Mathematics subjects, those which are internationally audited, because of the premium on a 'knowledge based curriculum'. Warnings against a restriction of the school curriculum are many (e.g. Greene, 1981; Nussbaum, 2006, 2010; Benn, 2012; Pring, 2012; Ravitch, 2013).

Dewey stood for a humanistic curriculum that supported both individual development and social aims. In *My Pedagogic Creed*, his short statement of his beliefs regarding education, he tells us:

> I believe that education is a regulation of the process of coming to share in the social consciousness; and that the adjustment of individual activity on the basis of this social consciousness is the only sure method of social reconstruction. ... I believe that in the ideal school we have the reconciliation of the individualistic and the institutional ideals. (Dewey, 1897, p. 93)

The current context of performativity in education takes the focus away from societal development. We draw on Dewey's philosophy of education in the book to expand on our notion that commitment to fighting back against such a technicist view of education is necessary. The book is structured around three key areas, all related to Dewey's philosophy of education – the first concerns technology; the second, embodiment and the third, democracy and development.

Part One – Dewey and Technology

That Dewey had something to say to our times is clear in the first part of this book, concerned with technology and the issues and controversies that digital technologies raise in our time. Is the fear of young people engaged in social media justified? What are the dangers of life in a networked era and how does living in a technologically mediated world impact on social life, the development of individuals, education and culture? How can digital technologies support educational developments? These large questions are discussed in the chapters of this part.

Bob Coulter, in Chapter 1, tackles the familiar fear of young people spending much of their time on social media and the argument that this distances them from real-life experiences and is a bad influence on their development. In contrast to these fears, many adults, educators and parents think that young people must have access to these technologies and be familiar and at ease with their use, since the twenty-first century has increasingly complex information systems and social means of communication. He draws on Dewey's frame of experience as articulated in *Democracy and Education* and *Experience and Education* 'to craft a framework by which uses of digital technology can be assessed for their educational value'. This framework, he argues, can support positive educational and personal development, in what he identifies as 'experience-rich, growth-promoting uses of technology'. Importantly, as his numerous examples illustrate, these positive uses of technology can be linked to broader concerns for young people developing the capacities needed for democratic citizenship.

In Chapter 2, Sally Eaves and Stephen Harwood continue this exploration of the social and creative possibilities of digital technology for young people in their account of 'makerspaces', which offer accessible and affordable venues within communities and which, in turn, can make a contribution to those communities. Makerspaces can provide a resource for people to explore and experiment, as well as share information and knowledge. Through explicating Dewey's views on what constitutes a desirable learning space and his view of the empowered individual, the authors analyse the value of makerspaces in educative processes, within a social learning community and this means outside formal learning environments, which have certain limitations. Eaves and Harwood are optimistic about the educative and social possibilities that such makerspaces afford, and the chapter suggests how individuals using these spaces are enabled to be creative and innovative.

The final chapter in this part of the book, Chapter 3, by Gonzalo Jover, Rosario González Martín and Juan Luis Fuentes further illustrates how Dewey's ideas are pertinent to our generation of students and educators. In an innovative project, they have developed a course, studying classic texts using the Internet, with secondary education students from three schools in Santiago (Chile), Madrid and London. The project is based on an open reading of Sophocles's *Antigone* through an online application that enables students from the participating schools to interact. The chapter explicates the theoretical bases of the project. The first two sections of the chapter analyse the interpretation that Martha Nussbaum and Dewey each made of *Antigone*. The final section presents the Antigone project as a learning experience, promoting what Dewey called a creative democracy.

Part Two – Dewey and Embodiment

One of the long-standing battles that Dewey fought throughout his work concerned the societal tendency to divide and 'dis' integrate features of humanity. He pursued a holistic view of human experience, stressing the need to understand persons as integrated and situated within their environment and in association with others. He famously argued against dualisms such as theory/practice or subject/object not necessarily because these are false starting points in philosophy but because sharp, fundamental splits 'oblige us to reach for antithetical principles to make sense of the world' (Fesmire, 2015, p. 46) creating inevitable consequences for our capacity to understand. Of these dualisms, mind/body was one split that is repeatedly challenged at a profound level in his work. Dewey suggests that 'false notions about the control of the body ... extending to control of mind and character, is the greatest bar to intelligent social progress' (Dewey, 1922, p. 23).

To signal the inclusivity he wanted to stress, Dewey coined the notion of body–mind but then amplified how he used the terms. At one level, he claims that embodiment is a straightforward indication that mind does not exist without body and that in health, the body does not live without mind. But the extent of this is far-reaching: 'body-mind simply designates what actually takes place when a living body is implicated in situations of discourse, communication and participation' (Dewey, 1925, p. 217).

Dewey is not combining the physical with the mental here but is suggesting that the body is not a 'thing' but rather our centre and source of situated activity with mind intrinsic to activity as a way of making sense of our transactions with the world. Our initial transactions based on impulse, in time, become habits of both mind and action. Thus, as Sharon Sullivan explains, Dewey sees the:

> ... organic body as a collection of activities, characterized by habit and grounded in physicality that is constituted by its relationships with its various environments. For human bodies in particular, this means that bodies give rise to and participate in the meanings provided by their transactions. As transactional participants in meaning, human organisms often help secure existing habits and cultural customs but they are also capable of transforming them. (Sullivan, 2001 p. 40)

In Western culture, there has recently been a surge of interest in health and well-being associated with care of the body and mind. For example, the growth in practices such as yoga and mindfulness mark renewed interest in how breath and body awareness can have profound psychological effects. Schools have not been immune to this trend and a number of educational institutions now give space and credence to these activities, often as a gesture towards the well-being of students and staff. However, the extent to which education itself is seen as an embodied experience is much more limited. For Dewey, embodiment is highly significant for our understanding of educational experience and learning. Therefore, the implications for education reach far beyond an additional class in mindfulness. Enquiry and the capacity for growth are embedded in the situations and activities that create educational experience; therefore, the stress on action cannot be understood without acknowledgement of the importance of the body. In the current technicist climate, the worth and extent of this awareness for the quality of educational experience becomes invisible – hence the struggle in many schools becomes one of 'what can we add on to our already crowded curriculum', rather than 'how should we think differently about the transformative experiences we give in the name of education.'

The chapters in this collection, which focus on the importance of understanding our lives as embodied, offer a number of clear calls for significant transformation, but all show an appreciation of the depth of Dewey's ideas on embodiment. We bring together three different perspectives that indicate some of the transformative relevance of due consideration of embodiment. These range from the extensive possibilities of the Alexander Technique, the very practice that helped Dewey deepen his own thinking related to the body, to the centrality of the body in racial inequality and its significance for democratic practice.

The theme of embodied habit emerges as a central tenet of Chapter 4 by Charlotte Woods, Malcolm Williamson and Jenny Fox Eades. They are practitioners of the Alexander Technique and, attracted by Dewey's own belief in the technique, they join Richard Shusterman in advocating that we should fight the academic dominance of the mind over the body in educational discourse and practice. This chapter reminds us of Dewey's beliefs and the somatic philosophy underpinning the Alexander Technique. Unconscious habits of the body that can be drawn into awareness and changed or corrected have transformational dimensions for our thought and receptivity to experience. This is part of the plasticity in our way of living that is so essential for growth and receptivity to other ways of being. Dewey was not only committed to his own practice of the Alexander Technique, but the writers suggest that his own regular experience helped him to articulate more clearly, the central role of body—mind throughout their work. The challenge to the anti-somatic stance of most educational discourse and practice is another dimension of seeing Dewey's work as a way of fighting the current dominant culture in education.

Corporeality resonates throughout Kathleen Knight-Abowitz's and Sue Ellen Henry's chapter (Chapter 5) and the need for transformation is all too clear. Their analysis of African American experience and disenfranchisement and the reality of 'fundamental plunder' of White classes over Black citizens, highlighted by Ta-Nehisi Coates, offers a striking and timely lens into the reach and subtlety of Dewey's sense of deep democratic participation in *Democracy and Education*. 'Black Bodies in Schools' reminds us how significant situated experience is for educating but also how the habitual and long-standing cultural environment of schools can unintentionally solidify racial constructs. Following Dewey, the writers see hope in that habits as 'embodied intelligences that typically harden into unconscious action and thought (that) can be brought to the light of reflective consciousness through the use of the mind'. They argue that the contemporary reality of the somatic experience of African Americans is a significant spur and resource for education and social justice, for 'inquiry around the status of bodies in any system, reveals personal and cultural truths'.

Christine Doddington's chapter in this part, Chapter 6, begins by looking at spaces and current trends that also offer alternatives to approaches that over-intellectualize the nature of education. The main focus is on a distinctive change of physical environment for educational experience — that of taking education into the open, to places outside of rooms, walls and buildings. Dewey's work on experience and habit is used to show how, building on the significance he gives the body, this change of place has richer potential than what mere physical relocation suggests. In particular, Dewey's later stress on the aesthetic nature of experience comes into play so that 'open' situations can be seen to have increased value for growth. An understanding of the value and nature of aesthetic experience is a further move in fighting the dominance of technicist views, which can infect outdoor, just as much as indoor, education.

Part Three — Democracy and Development

In recent years, the traditional versus progressive debate has been reinvigorated by interpretations of the work of an American scholar of Literature, E.D. Hirsch, by academics and teachers. In his 1988 book, *Cultural Literacy*, he criticizes Dewey's claim that 'accumulating information in the form of symbols' devalues education; he argues that the progressive focus on student-led learning in primary education that Dewey helped inspire leads to divergent knowledge that fuels 'cultural fragmentation'. The poor lose out the most because the curriculum does not require that they learn basic facts at home that enable more sophisticated participation within society — unlike their wealthier counterparts — putting them in a disadvantage in secondary and tertiary education. This has in turn shaped the rise of academies and charter schools in the United Kingdom, the United States and elsewhere with a focus on traditional curricula and discipline as a foundation for academic and personal success. In a nutshell, they suggest that there is a core of 'powerful knowledge', in Michael Young's phrase, that inducts young people into language and culture without which they will be unable either to fully comprehend or to make effective connections between the things they learn. This core symbolic knowledge, it is claimed is best learnt within clearly defined subject disciplines, enabling students to think critically once the foundations are secure. Innovatively, this movement links the return to a traditional curriculum with reducing social inequality by promising to give all students a chance to a form of education which is traditionally the preserve of the elites.

To date this traditionalist stance has been held by relatively few — but catalysed to significance by two factors. First, the passion with which it is advocated in the face of a perceived progressive stranglehold over teacher training institutions and wider school cultures; second, the huge support it has received from conservative politicians who see it as justifying their long-held views that the elite education that most of them received should be the standard for others. This support is more than ideological: the recent round of the 'Teaching and Leadership Innovation Fund' in the United Kingdom revealed that nearly all of the £74 million allocated was to a range of companies, academy chains and teacher training organizations that promote highly directive approaches to the curriculum such as compulsory phonics, and highly prescriptive approaches to classroom behaviour emphasizing transmission and low student participation. In the United States, this process has progressed further. Doug Lemov's *Teach like a Champion* — a book that advocates teachers setting up a regime of military strictness and uniformity within the classroom to create the best conditions for efficient transmission of knowledge — has been adopted as the basis of the curriculum for the Relay Graduate School of Education, a rapidly expanding teacher training programme that eschews college-based learning about education in favour of teacher techniques for behaviour and content control, and judges students principally on the basis of their students' grades. Alongside this goes an increased blurring of the lines between public and private provision, with the justification that the money must follow the innovation, be it in the public or private sector, and that, by implication, the ossified progressive majority in the state system must be shaken up from the outside.

However, a deeper study of *Democracy and Education*, such as the authors in Part Three provide, shows us that Hirsch's analysis of Dewey is flawed, and that the form of equality promised by this movement is both unrealistic and undemocratic. First, Dewey explicitly distances himself from key tenets of progressive pioneers such as Froebel and Montessori, despite his sympathy towards their intentions: for example, he rejects their naturalism (the belief that children's true and unique nature is already embedded within them) and idealism (that there are perfect forms of knowledge that are 'recognised' and adopted by learners). Instead, he delineates a distinctive, pragmatist position that sees growth as the product of ongoing negotiation between teachers, students and society focused on real problems in a mutable world.

Second, chapter 21 of *Democracy and Education* (Dewey, 1916) gives a historical analysis of traditional divisions between 'academic' and 'vocational' curricula going back to the mind/body distinction made in ancient Greece, demonstrating how curricula for the elite have prized abstract knowledge as a positional good rather than for its practical utility. It is thus valued substantially because of its deliberate separation from vocational focuses on uses of knowledge, which has formed curricula for the majority. Aiming for 'an elite education for everyone', in the former UK prime minister David Cameron's oxymoronic phrase, is thus not only politically implausible, but damaging for all parties since both educational routes are diminished in personal and social value by their separation. The increasing focus on transmitting and measuring the uptake of 'powerful knowledge', and the competitiveness, prescriptiveness and narrowing of the curriculum that it has promoted, has only increased such divisions – with the children of the wealthy and educated always at an advantage from the start. Further, it changes the nature of that knowledge from its inherent value, enabling students to act more powerfully in their everyday lives through its application, to instrumental value, where the principal use of knowledge is to demonstrate one's superior command of it in examinations that lead to advancement at others' expense. Finally, it normalizes equality of opportunity in education over more genuine equality: the belief that as long as a child has 'had a chance' to succeed academically and to join, say, an elite profession as a result, then the failure of the majority to do so is their own fault, and perhaps that of their teachers and families too. This is a recipe for the continued segregation of classes that Dewey fought against. He recognized that school-based education cannot overcome such inequalities alone, but can only do so as part of a wider society in which a diversity of unique, incommensurable interests and connections between people are promoted and enabled from the start, leading to personal and collective growth.

In this ongoing coup against broad-based, public sector teacher education, Dewey has been recast as bogeyman instead of talisman. His work, however, offers us ways to fight back that are not stereotypical of a romantic and insufficiently rigorous progressivism. Moving beyond such misinterpretations, the authors in Part Three draw on different aspects of Dewey's work to demonstrate how a broader and forward-looking understanding of the curriculum can develop both students' motivation to learn and the social bonds essential to a healthy democracy.

In Chapter 7, Neil Hopkins states that control of the curriculum is always political – and that Dewey leads a long line of educational thinkers who have argued against national governmental control over the curriculum. Hopkins explores the English context, where a zeal to drive up 'standards' as measured by quantified tests has refocused teaching onto boosting performance both nationally and, through an increasing focus on the Programme for International Student Assessment, internationally. This, he argues, has both narrowed and homogenized the curriculum, sifting out the opportunities for adapting learning to local contexts and to individual students. Furthermore, it reimagines educational performance as an international currency in a competitive economic sphere. Students, if graded as comparable units, are stymied in the development of their unique agency. Instead, he gives examples of where ownership of the curriculum has been shared within the community, promoting a dialogue among all stakeholders about what should be learned collectively and individually. The resulting curriculum is a living, context- and problem-orientated agreement, rather than a top-down directive of approved content, which engages all parties in a democratic process that is educative in itself.

Brian Dotts (Chapter 8) deftly explores Dewey's radical understanding of democracy as a living process, rather than a desirable form of state. He takes us on a highly informed tour of early modern political thinkers, drawing parallels between Dewey's critique of their rigid conceptions of democratic states and Habermas' analysis of how the individual is captured and restricted by bureaucracy. Dewey's interpretation of democracy as an evolving framework for promoting diverse communication within and across societies, he argues, not only prefigured and influenced Habermas's communicative action theory but went beyond it by extending this principle of humane and expansive communication to all fields of human life – not just political institutions. Dotts highlights that education requires the foundations of shared ways of life, language and values in order to operate – but must encourage learners to always be ready to question and reshape those foundations as part of their critical engagement with the unique present situation. Thus, democratic education, when it becomes a passive and factual topic, is stultified; this parallels exactly a fixed curriculum that does not encourage learners to see its precepts as ultimately fallible and adaptable.

In Chapter 9, Victoria Door and Clare Wilkinson build on this theme by exploring Dewey's synthesis of relationships, attitudes and behaviour in education. Values and dispositions are not transmitted but rather learned through example, with teachers as powerful and vital role models for children. In particular, teachers have a duty to model openness to, and placing value on, the distinctive perspectives, knowledges and activities of each student, as this 'enlarges and enlightens experience, it stimulates and enriches imagination; it creates responsibility for accuracy and vividness of statement and thought'. Through the example of students' challenging behaviour and personalized learning, they advocate teachers engaging with students' subjectivities rather than imposing an inflexible line; through exploring underlying causes and consequences, the interaction becomes educational for both, and a model for how to engage with others in a democratic society. This open-mindedness is not a licence for poor behaviour or idiosyncratic tangents but a commitment to mutual realignment within a community's members that respects the interests of all; it requires the cultivation of 'intelligent sympathy for others'. It enables all parties to break the habits of thought and action that render relationships objective and mechanical, instead ingraining the desire to continue to grow through interacting with the distinctive qualities of others – which themselves form a substantial strand of a situated democratic curriculum.

Finally, in Chapter 10, Valentine Ngalim, exploring Dewey's concept of 'interest' in the realm of mathematics education, explains that this does not mean that students should learn what they like, but that they should and must be helped to discover the power of mathematical thinking through tasks that provide rich and engaging experiences. He gives the use of maths to calculate the shapes, angles and sizes of plots on a school farm, overcoming the false division between abstract processes and embodied activity. This multidisciplinary activity exemplifies 'interest' as a goal-orientated, intersubjective social phenomenon. Growth in education is thus the fruit of rich experiences that integrate the shared abstractions of our cultural heritage with unique students and situations. The value of mathematics need not be proven through the promise of equal engagement with elites, but with its power to enhance one's understanding and actions in the present.

Epilogue

We conclude the book with a cautiously optimistic and forward-looking text by Gert Biesta, 'The Persistence of Dewey's Pragmatism: On Possibilities and Risks'.

Biesta believes that 'the return of Dewey as an educational thinker has perhaps less to do with the intellectual dynamics of 20th century educational thought and more with the politics of education', and he queries how far the use of Dewey's name coincides with the actual substance of his thought. Biesta points us in the direction of the value of Dewey's work in providing an outlook very different from the reliance on economic outcomes. As such, Dewey remains a source of inspiration. Biesta sees contributions to educational debates, such as the chapters in this book as important in providing a thoughtful antidote against the direction of conservative policy in education.

Nevertheless, we should be mindful of the pitfalls of uncritical enthusiasm for Dewey's educational ideas. Biesta analyses these pitfalls as first a non-questioning acceptance of Deweyan pedagogy in a way which becomes dogmatic and rigid. This is counter to Dewey's own critique of 'the quest for certainty'. Biesta reminds us that Dewey's thought is 'not a set of (ontological) claims or beliefs, but a collection of specific answers to highly contextual questions and problems'. Further, there are issues arising from the fact that Dewey's is more a theory of learning than an educational theory. Biesta claims that a theory of learning is not automatically and not out of itself also a (sound) theory of education. 'The learning question is, in other words, not the same as the education question'.

We end the book with Biesta's words, with which the editors heartily concur, that 'the return to Dewey's educational thought cannot be a matter of repetition but requires thoughtful reconstruction – and Dewey would probably be the first to agree with this'.

References

Apple, M. W. (2004), Schooling, markets and an audit culture. *Educational Policy*, 18 (4), 614–621.

Apple, M. W. (2005), Education, markets and an audit culture. *Critical Quarterly*, 47 (2), 11–29.

Ball, S. (2001), Performativities and fabrications in the education economy: towards the performative society. In D. Gleeson and C. Husbands (Eds.), *The Performing School: Managing Teaching and Learning in a Performance Culture*. London: RoutledgeFalmer.

Ball, S. (2012), The making of a neoliberal academic. *Research in Secondary Education*, 2 (1), 29–31.

Benn, M. (2012), *School Wars: The Battle for Britain's Education*. London: Verso.

Bruno-Jofré, R. (2010), To those in "Heathen Darkness", Deweyan Democracy and Education in American Interdenominational configuration – the case of the committee on cooperation in Latin America. In R. Bruno-Jofrê, J. S. Johnston,

G. Jover and D. Tröhler (Eds.), *Democracy and the Intersection of Religion and Traditions*. Montreal: McGill-Queen's University Press, pp. 131–170.

Bruno-Jofré, R. and Schriewer, J. (2012), *The Global Reception of John Dewey's Thought: Multiple Refractions Through Time and Space*. London: Routledge.

Davies, B. (2003), Death to critique and dissent? The policies and practices of new managerialism and of 'evidence-based practice'. *Gender and Education*, 15, 91–103.

Dewey, J. (1897), My pedagogic creed. In J.-A. Boyson (Ed.), *The Early Works of John Dewey, 1882–1898* (2nd Release e-edition), vol. 5. Carbondale, IL: Southern Illinois Press.

Dewey, J. (1916), Democracy and education. In J.-A. Boyson (Ed.), *The Middle Works of John Dewey, 1899–1924* (2nd Release e-edition), vol. 9. Carbondale, IL: Southern Illinois Press.

Dewey, J. (1922), Human nature and conduct. In J.-A. Boyson (Ed.), *The Middle Works of John Dewey, 1899–1924* (2nd Release e-edition), vol. 14. Carbondale, IL: Southern Illinois Press.

Dewey, J. (1925), Experience and nature. In J.-A. Boyson (Ed.), *The Later Works of John Dewey 1925–1953* (2nd Release e-edition), vol. 1. Carbondale, IL: Southern Illinois Press.

Dewey, J. (1937), The Leon Trotsky Inquiry. In J.-A. Boyson (Ed.), *The Later Works of John Dewey, 1925–1953* (2nd Release e-edition), vol. 11. Carbondale, IL: Southern Illinois Press.

Dewey, J. (1940), The case for Bertrand Russell. In J.-A. Boyson (Ed.), *The Later Works of John Dewey, 1925–1953*, (2nd Release e-edition), vol. 11. Carbondale, IL: Southern Illinois Press.

Fesmire, S. (2015), *Dewey*. London: Routledge.

Greene, M. (1981), Aesthetic literacy in general education. In *80th Yearbook of the National Society for the Study of Education* (Ed.). Chicago, IL: University of Chicago Press, pp. 115–141. Available at: http://www.scribd.com/doc/26620361/Greene-Maxine-Aesthetic-Literacy-in-General-Education#scribd (accessed 07.08.15).

HMSO (1967), *The Plowden Report, Children and their Primary Schools: A Report of the Central Advisory Council for Education (England)*. HMSO, London.

Murray, J. (2012), Performativity cultures and their effects on teacher educators' work. *Research in Teacher Education*, 2 (2), 18–23.

Nussbaum, M. (2006), Education and democratic citizenship: capabilities and quality education. *Journal of Human Development and Capabilities*, 7 (3), 385–395.

Nussbaum, M., (2010), *Not for Profit: Why Democracy Needs the Humanities*. Princeton, NJ: Princeton University Press.

Oakeshott, M. (1972/1989), Education: the engagement and its frustration. In T. Fuller (Ed.), *The Voice of Liberal Learning*. New Haven, CT: Yale University Press.

Peacock, A. (2016), *Assessment for Learning without Limits*. London: Open University Press.

Pring, R. (2012), *The Life and Death of Secondary Education for All*. Abingdon: Routledge.

Ravitch, D. (2013), *Reign of Error: The Hoax of the Privatization Movement and the Danger to America's Public Schools*. New York, NY: Alfred A. Knopf.

Stengel, B. (2016), *We Can Make Mistakes and We Can Fix Them: Countering Cruel Optimism to Promote Public Education*. Available at: http://www.educ.cam.ac.uk/events/conferences/dewey2016/eresources/FixMistakes.doc

Stone, L. (2016), Re-thinking Dewey's democracy: shifting from a process of participation to an institution of association. *Journal of Curriculum Studies*, 48 (1), 78–93.

Sullivan, S. (2001), *Living across and Through Skins: Transactional Bodies, Pragmatism, and Feminism*. Indianapolis, IN: Indiana University Press.

PART 1
DEWEY, EXPERIENCE AND TECHNOLOGY

Chapter 1

Preserving Rich Experience in the Digital Age

Bob Coulter

Abstract

Many educators fear that proliferating digital technologies in school and at home create an artificial barrier to young people from having a meaningful direct experience with the world. At the same time, others argue that ubiquitous access to these same technologies is essential if young people are to make sense of the increasingly complex information space characteristic of the twenty-first century. In an attempt to bridge this gap, the chapter draws on Dewey's frame of experience as articulated in *Democracy and Education* and *Experience and Education* to craft a framework by which uses of digital technology can be assessed for their educational value. Characteristic features of experience-rich, growth-promoting uses of technology include support for both the active and passive dimensions of experience, as well as the ability to support continuity, interaction, purpose and progressive organization of experience. These (arguably) better uses of technology are in turn linked to broader concerns for young people developing the capacities needed for citizenship in a creative democracy. Numerous examples of youth projects facilitated by the author are provided to illustrate how the framework is applied in practice.

Keywords: Dewey; experience; digital technology; creative democracy; growth

Introduction

Many educators and parents fear that children today suffer from an increasingly sterile form of experience. With less direct engagement with the natural world (Sobel, 2008), and with increasing screen time (American Academy of Pediatrics, 2015), they feel that we are fledging children ill-equipped to grow into contributing citizens. To borrow a cute turn of phrase, these critics fear that we are creating a generation of game-obsessed 'homo zappiens' (Veen and Vrakking, 2007) very different from ourselves. With this, there is often a sense of alarm, captured in apocalyptic images such as that generated by the book titled *Grand Theft Childhood* (Kutner and Olson, 2008). Even if we don't run to media-fuelled extremes like this, there is still a pervasive sense that something is different – that growing up in the twenty-first century is qualitatively different than it was 'when we were young'. One of the most common distinctions drawn in this regard is between young people who are thought to be 'digital natives' who run ahead of us into a technological future and the rather troglodyte-like 'digital immigrant' adults destined to be left behind (Prensky, 2001). In my experience, this distancing between the generations is too easily drawn in the face of clear evidence to the contrary, as evidenced by the many kids who struggle with technology, and the many adults of all ages who are quite proficient with a range of technology skills. Still, it's a pervasive and persistent image that creates an artificial divide between generations that we will need to bridge if we are to carry out the age-old – and very necessary – process of acculturating the young and guiding them toward a responsible citizenship. Quite simply, children mustn't be seen as an alien species if we are to nurture their growth effectively.

Fortunately, there are many positive models of technology use that enable rich learning opportunities and which counter the generational separation. With careful planning, digital tools can be an integral part of a fertile, experience-based learning environment. Used in the right context and for pedagogically sound reasons (and not simply for their own sake in pursuit of some vague idea of being a 'twenty-first-century learner'), tools such as data visualizations (MaKinster et al., 2014) and computer simulations (Begel and Klopfer, 2005) can be essential learning resources. Specific benefits that might be realized include enhanced engagement with the phenomena at hand, stronger connections with peers and adults (both locally and beyond), scaffolding that supports reflection on what is being experienced, and with this scaffolding, opportunities to revise and extend emergent thoughts. While each of these benefits can, of course, happen without digital adjuncts, we will see in the discussion below how strategic use of digital tools can actually enhance students' experience in ways that are harder to achieve without the technology. But, this will only happen with nuanced judgement.

In an effort to better guide our use of technology in educational settings, I offer a framework for preserving rich experience in a digital age. More specifically, in the pages ahead I will sketch a path showing how a Dewey-inspired approach toward experience and thinking enables us to support young people as they engage with the world around them. Working within this framework, aesthetically enriched experience is not only preserved but also in fact extended through positive use of technology. With this, deep and complex thinking can be scaffolded with strategically deployed technology resources. When these threads of experience and thinking converge, we can nurture active youth participation, with a goal of setting them on a path toward fulfilling the challenge toward democratic living that Dewey (1939) issued in his essay 'Creative Democracy–The Task before Us'.

Framing Experience

Starting at the most foundational level, Dewey's (1916/1966) framing of experience in *Democracy and Education* offers a benchmark against which uses of digital resources can be assessed. By defining experience as 'an active and a passive element peculiarly combined' – or in other words, as an iterative process of doing something intentional and then experiencing the results before staking out a next action – we can start our analysis. As Dewey points out, neither activity done for its own sake nor passive reception of information conveyed to us constitutes an experience. It's the intentional fusion of the two that we need to be working toward. Phrased more simply, intentional action and a thoughtfully considered reaction need to work together to create an optimally engaging learning experience. While this pairing would seem self-evident based on our life experiences, the norm for too many schools is a curriculum designed simply to pass along information and to practice skills in contexts over which the students (and often the teachers) have no say. This lack of intention is well captured in the euphemism 'delivering the curriculum' and is raised to an art form in Pring's (2013) term 'deliverology'. In these dystopian learning environments, no one chooses. Rather, we just follow along in a perverse rendering of the etymology of the term curriculum as a course to be followed, all too often in a lock-step fashion with little consideration of whether this path is best for all students (or, for that matter, even good for any students). Within this sterile process, we assess students' progress and then rank them (and in turn, their teachers and schools) by testing for recall on demand, almost always in the absence of meaningful context. In a school we work with, I've actually had an administrator challenge me about why we spend so much time trying to get the kids thinking when it is more efficient just to tell them what they need to know for their tests. Fortunately, many teachers push against this approach and try to go beyond the dull litany of deliverology by jazzing up the learning environment a bit. Still, this poses a problem if they resort to projects that privilege activity over experience, a phenomenon Moscovici and Nelson (1998) have aptly described as 'activitymania'. Viewed in a Deweyan context, if too much priority is placed on the doing without the associated reflecting, little growth is nurtured. In fact, holding kids' attention through contrived means deflects their attention away from having real experiences. As Dewey (1938/1963) described them in *Experience and Education*, these overwrought activities are 'miseducative' in that they serve to block future growth. Common examples might include science classes which are populated by pseudo-events like fake volcanoes made with baking soda and vinegar, or math classes in which students collect meaningless data simply to check off 'making graphs' from the curriculum scope and sequence. We can – and need to – do better if we want to build positive learning environments.

In some ways, forging an alternate path is not hard, in the sense that moving toward an experience-driven learning environment resonates more fully with normal human behaviour. Anyone who works with kids know that they are capable of much more creative and thoughtful engagement with the world than one might expect from looking at scripted curriculum paths or from observing poorly thought-out lurches into activity. Unless they have been schooled into disengagement (which, sadly, is a common affliction of the young), the vast majority of kids want to be involved and want to be challenged. Working toward increased competence is an integral part of being a human. As educators, we need to leverage and channel this impulse, not work to stifle it. To see the contrast in how people act in different contexts, notice the passive students who miraculously come alive after school as they play (and perhaps design) complex games. Even within school, there can be quite a range in levels of engagement depending on how effectively we invite participation. The following vignette shows students actively engaged in a digital experience which fostered deeper and more complex thinking than their normal curriculum allowed.

Like Clockwork: Digitally Enriched Experience in Action

A colleague and I were recently working with a group of 10 and 11 year olds as they worked to design simulated clocks using computer modelling tools. As part of this, the kids worked as a class to act out the motions of the minute and hour hands of an analogue clock. From there, the kids worked to create models of that motion on screen. As they did this, they had to draw on several key math concepts such as the radius, diameter and circumference of their clock face, and use this information skilfully as they encoded formulas within their models. Key questions the students faced included: *How long of a distance does the tip of the minute hand travel as it goes around the clock face?* and *How can we model that movement on screen?* While each student was working on their own clock, they readily shared strategies with their peers – offering ideas and responding thoughtfully to what others suggested. As the project progressed, the students employed relatively complex skills such as computational thinking as they broke the problem down into small steps, and proportional reasoning when they had to figure out how to programme the hour hand to travel in a path similar to the minute hand, but exactly $1/12$ as quickly. The only evaluation of their work was self-imposed: Did the hands move (literally) 'like clockwork', and did the hour hand move one hour on the clock face for each sweep around the clock face by the minute hand? If not, something needed to be fixed. Recall here the fundamental premise of an experience: a pairing of active and passive elements. More colloquially, the students' clock-making interwove action and reaction as ideas were developed, tried out and revised based on how well they served the purpose. Animated by the challenge of designing a clock that mimicked real-world ones, student engagement was quite high throughout the process. And, most strikingly, not once over the course of several work sessions did a student ask about project requirements or a grade. Instead the kids were internally motivated, basing their work on higher standards than they would face in their normal curriculum. This contrast with their regular school environment became clear one day when they had to leave the computer lab to go to math class, which the kids characterized as dull and repetitive, 'doing the same things we've done since third grade'. These are kids who were leaving an experience where they were challenged to apply a set of math skills well beyond the expectation for their grade level, dreading having to return to a math environment where they will be less challenged, and with that, less fully invited to participate in their own learning and growth.

Framing the Work in Broader Contexts

My experience with the clock project largely mirrors what Melissa Gresalfi and her colleagues (2012) found when she compared the learning environment in two middle school classes in the same building, who were using the same curriculum. Given this pairing, the student ability and curriculum variables were about as controlled as you will get in a natural setting. The striking findings were in the ways in which the students seem to have absorbed very different norms for learning within each class. In the class where the teacher held expectations for higher-level inquiry, students rose to the challenge and asked comparatively higher-order questions. Overall, they displayed a level of real engagement. In the other class, where simply covering the curriculum seemed to be the primary goal, students adopted a much more passive demeanour in keeping with the norms established within that class. Instead of active engagement, classroom interactions followed a much more traditional pattern of teacher-initiated, low-level questions to which the students gave pro forma responses. In both of these classes, the students were smart enough to 'play the game' that they were being offered. Our challenge as educators is to be sure that the game we give them is worthy of their engagement.

Before moving forward, I feel compelled to offer a cautionary note here. While I have been critical of some of the classroom environments described in the previous pages, I'm well aware that they don't emerge out of nowhere. They get that way for complex reasons and are quite challenging to change. In an earlier study – *No More Robots: Building Kids' Character, Competence, and Sense of Place* (Coulter, 2014) – I reported on how teachers go at their work in very different ways, often emerging from very different ways of seeing learning and even the fundamental nature of childhood. Aside from these individual differences in how teachers approach their work, many operate within a system that makes it very hard to break out of the mould. Where test scores and other discrete, context-free measures are used to rate and rank schools (and with that, the teachers and students who make up the school), there is great pressure to conform with established models of teaching. In these settings, following the curriculum script with fidelity to pre-approved teaching techniques offers a degree of cover that isn't there if the class goes off-script. If you innovate and the scores aren't good, teachers assume – often with good reason – that dire consequences will follow. When this narrowing of pedagogy happens, teaching is reduced to a technician-level task with no room for nuanced judgement. Echoing Pring's deliverology imagery noted earlier, teaching moves uncomfortably close to the work of a delivery driver who is being monitored and rated for efficiency in driving and in getting a load of packages delivered. Just as drivers are rated on how they use every minute of the day based on an wide array of sensor data embedded in their trucks (Goldstein, 2014), I've seen teachers rated in a single observation session on more than 40 discrete ticks such as whether they use pre-approved words to secure their students' attention. If we are to move forward toward improved learning environments, we need a better path. Following the advice of Collini (2012), we need to move past facile forms of measurement toward nuanced expert judgement of what is of most worth.

As hard as the work may be, I will argue that the foundation of our effort toward improved learning spaces is best laid in working on students' experiences. Instead of marching through an assigned set of topics and skills (even if they are jazzed up with an occasional activity), we need to remember that the educative benefit is realized in the continuous interplay of the active and passive elements. For the clock project, the kids were probably drawn in initially by the chance to use modelling software that was still new to them, and a chance to get out of the classroom. Even if we grant this, what sustained their engagement over the multiple sessions of our work together was the interplay between the active doing and the passive undergoing that is at the core of experience. They had to act out the motion of the clock, reflect on how they could represent that motion by sequencing the on-screen 'blocks' that made up the computer code, implement the code as they built their programmes and make adjustments as needed to improve their clock's functioning. Throughout, there was an iterative process of trying something, reflecting on how well it worked and then charting out their next steps. Over time, this work helped all of the students to develop a level of competence and confidence with the modelling tools for which they were rightly proud, and which they can now use in a variety of other projects, both within their curriculum and in freely chosen pursuits such as designing original games. Lest this effort be written off simply as an enrichment (and thus, not part of the 'core' curriculum), note that they deepened a range of math skills including mental computation, measurement, proportional reasoning and use of a variety of geometry formulas. Any stereotype that spending time on computers inherently dumbs kids down or turns them into zombies is too simple. On the other hand, we also need to steer clear of the equally ill-founded notion that use of technology is inherently good – a claim that is often used to justify the significant expenses that go with buying educational technology. We need better thinking in the field and, ironically, a man who never used a computer holds the key to moving forward. Later in the chapter, we'll be taking a closer look at specific Dewey-inspired criteria that can guide our decision-making.

Before going further, though, I'd like to spend a minute looking at the social dimension of technology use. While common images of kids assume that screen time limits interpersonal exchanges, or that communication is reduced to text messaging, this doesn't have to be the case. Well-deployed technology can be a catalyst toward enhanced communication. Again, it's all in how it is used. While the clock project described earlier was mostly a 'solo' venture for each student (enhanced by some collaboration as students shared strategies for what worked), it's important to note that digital tools can also support projects which are fundamentally collaborative in nature. For a simple example, many students these days have easy access to digital cameras, most often in their cell phones. While a simple activity-level use of the cameras might involve a task such as having students make a photo album of their field observations, much more can be done if the work is intentionally structured to be an experience. Imagine if instead of simply taking a series of snapshots, students were challenged to record seasonal change through photo monitoring of specific locations done at regular time intervals. This shift in the structure of what they are photographing – changing from haphazardly taken snapshots to a sustained and intentional effort to document change over time – lets the work become an experience through ongoing reflection on what the sequential photographs reveal. As students take new photos as part of each monitoring effort, trends become apparent. This feeds a reflection cycle, which astute teachers can leverage to promote discussion about what has happened, and to draw out evidence-informed predictions as to what is likely to happen next. Again, to draw the contrast, simply taking photographs to document a field trip would be an activity, but such an effort would be missing the passive side of reflecting on the collected evidence. In fact, as a collaborative effort, the discussion about the collected set of images itself becomes a form of experience as students formulate an observation or a hypothesis, respond in a critical and constructive manner to what others offer and jointly reflect both on what has happened so far and on what is to come. Over time, this iterative process nurtures growth in evidence-based understanding which occurs best through high-quality experience. This growth in turn leads to the development of a more detailed and complex understanding of the specific issues associated both with seasonal change and with broader concepts of ecosystem dynamics. Moving from this specific example to general principles, collaborative ventures like this involving groups sharing a common purpose helps to enhance the value of the experience at hand, and more broadly to support students in developing the social skills needed to be collaborative, contributing members of society. Traditional models of education premised on individual work completed in isolation, and on classroom 'discussion' which amounts to teachers posing a question, calling on a student to respond and evaluating the accuracy of the response – the so-called I-R-E model – simply can't achieve this higher level of collaboratively shaped inquiry.

Specific to the focus of this chapter, note how the technology used in these examples has proven to be an integral part of the students' experience, and not a distraction that needs to be regulated, or offered as a sugar-coated incentive for students who 'get their (real) work done.' After a brief interlude, I'll resume this argument and lay out a set of criteria which can help in using technology in ways that foster meaningful experience.

Lasting Impact of Experience

Before moving forward into a closer analysis of just how we can preserve experience in the digital age, I'd like to take a brief interlude to consider why this is important. While the vignette I shared earlier with the administrator advocating that we simply tell the students what they need to know was a bit extreme, it's not out of line with dominant ways of thinking about education. Throughout my career I've been chided about why we don't hold off on higher-order thinking until the kids are older 'once they have mastered the basics' or 'after they know more.' In fact, during my past couple of years as a classroom teacher of eight and nine year olds, I had a few parents who paid a good bit to an after-school tutorial company each week since I wasn't teaching in my class 'the math they needed to know'. (In fact their test scores were among the best in the school's history, but facts can be very inconvenient at times.)

While this choice to pursue different paths toward math learning could simply be ascribed to a difference of opinion between the parents and me as to the best way for kids to learn, emerging research on neuroplasticity and cognitive development suggests otherwise. It is becoming increasingly clear that inquiry that unfolds in a manner like the examples I've shared nurtures a particular (and lasting) form of cognitive development. There is no hubris in this claim, since the claim is equally true for the more traditional, rote approaches I've used as points of contrast. Both approaches have a lasting and significant impact. This seeming contradiction can be traced to Dewey's intuition about the plasticity of the brain (1916/1966) in response to experience – an idea which presupposed modern concepts of neuroplasticity (Eagleman, 2015). While the terminology may be off-putting, the idea is comparatively simple: our experiences help to sculpt the neural pathways that over time come to shape our thoughts. Based on what we do, certain parts of our brain develop rich connections. Areas that are less used don't develop as well and in fact may atrophy in comparison with the pathways that are better supported. What we do has impact well beyond the moment. With all of this, timing is important. Wexler (2008) documents the age sensitivities involved. When we are young, our plasticity is the highest. Implicitly, this favours laying groundwork for experience now, rather than waiting until the kids are older. In fact, consistent with Dewey's idea of each experience feeding into the success of the next venture, cumulative growth from our youngest years is critical and can't just be 'jump started' after the fact. This becomes particularly important when we recognize that learning as an adult involves more adaptation to the structures we have, and less on forging our neural structures up front.

Paired with this focus on individual cognitive growth, we also need to be attentive to group contexts and the impact of culture on brain development. While space here precludes any deep consideration of the issues, there are some intriguing ideas in this regard being documented in the emerging field of neuroanthropology (Lende and Downey, 2012). Group norms for how we pursue our work, and what counts as good thinking, will inevitably have a lasting impact on the individuals who make up that group. It seems counterproductive to have students work as individuals throughout their school careers and then send them off to their workplace where they will need teamwork development activities. Pre-wiring for experience, inquiry and collaboration seems so much more efficient.

Pulling all of this together, focusing on experience is more than a simple matter of choice or preference for what we do. Different paths have lasting impact on our cognitive structures, and thus are supportive of different developmental trajectories. In the remaining pages, I will be focusing on how we can best leverage the affordances of technology to achieve these goals while avoiding facile substitutes.

A Framework for Experience-Based, Technology-Enhanced Thinking

As a start toward a planning model, I suggest that we build from the premise discussed above — that experience grows out of engagements with the world that include both an active and a passive component. Given this foundation, when we analyse an experience, we need to attend simultaneously to the ways in which learners are able to take on an active role in their exchange with the world, and the ways in which learners attend to the *re*action which follows. Without the action, we are passive vessels; if not for the reaction, we too easily lapse into 'activitymania' where action is pursued for its own sake. Each of these considerations is particularly apt in looking at technology, where we need to guard against either extreme — becoming enraptured with glitzy new features which prioritize action or being lulled into becoming passive consumers of information. Recall the administrator I described earlier who was most interested in efficiently conveying needed information to the students. While the Internet has many uses, there is much more to experience than looking up facts or watching canned tutorials.

Assuming that we do find spaces with the right interplay of the active and the passive, we also need to attend to an assumption Dewey explicitly embedded within in all of this: any particular active–passive interchange has its real value in the ways in which it enhances the potential for future experiences to be beneficial. One way of envisioning this might be to think of an increasing spiral, where each experience feeds the next in a progression toward greater heights. Or, you could reverse the metaphor and drill more deeply into the phenomena of interest. In either case, the key to the imagery is to see that experience takes us someplace different and is not just an accumulation of facts and skills that feeds the banking or warehousing metaphors that are all too common in conceptions of education. With this expansion in perspective and capacity for meaningful engagement, learners gain more agency in their own lives and with it, greater potential to do good in the community.

Moving ahead, we need to consider what happens within experiences that give the active–passive interchange its value. Here, a critical look at thinking comes to the fore. Dewey (1916/1966, p. 151) offers a useful structure for this when he argues that thinking involves four interrelated acts: '(developing) a sense of the problem, the observation of conditions, the formation and relational elaboration of a suggested conclusion, and the active experimental testing'. While at first glance these four components seem to give undue weight to the active component of an activity, there is also a passive element embedded in each that is essential to the success of the endeavour. Figuring out what is going on and what might be causing it, and from there trying to determine what sort of relationships underlie what is being observed (and how they might be tested) all require rapid loops of observing, processing and drawing from previous experience. In that, the active and passive conjoin toward a successful venture.

To be clear in this, we have to be sure we are working from a sufficiently broad conception of thinking. While standard images tend to frame thinking as a singular and rather cerebral venture, I have no doubt Dewey would enthusiastically recognize emerging understandings of embodied cognition (Clark, 2008) and social epistemology (Kotzee, 2013). Obviously, we think with our minds, but our bodies are an integral part of that work. Space limits preclude going into much detail here, but acknowledging the skill of an artist or craftsman deftly using his or her hands as part of coming to know a situation, sizing up the possibilities and the like should be sufficient to decentre us from considering thinking to be entirely brain-based. Part of this extended cognition has to include social interaction as well. While each of us is responsible for forming our own thoughts, these thoughts are deeply influenced by the interactions we have with each other. Echoing John Donne, none of us is an island. The challenge we face in building rich experience is in being sure that we have structured dialogue (Gallas, 1995) and informal collegial interaction (Collini, 2012) that brings in different perspectives and that challenges us to continually reimagine our perceptions and rethink our beliefs.

Tool Selection and Use

Building from these foundations of experience and thinking, Dewey (1938/1963) offers a set of concepts which can be used as selection criteria when considering applications of educational technology. For each, we need to be sure that both the affordances of the technology and the ways in which it is actually being used meet the criteria. Simply having the technology won't suffice. With that caveat, I will draw directly on Dewey and argue that appropriate uses of technology need to support:

- *Continuity*: Does the technology foster continuity from prior experience to the task at hand and beyond?
- *Interaction*: Does the technology encourage greater interaction with the physical and social world?
- *Purpose*: Does the technology enhance pursuit of a significant purpose, or is the apparent engagement simply an example of the Hawthorne effect?
- *Progressive organization of experience*: Does the technology enable students to develop increasingly elaborate and intricate understanding?

An event less experiential in a Deweyan sense – such as viewing an online tutorial presenting steps used to apply the Pythagorean theorem, followed by a set of rote textbook exercises graded by the computer simply as correct or incorrect – would fail the test for conjoint active–passive involvement. This example illustrates students serving as 'theoretical spectators' (Dewey, 1916/1966, p. 140) rather than as full participants in an experience. No matter how engaging the tutorial may be, the absence of a context that challenges students to make meaningful use of the Pythagorean theorem limits the activity's potential. Another context requiring that a student uses the Pythagorean theorem could have experiential value. In this case, active engagement in learning and applying the formula is paired with the passive component of reflecting on the utility of the solution: *Did it meet my need? How might my effort be improved?* Eleven-year-old Ross Stauder captured the difference between an authentic task and an assignment while reflecting on his experience at a game design camp. As he noted, 'Making handheld games is a lot different than school because it requires smarter thinking and trial and error × 17. In school you don't get a second trial because when it's done it's done and that's your grade' (Coulter and Stauder, 2015, p. 144).

As these examples illustrate, the critical issue is the intended use of the technology, not the tool in itself. Photography can be a meaningful data collection tool, or a way to grab souvenirs quickly forgotten. An online tutorial can be rote activity, or a targeted resource providing the information needed to address an authentic problem. To preserve rich experience, we need to do more than simply adopt the latest technologies and then look for applications. Instead, we need to refocus our efforts on creating fertile learning spaces and from there, select applications of technology that enable the kinds of experiences which extend students' thinking.

Closing Thoughts: Is This the Right Way to Use Technology?

I offer for your consideration the premise that uses of technology are most worthy of consideration when they:

- enable students to better engage in Dewey's conjoint active–passive criteria for experience;
- support Dewey's four dimensions of thinking (developing a sense of the problem, observation of conditions, formation and relational elaboration of a suggested conclusion and the active experimental testing) and
- enable continuity with what has come before, support interaction with materials and each other, foster a real sense of purpose (which the learner embraces) and contribute to the progressive organization of experience.

When these criteria are met, we are well on our way toward preserving experience in the digital age.

Acknowledgements

The work described here was supported in part by the U.S. National Science Foundation and the Litzsinger Road Ecology Foundation.

References

American Academy of Pediatrics (2015), *Media and Children*. Available at: https://www.aap.org/en-us/advocacy-and-policy/aap-health-initiatives/pages/media-and-children.aspx (accessed 10.10.17).

Begel, A. and Klopfer, E. (2005), StarLogo: a programmable complex systems modeling environment for students and teachers. In A. Adamatzky and M. Komosinski (Eds.). *Artificial Life Models in Software*. New York, NY: Springer-Verlag.

Clark, A. (2008), *Supersizing the Mind: Embodiment, Action, and Cognitive Extension*. Oxford: Oxford University Press.
Collini, S. (2012), *What Are Universities for?* London: Penguin.
Coulter, B. (2014), *No More Robots: Building Kids' Character, Competence, and Sense of Place*. New York, NY: Peter Lang.
Coulter, B. and Stauder, R. (2015), 'To have fun and display our awesomeness': mobile game design and the meaning of life. In C. Holden (Ed.). *Mobile Media Learning: Innovation and Inspiration*. Pittsburgh, PA: ETC Press.
Dewey, J. (1916/1966), *Democracy and Education*. New York, NY: Free Press.
Dewey, J. (1938/1963), *Experience and Education*. New York, NY: Collier Books.
Dewey, J. (1939/1976), Creative democracy: the task before us. In J. Boydston (Ed.). *John Dewey: The Later Works, 1925–1953*, vol. 14. Carbondale, IL: Southern Illinois University Press.
Eagleman, D. (2015), *The Brain: The Story of You*. New York, NY: Pantheon Books.
Gallas, K. (1995), *Talking Their Way into Science: Hearing Children's Questions and Theories, Responding with Curricula*. New York, NY: Teachers College Press.
Goldstein, J. (2014), *To Increase Productivity, UPS Monitors Drivers' Every Move*. Available at: http://www.npr.org/sections/money/2014/04/17/303770907/to-increase-productivity-ups-monitors-drivers-every-move (accessed 0.10.17).
Gresalfi, M., Barnes, J. and Cross, D. (2012), When does an opportunity become an opportunity? Unpacking classroom practice through the lens of ecological psychology. *Educational Studies in Mathematics*, 80 (1–2), 249–267.
Kotzee, B. (Ed.) (2013), *Education and the Growth of Knowledge: Perspectives from Social and Virtue Epistemology*. Oxford: Wiley-Blackwell.
Kutner, L. and Olson, C. (2008), *Grand Theft Childhood: The Surprising Truth about Violent Video Games and What Parents Can Do*. New York, NY: Simon & Schuster.
Lende, D. H. and Downey, G. (Eds.) (2012), *The Encultured Brain: An Introduction to Neuroanthropology*. Cambridge, MA: MIT Press.
MaKinster, J., Trautmann, N. and Barnett, M. (Eds.) (2014), *Teaching Science and Investigating Environmental Issues with Geospatial Technology*. New York, NY: Springer-Verlag.
Moscovici, H. and Nelson, T. H. (1998), Shifting from activity mania to inquiry. *Science and Children*, 40 (1), 14–17.
Prensky, M. (2001), *Digital Natives, Digital Immigrants*. Available at: http://marcprensky.com/writing/Prensky%20-%20Digital%20Natives,%20Digital%20Immigrants%20-%20Part1.pdf (accessed 10.10.17).
Pring, R. (2013), *The Life and Death of Secondary Education for All*. Abingdon: Routledge.
Sobel, D. (2008), *Childhood and Nature*. Portland, ME: Stenhouse.
Veen, W. and Vrakking, B. (2007), *Homo Zappiens: Growing Up in a Digital Age*. London: Network Continuum Press.
Wexler, B. E. (2008), *Brain and Culture*. Cambridge, MA: MIT Press.

Chapter 2

The Emergence of Makerspaces, Hackerspaces and Fab Labs: Dewey's Democratic Communities of the Twenty-first Century?

Sally Eaves and Stephen Harwood

Abstract

A new form of learning space has emerged across the world, marking a shift from Do-It-Yourself to Do-It-Together. This space, generically known as a makerspace, is located in accessible and affordable venues, both within communities and serving communities. It offers a resource that allows people to discover their latent capabilities through exploration, experimentation and iteration, alongside the knowledge openly shared by those around them. The underlying rationale is found in the work of John Dewey, notably *Democracy and Education* (*D&E*, 1916). This chapter examines this newer form of space to gain insight into what it implies for learning and education. It commences with a reflection of salient aspects of Dewey's *D&E* (1916) and how this informs understanding on what is desirable in a learning space. This is followed by a reflection upon research on makerspaces to establish how they can be conceptualized. A case study provides rich insights into characteristics, ethos and practices, while acknowledging that each space is unique and not representative of them all. Nevertheless, it foregrounds the essence of what defines a makerspace. The chapter closes with discussion of the implications and what may be concluded.

Dewey and Education in the 21st Century: Fighting Back, 37–59
Copyright © 2018 by Emerald Publishing Limited
All rights of reproduction in any form reserved
ISBN: 978-1-78743-626-8

Whatever has transpired between the publication of Dewey's *D&E* (1916) and the present, his vision of the empowered individual clearly manifests in the makerspace. It allows individuals to break free from the limitations of the formal educational system and, as part of a social learning community, discover their potential in new, natural, non-linear and often unexpected ways. Further, and perhaps only just beginning to be understood, is its wider potential to ignite alternative approaches on how to contribute to society and catalysing new directions for the future of work. With increasing research insights alongside broadened awareness of the possibilities, individuals can gain the capability to design and build for their future – that is only limited by their capacity to imagine it.

Keywords: Makerspace; hackerspace; Dewey; experiential learning; creativity; informal education

Introduction

Traditional forms of domestic space that enable 'doing' (garages, garden outbuildings) have re-emerged as new forms of active space in communities. Hobbies and Do-It-Yourself (DIY) (Atkinson, 2006) have been transformed from something undertaken in isolation, perhaps accompanied by membership of a local or national club, to something done in a shared space – a makerspace. This represents a move towards a DIT or 'Do IT Together' ethos and approach that is self-organizing, creative, entrepreneurial and interconnected.

The term 'makerspace' is an encompassing designation to denote those locales whereby members of the community are empowered to be creative and can do/make something. What was once limited in terms of resources and knowledge afforded at an individual level has been expanded to what the community can afford. Underpinning these spaces is the nature of the learning that they foster. Learning is iterative and experimental – the endeavour to make something work, failing and learning from mistakes, all supported by peers who openly share skills and expertise.

The rationale for this community grounded and social learning experience can be found in the work of John Dewey, most particularly, in the seminal work of *Democracy and Education* (*D&E*, 1916). Dewey argued against the contemporary forms of learning that required a prescriptive consumption of facts, demanded compliance and stifled curiosity and creativity. By contrast, he proposed an experiential and organic form of learning which is grounded in the everyday of the community. This resonates strongly with today's makerspaces and how participants in these settings enrich their lives, individually and collectively, through learning and sharing practices.

The chapter examines this newer form of DIY or DIT space with a view to understanding what it implies for learning and education. It commences with a reflection of relevant aspects of Dewey's *D&E* (1916) and how this informs understanding on what is desirable in a learning space. This is followed by an evaluation of research on makerspaces to establish how they can be conceptualized. A case study is then presented which provides insight into the realities of such spaces, acknowledging that each is unique and not representative of them all. Nevertheless, the case draws attention to the essence of what defines a makerspace. The chapter closes with discussion of the implications of the insights presented and what can be concluded.

Formally or Naturally Occurring Education

John Dewey's *D&E* (1916) offers a critique of the then contemporary formal educational system, which is contrasted with the informal education that arises from social engagement (Figure 1). This provides a basis for an argument which can view education in terms of something externally imposed with development in compliance with the rules of society (traditional) or something that specifically meets the needs of the learner, personal growth and preparation for membership of society (experiential).

The traditional view of education invokes a formal process, which takes place within the specially constructed environment of the school 'with the express reference to influencing the mental and moral disposition of their members' (Dewey, 1916, p. 22). The role of education is to guide, to control or to direct on a particular course. While guidance supports the compliant, control is exercised upon the non-compliant, who are made to submit. This disregards natural instincts, suppresses 'obnoxious traits' and brings all into conformity and uniformity, with an aversion for novelty, progress and uncertainty. There is a 'common subject matter' codified into an abstract form and distant from the reality of 'life-experience'. Knowledge concerns the acquisition of information, that is the 'body of facts and truths

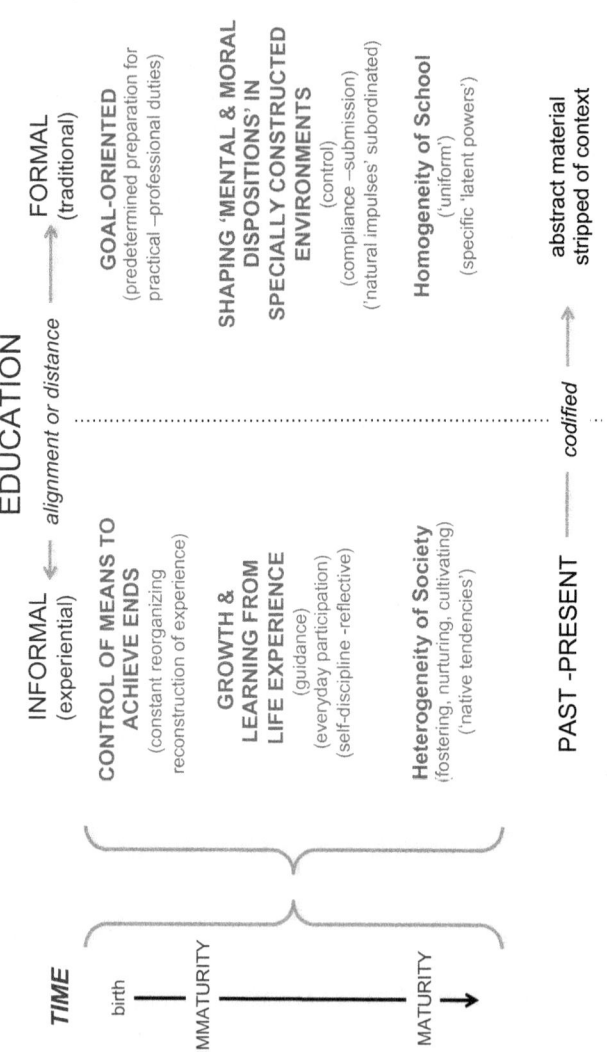

Figure 1: Education as Experienced Naturally in Contrast to the Traditional View.

ascertained by others' (ibid., p. 220), independent from the process of inquiry that brought it into being as material for further inquiry. The use of knowledge is therefore mechanical. Within this view, the aim of education is to prepare children for society through the development of specific latent powers (e.g. perceiving, retaining, recalling) to accomplish 'practical and professional duties'. Through repetition in practice, the mind can be trained. It serves the goals of a higher body, that of the state?

In contrast, Dewey presents an experientially oriented view of education. Learning is part of the experience of being a member of a community. Education is a social function: 'the education which everyone gets from living with others' (ibid., p. 7). In this sense, education is informal and supports personal growth, which commences at birth. 'Immaturity' is the 'ability to grow' and learn from experience. Education enables people to develop both an intellectual disposition and the ability to handle novel situations, adapt to changes and continually grow. It is surmised that, if life is development, then growth (development) is life. Thus, the educational process is its own end; it is one of 'continual re-organizing, reconstructing, transforming' (ibid., p. 59). Thus, it can be argued that education does not end upon leaving school but should be ongoing, learning from life itself with the 'finest product of schooling' being the making of 'conditions of life such that all will learn in the process of living' (ibid., p. 60). Education is not about '"telling" and being told, but an active and constructive process' (ibid., p. 46). It involves 'fostering', 'nurturing' and 'cultivating', but, this draws attention to the conditions in which this growth takes place, that is those conditions 'that promote or hinder, stimulate or inhibit' (ibid., p.13). These conditions involve others and so constitutes the social environment, which is educative by virtue of how it shapes behaviour.

Experience and reflection are important features of education. Experience is 'trying' (ibid., p. 163) where, through experiment, meaning is made explicit, i.e. is active. Alternatively, experience is 'undergoing', something is done which does something in return, by which we undergo the consequences of our action, i.e. is passive 'when the change made by action is reflected back into a change made in us, the mere flux is loaded with significance. We learn something' (ibid.). Meaning emerges as a consequence of our actions. Both imply learning. However, 'mere activity does not constitute experience' (ibid.). This reveals the importance of 'reflection', which relates to how we discern the relationship between 'what we try to do and what happens in consequence' (ibid., p. 169). In experiences characterized by experimentation ('trial and error'), different things are done until it works, which then becomes the 'rule of thumb' method for subsequent actions. Through our reflection (intentional thought) about our experimentation, we make explicit the 'specific connections' between what we do and the resultant consequences.

This results in Dewey's proposal about how these insights into an informal experientially oriented education can inform a formal educational experience (Figure 2).

Dewey concludes that the key to the 'present educational situation' is to reconstruct the 'materials and methods', 'relegating' literary approaches (e.g. textbooks) to 'necessary auxiliary tools'. This implies embedding what goes on outside school into the curricula, and not viewing school as a vehicle to technically prepare students for work:

> The problem is not that of making the schools an adjunct to manufacture and commerce, but of utilizing the factors of industry to make school life more active, more full of immediate meaning, more connected with out-of-school experience. (ibid., p. 369)

The aim is to allow people to develop into valued members of the community:

> It signifies a society in which every person shall be occupied in something which makes the lives of others better worth living, and which accordingly makes the ties which bind persons together more perceptible – which breaks down the barriers of distance between them. It denotes a state of affairs in which the interest of each in his work is uncoerced and intelligent: based upon its congeniality to his own aptitudes. (ibid., pp. 369–370)

The emphasis is upon the ability to use knowledge in doubtful situations and thereby deal effectively with problematic situations. Thus, the instructor should be less concerned with the subject matter and instead be more focused on how the learner is engaging with the material. Further, it is important to learn from the past, but a past not disconnected from the present: '… knowledge of the past is the key to understanding the present … [with the] true starting point of history is always some present situation with its problems' (ibid., p. 251). This draws attention to the 'permeating social spirit' underpinning how the school

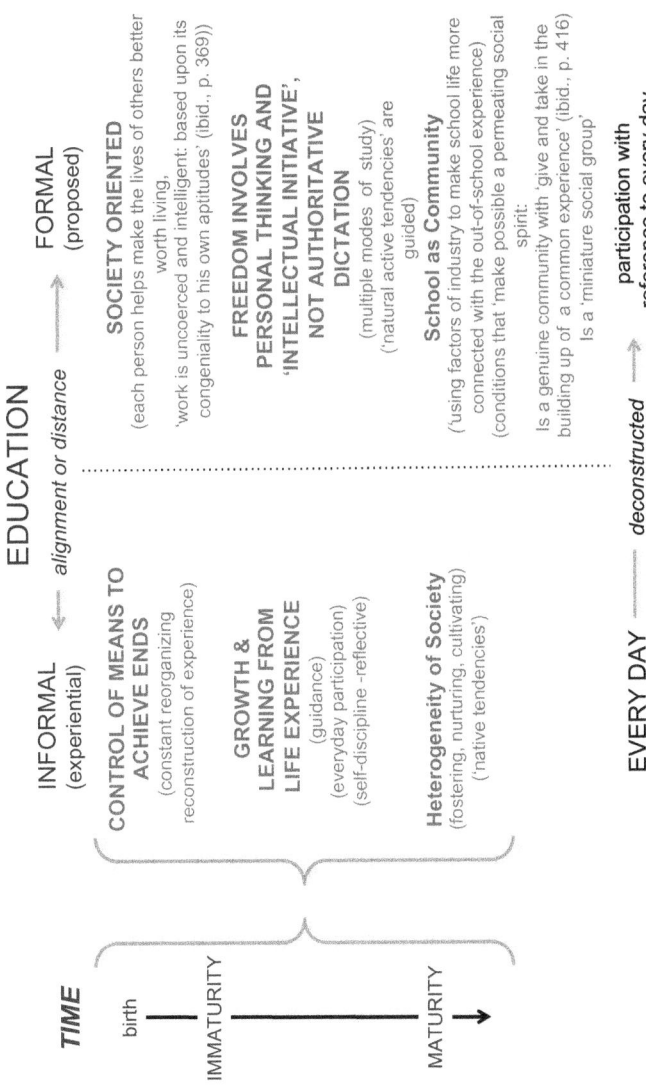

Figure 2: Education as Experienced Naturally and Its Feed into a Formal Setting.

is administered, the curriculum and its methods of instruction. This requires the school to be a genuine community, a 'miniature social group'. There is ongoing entanglement between school and out-of-school with a common social life as opposed to 'the proverbial separation of town and gown, the cultivation of academic seclusion, operate in this direction' (ibid., p. 416).

At the heart of this enterprise is the concept of democracy. Dewey's view of the role of democracy in education is captured in the statement whereby democracy is

> ... a mode of associated living, of conjoint communicated experience. The extension in space of the number of individuals who participate in an interest so that each has to refer his own action to that of others, and to consider the action of others to give point and direction to his own, is equivalent to the breaking down of those barriers of class, race, and national territory which kept men from perceiving the full import of their activity. (ibid., p. 101)

Activity is considerate and respectful to others; it is accessible, inclusive and participatory, orientated towards shared social goals. This social element pervades education. Education is about the 'freeing of individual capacity in a progressive growth directed to social aims' (ibid., p. 115). It is orientated to enabling 'an individual to make his own special contribution to a group interest, and to partake of its activities in such ways that social guidance shall be a matter of his own mental attitude, and not a mere authoritative dictation of his acts' (ibid., p. 352). In this sense, education is not about authoritative dictation, rather that the individual has freedom to engage in personal thinking and 'intellectual initiative', but within a social context.

Newer Forms of Space – The Makerspace

There is no definitive definition of a 'makerspace' reflecting its heterogeneous dimensions and newness of spatial form. It is not a word found in the *Oxford English Dictionary*. Moreover, definitions in scholarly materials are rare. Sleigh et al. (2015) define a makerspace as

> ... an open access space (free or paid), with facilities for different practices, where anyone can come and make something. (ibid., p. 2)

However, this is a very generic statement which reveals little about those who are 'anyone' and why they have an ongoing engagement. Instead, it is to the practising makerspace community that one needs to turn. An online search reveals the website www.makerspace.com. This explains that a makerspace is

> ... a collaborative work space inside a school, library or separate public/private facility for making, learning, exploring and sharing that uses high tech to no tech tools. These spaces are open to kids, adults, and entrepreneurs and have a variety of maker equipment including 3D printers, laser cutters, cnc machines, soldering irons and even sewing machines ... It's more of the maker mindset of creating something out of nothing and exploring your own interests that's at the core of a makerspace ... Makerspaces are also fostering entrepreneurship and are being utilized as incubators and accelerators for business startups. (Makerspaces.com, 2014–2017)

It also presents over 15 other definitions, drawing attention to activities such as build, create, 'make meaning', risk-take, craft, tinker, wonder, experiment, collaborate, explore and socialize. A further online search reinforces this diversity of interpretation with additional operative concepts including dream, fail, problem-solve, innovate, share and play. The message is that, since such spaces are so diverse, then it is perhaps unproductive to attempt a precise definition of makerspace. Instead, it is considered more important to think of makerspaces in terms of a physical space, operated collectively, in which people do things in accord to the spirit created for the space, irrespective of what this is called (e.g. hackerspace, hackspace, fab lab, techshop, repair café, refab space).

The ethos of this space is liberating, social, non-judgemental and non-conformist. Individuals can be true to themselves in what they are doing, working with people they can trust. Venue is important in the sense of how it shapes the learning of those engaged in the space. While a hackspace in a rented property may support informal learning, exploration and the making of mistakes, an institutional setting may impose a more structured approach (Halverson and Sheridan, 2014; Hsu et al., 2017). Lande and Jordan (2014) categorize the different types of makerspaces as shared co-working, collaborative clubhouse, library community centre, school innovation space, science museum for informal education and for-profit shops (e.g. TechShop).

Further, the interplay of the physical space with the affordances of Web 2.0 should not be overlooked and moreover can be considered a key contributor to their growing global reach and development. The majority of makerspaces operate with a parallel online virtual environment (Eaves, 2014a, 2014b; Davies, 2017), which may include websites, social media pages, image sites (e.g. Flickr) and wikis. These typically provide advice to would-be makers on starting new spaces, and make public key information on current projects, events, membership options and opening hours for those already operating. They also provide key conduits for makers within a space, or across spaces, to communicate, make decisions and share design schemas. The core communication devices are email listings, often split into multiple lists grouped by the nature of the discussion (finance, event planning, etc.) and which enable a continuation of in-person conversations and use of the IRC – internet relay chat.

The transformational nature of makerspaces has led to the proposition that they characterize a 'new industrial revolution' (Gershenfeld, 2012) which connects to broader developments in society. Naboni and Paoletti (2015) claim that this is the 'third industrial revolution'; the first industrial revolution characterized by mechanization, the second by mass production, while the third is 'characterized by affordable manufacturing tools connected to the internet' (ibid., p. 16). While the twentieth century saw the democratization of information, Bull et al. (2010) proposed that the twenty-first century symbolizes the 'democratization of production through personal fabrication' (Bull et al., 2010, p. 331).

A comparable view is presented by Fox (2014), which views the makerspace and previous developments in terms of their DIY aspects. The first wave (subsistence DIY) reflects what is grown and made, without recourse to markets. The second wave (industrial DIY) is characterized by bought kits for self-assembly (e.g. furniture). The third wave (new DIY or Do-It-Together [DIT]) exploits the functionality of online digital domains with their interactional capability and the mobility of newer digital forms of production technologies (e.g. three-dimensional [3D] printing). This is a field of rapid emergence – four-dimensional printing adds the additional dimension of time, enabling users to build from multiple materials with parts capable of transforming from one shape to another on their own. The capacity to self-assemble, self-fold and shift shape offers an array of new opportunities for DIY and DIT personalized manufacturing alongside new conduits for their distribution (Mao et al., 2015).

While first wave DIY emphasized production for self-consumption, the second wave is characterized by pre-designed goods, lack of access to production capability and limited technical knowledge. The third wave is characterized by sophistication in knowledge, accessible production technologies and entrepreneurial opportunity, though its financing can present a challenge. Within the educational community (e.g. schools, museums, libraries) makerspaces may encourage interest in STEAM (science, technology, engineering, arts and mathematics) (Halverson and Sheridan, 2014; Vossoughi and Bevan, 2014; Bevan et al., 2015; Hsu et al., 2017). Further, their discursive nature and the capacity of advance thinking is emphasized in Brooke's description of such spaces as the 'digital-age equivalent of the English Enlightenment coffee houses' (Brooke, 2012, p. 22).

Makerspaces have emerged in a variety of established venues: public libraries (Slatter and Howard, 2013; Boyle et al., 2016), schools (Blikstein, 2013; Vossoughi and Bevan, 2014; Halverson and Sheridan, 2014), universities (Barrett et al., 2015; Burke, 2015; Wong and Partridge, 2016; Shapiro, 2016) and museums (Bevan et al., 2015). This reflects the growing awareness of the potential for public spaces to attract members of the local community. They provide opportunities for co-creation and knowledge sharing ('open design') (Neves and Mazzilli, 2013) as well as for professional development (Paganelli et al., 2016) and entrepreneurship (Mortara and Parisot, 2016, 2017). However, these spaces have been questioned with regard to barriers to women giving rise to gender bias (Lewis, 2015; Richards, 2016) as well as having limited accessibility for the disabled (Brady et al., 2014). To add are debates on whether makerspaces contribute to sustainability and, if so, how they do so (Maldini, 2016; Nascimento et al., 2016). Particular type of events associated with makerspaces are hackathons and Maker Faires (Dougherty, 2012; Johnson and Robinson, 2014; Komssi et al., 2015; Irani, 2015; Criado and Otárola, 2016). While the latter offer opportunities for people from different makerspaces to share, the former are intensive experiences where, over a few days, groups of people can creatively address specific challenges. This introductory overview of makerspaces highlights some of the core discussions about their inclusivity and how the concept of a makerspace has shifted from an exclusive domain for like-minded persons into a more inclusive community through public venues. More importantly, it hints at the diversity that characterizes the makerspace community.

This diversity is revealed further in a detailed empirical study of the 97 UK makerspaces identified at the time, conducted by Sleigh et al. (2015), which led to a publically available rich dataset (Nesta, 2015). Our analysis of this dataset suggests that there is a generic conceptual model which characterizes these spaces (Figure 3). Central is the notion of a space which is occupied with the facilities, tools, materials and people that combine to support the activity of the maker, typically complemented by the affordances of virtual space.

Second is the manner in which the space is controlled or regulated (i.e. governance), drawing attention to such issues as funding (e.g. sponsorship or membership fees), management (e.g. legal structure) and ownership (i.e. influence upon activity or ability to withdraw space) — each of which play a role in the survival of the space and its development over time. Third is the relationship between the local community and the space and whether there are explicit or veiled issues about who can and cannot become a maker. Finally, is the nature of the experience itself (e.g. empowering, learning, making, socializing) and the norms that govern what is and what is not acceptable. Collectively this creates the culture — the defining spirit in which learning and creativity is encouraged to foster and what this might lead to. Identity and ideology is central in this determination of what a space is and what it may evolve to, establishing its uniqueness.

Case Study

The object of this longitudinal study is urban and well-established makerspaces across the United Kingdom, with more recent expansion into developing nations. The aim is to provide insight into the characteristics, ethos and practices of these spaces, notably with respect to the nature of the individual and social learning experiences that can be fostered, and their implications for more formal learning environments. It offers an accumulative and reflective account of the empirical mixed methods research undertaken, alongside active participation as a mentor in several settings. The approach is considered highly illustrative of the heterogeneity of the community, with experience gained in independent spaces located in the creative quarter of a city, to spaces embedded or affiliated to a university or council regeneration programme.

Thematic vignettes are drawn from this depth and breadth of research and experience as gained over more than five years, endeavouring to enable the voices of the participants to be foregrounded and

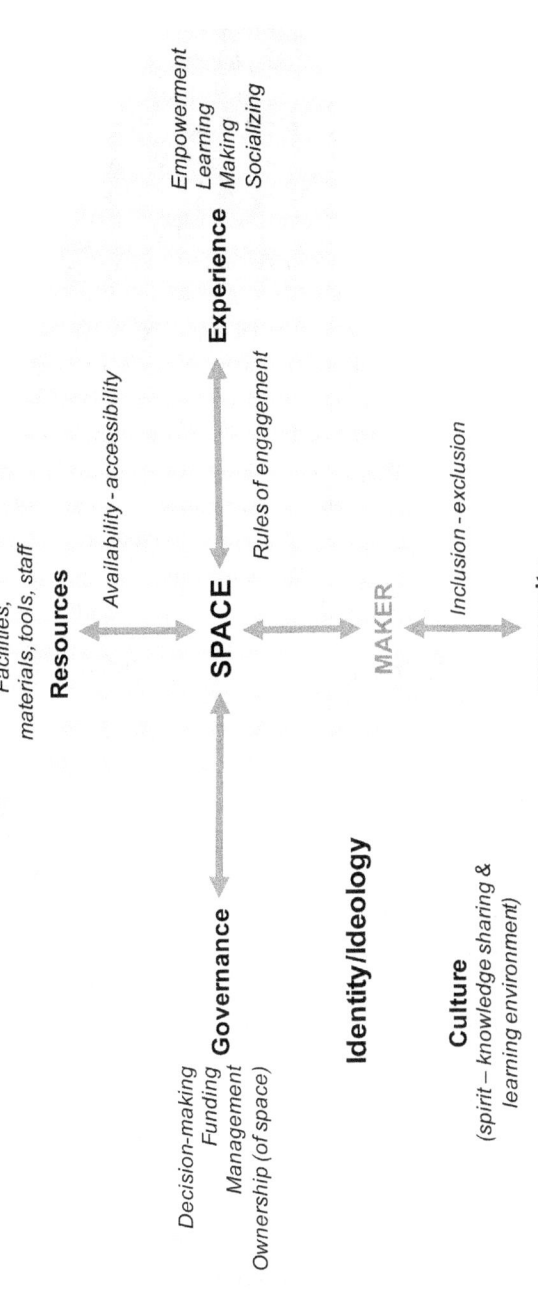

Figure 3: Conceptualizing Makerspaces (Based upon Analysis of NESTA, 2015). (The solid area denotes the space of an individual within the collective space of the makerspace — semi-shaded area — characterized by its identity, culture and governance mechanisms.)

elucidating the core realities of such spaces, while acknowledging that each is unique. Drawing on 'experience-near' methods (Estrella and Forinash, 2007, p. 382) and in the spirit of Dewey, this approach also responds to increasing calls to 'relocate academic inquiry within the realm of local, personal, everyday places and events' (Finley, 2008, p. 72).

Particular focus is afforded to Access Space (2017) in Sheffield, given its pivotal role and pioneering position within the United Kingdom, first opening in 2000 and remaining the longest running and open access media lab in the country. There are no cost or entry requirements for interested participants – it is available so that *anyone can take part*, perhaps making this one of the purest forms of makerspace observed to date. Indeed, operating under registered charity status by volunteers and with a keen interest in local social action outcomes, 50 per cent of participants at activities run at the space have been in 'danger of exclusion and are on the margins of society'. Access Space provides resources and skill development across a spectrum that includes open source software, web development, photography, art, audio/visual digital skills and fabrication, notably 3D printing and laser cutting.

The second space drawn on in depth is Bristol Hackspace (2017), which was founded in 2009 as a limited company before becoming a social enterprise in 2011. Its stated aim is to 'open up technology to anybody who takes an interest in it'. In common with Access Space, this lab is committed to an ethos of encouraging making and unmaking to understand how things work and to the open sharing of the knowledge gained in doing so. In contrast to Access Space, aside from a weekly public open evening, a monthly subscription (typically £10–20) is required to become a member with 24-hour access to the hackspace. Activities are primarily individual- and project-based and cover areas such as electronics, robotics, metalwork, woodwork, bike maintenance and crafts, particularly knitting and jewellery making. Strong links are maintained with local technology groups and the wider hackspace community.

The Nature of Learning and a Space to 'Be'

After the triangulation of a depth and breadth of data sources, it is the nature of learning, unlearning and open knowledge sharing that emerges as the central characteristic and enduring ethos of all makerspace forms. Indeed, the nature of the space itself can provide a conduit to becoming for its participants. Knowledge is shared primarily peer to peer, within a highly active, engaged and constructive local community.

This can create a virtuous circle of learning as elucidated by one Access Space member 'it is incredible to observe the "newbie" participant evolve to be a mentor themselves — a richly empowering experience'. Knowledge does not develop via a mechanical, linear or formal process towards very specific end goals, but by contrast, is typically a cumulative experience, acquired in a natural, informal and explorative way through iterative practices of making, taking apart and trying again:

> I try something and fail, I tinker a while, change some aspects of the set-up and try again ... the result may not be what I expected but I will notice something else instead and run with that ... it's so often a surprising new direction with expanded possibilities. Yes, that's the best way I can describe what it's like learning here ... It's all about being free to experiment, to tweak, it's fine to fail!!!! Just be curious, ask questions but always seek to find out the why yourself and keep on moving forward — sharing what you find along the way. (Bristol maker)

This reflects how an individual's development can be embedded within the active and facilitative social learning that is taking place as part of the everyday experience of being a community member. The processes of inquiry and of creation are as critical, if not more so, than the actual physical artefact/outcome that may be produced. As one contributor stated, 'My ideas just seem to flow better, things come together when I am working and reusing materials, reshaping and reconstructing them'. In essence, this describes an opening up of opportunity to explore, to experiment, to make and unmake, to build connections and, ultimately, to make meaning of the very experience of doing itself. This ethos is exemplified in the 3D-printed signage found at Access Space (Figure 4).

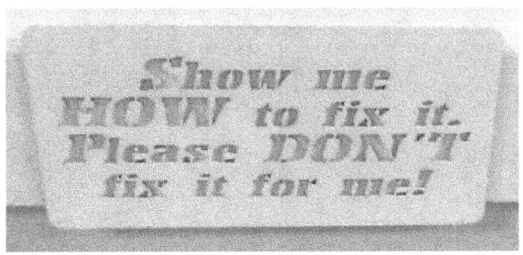

Figure 4:   Signage from Access Space Main Lab.

This acquisition of knowledge and expertise alongside personal growth acquires further legitimization from the prominent and everyday display of participant artefacts in many spaces. At Access Space, this is taken a stage further with dedicated exhibition evenings. These are occasions where contributors have literally taken an identical blank canvas and transformed it in any way that 'mattered to them' as illustrated in Figure 5. Both forms of showcasing make a difference – this is not a case of 'art for art's sake' (Abrams and Harpham, 2009, p. 4). The artefacts highlight the individuality of participant works: '*their* interests, *their* creativity and *their* priorities, congruent with a *do-ocracy* ethos' (Chen, 2009, p. 55). Further, meaning can be elaborated collectively within a social context, the intersubjective process of which can also support empowering participant transitions often associated with their sense of identity. As one participant stated, 'I never saw myself as an artist at all, nobody else would give me this opportunity. I can now say I have exhibited'!

Finally, the very nature of space is brought into sharp focus. With regard to physical design, features such as clearly identifiable activity zones, connective walkways to enable easy flow between areas and provision of informal seating can facilitate a balance between quiet individual working and opportunities for socialization and creative discovery which can 'bring the unexpected together'.

These spaces are much more than a specific local setting with practical affordances, even including the virtual space that typically provides

Figure 5: A 20×20 Canvas Exhibition at Access Space.

ongoing local support. It is the people within the makerspace and their shared sense of purpose which defines what a particular setting is all about, how it operates and the ways in which it can evolve over time. This can also prove an area of tension where a founder member(s) retain strongly held views regarding the ideology of a space and who can or cannot participate – yet a burgeoning community and the impact of new members may evolve the character, focus, aspirations and overarching trajectory.

This tension is evidenced online and offline, most explicitly via open discussion threads that provide a rich window into the development of these issues, and different approaches to mitigate them over time. Access Space, for example, was open to work alongside researchers to help surface the key themes and build towards a consensus around its underlying superordinate goal, while debating areas such as governance, structure and roles (Eaves and Walton, 2013). Today Access Space foregrounds inclusivity, bringing people from different backgrounds together to share and develop skills, working on creative, enterprising and technical projects. The founder left to establish a new making centre in the same city combining craft shop, facilities such as laser cutting and evening skills workshops, run by the crafters themselves.

Space therefore has highly emotive, cognitive, reflective, identity-linked and ideological dimensions which change with time and experience. It is associated with shared ownership and self-permission, with the cumulative voices of participants, suggesting that it scaffolds the process of 'letting-go'. Indeed, it is clear that makerspaces are highly liminal (Küpers, 2011) – offering a place to transition, to become and to simply just be.

> Nothing about our space is fixed or final – our future is driven by our members, by us. We are what we are because of the people here and we will grow as our people do. (Long-term Bristol participant)

Discussion and Conclusion

The case study reveals a particular form of space (makerspace) that breaks with the formal educational spaces that comprise today's schools, colleges and universities. Implicit is a form of learning that contrasts with the more traditional forms of education found in these formal settings. These newer forms of space are characterized by access to both resources and pools of knowledge, but of a form and use different from existing formal locales. Resources are not those typically found in formal spaces (e.g. texts) that are geared to the requirements of institutional educational demands, but instead, offer facilities to make things which cater to more personal motivations (e.g. 3D printer, laser cutter). The pools of knowledge are not those in authority whose role is to educate, but rather comprise the members of the community that constitute the space, where knowledge is openly shared as required.

Conditions have been created in these spaces to foster inclusivity, accessibility, sharing, opportunity and discovery of self. Importantly, these spaces are embedded in their local community. Like the formal spaces, these newer settings highlight the importance of learning, but in an informal and organic manner. Learning is by trying, tweaking, experimenting, fusing and failing, with no judgement or recrimination. Opportunities to explore one's (unconventional − impossible) ideas can lead to a transformation of self − the creation of something not thought possible and the realization of achievements. Exhibition of these achievements enables this discovered self to be better understood and expressed. These issues are revealed in Figure 3, where the space is the point of confluence whereby members of the community can engage with each other in shared experiences, and individuals can realize their self. However, no two spaces are the same. Each has a unique identity shaped by the way in which the space is owned, funded and managed (Governance) and the underlying ideology that guides how things are done (Culture) (Figure 6).

Figure 6: A Quiet Zone at Bristol Hackspace.

This insight into the nature of makerspaces appears to strongly resonate with Dewey's distinction between the formal traditional schooling system and how it may be informed by the more natural experience-grounded approach that typifies informal out-of-school learning. A makerspace is an experientially oriented learning environment, which should comprise a genuine maker community entwined within the larger community. It should be a safe trusting space, with a social spirit, where, though the sharing of expertise, people can make possible their imagination. It should allow personal development, so can foster education, but of a highly applied and engaged nature, with the maker active and constructive in trying to make things work – continually experimenting, reflecting and learning from mistakes. It is a mode of inquiry or a form of research, where trial and error are the norms in the search for a solution to whatever it is that is being attempted. Most importantly, it should be a democratic space that is accessible, inclusive and participatory, with its participants being considerate, open and respectful to others. It allows for the breakdown 'of those barriers of class, race, and national territory' (Dewey, 1916, p. 101).

The implications of the insight provided by Dewey's *D&E* (1916), the literatures relating to makerspaces and the case study itself are threefold. First, the implications for formal educational institutions. The growing recognition of the value of makerspaces has resulted in their emergence in schools (Blikstein, 2013; Vossoughi and Bevan, 2014; Halverson and Sheridan, 2014), colleges and universities (Barrett et al., 2015; Burke, 2015; Wong and Partridge, 2016; Shapiro, 2016). However, do these offer a complement to the more traditional curriculum or should they be embedded as part of the curriculum? For example, makerspaces can provide facilities to do things that can be related to project and coursework and naturally support interdisciplinary learning.

Second, Dewey makes the distinction between the development of a person's latent powers to accomplish 'practical and professional duties' and the development of the independently thinking individual, as a member of a community. The makerspace offers the individual the opportunity to engage in learning to make something using the latest of technologies, which has the possibility of providing self-employment. While makerspaces can satisfy personal interest, they also offer entrepreneurial avenues to sell and scale what is built (Mortara and Parisot, 2016, 2017). Are makerspaces the incubators of the 'third industrial revolution' (Naboni and Paoletti, 2015), which can thereby play a pivotal role in the much-debated future of work itself?

The third issue relates to inclusivity. A perennial concern relating to science and technology fields is the perceived exclusivity of these domains to women – they remain male-dominated environments (UNESCO, 2017). This can extend to makerspaces with their hands-on orientations utilizing newer forms of technology as discussed by Lewis (2015) and Richards (2016). As community-embedded ventures, such as in public libraries (Slatter and Howard, 2013; Boyle et al., 2016) museums and schools, by virtue of these being inclusive community spaces, they offer the opportunity to break down this perceived exclusivity and encourage, not only women and girls, but others from disadvantaged social groups, to engage in STEAM activities (Halverson and Sheridan, 2014; Vossoughi and Bevan, 2014; Bevan et al., 2015; Hsu et al., 2017).

To conclude, whatever has transpired between the publication of Dewey's *D&E* (1916) and the present, his vision of the empowered individual clearly manifests in a space perhaps not envisaged by Dewey. This space, the makerspace, allows an individual to break free from the limitations of the formal educational system and as part of a social learning community, discover their potential in new, natural and perhaps unexpected ways. This raises an important point to reflect upon – are these new learning spaces becoming the catalysing incubators of a new renaissance for prosumers and for a democracy of production? If this is the case and with increased awareness of these spaces, individuals have a capability to design and build for their future that is only limited by their capacity to imagine it.

References

Abrams, M. and Harpham, G. (2009), *A Glossary of Literary Terms*. (9th Ed.). Boston, MA: Wadsworth Cengage Learning.

Access Space (2017), *Making and unmaking* [online]. Available at: http://accessspace.org/ (accessed 30.03.17).

Atkinson, P. (2006), Introduction: do it yourself: democracy and design. *Journal of Design History*, 19 (1), 1–10.

Barrett, T., Pizzico, M., Levy, B. D., Nagel, R. L., Linsey, J. S., Talley, K. G., Forest, C. R. and Newstetter, W. C. (2015), *A Review of University Maker Spaces*, Georgia Institute of Technology, Atlanta, GA [online]. Available at: https://smartech.gatech.edu/handle/1853/53813 (accessed 30.03.17).

Bevan, B., Gutwill, J. P., Petrich, M. and Wilkinson, K. (2015), Learning through STEM-rich tinkering: findings from a jointly negotiated research project taken up in practice. *Science Education*, 99 (1), 98–120.

Blikstein, P. (2013), Digital fabrication and 'making' in education: the democratization of invention. In J. Walter-Herrmann and C. Büching (Eds.), *FabLabs: of Machines, Makers, and Inventors*. Bielefeld: Transcript Publisher.

Boyle, E., Collins, M., Kinsey, R., Noonan, C. and Pocock, A. (2016), Making the case for creative spaces in Australian libraries. *The Australian Library Journal*, 65 (1), 30–40.

Brady, T., Salas, C., Nuriddin, A., Rodgers, W. and Subramaniam, M. (2014), Makeability: creating accessible makerspace events in a public library. *Public Library Quarterly*, 33 (4), 330–347.

Bristol Hackspace (2017), *Welcome* [online]. Available at: http://bristol.hackspace.org.uk/ (accessed 30.03.17).

Brooke, H. (2012), *The Revolution Will Be Digitised: Dispatches from the Information War*. London: Windmill Books.

Bull, G., Maddox, C., Marks, G., McAnear, A., Schmidt, D., Schrum, L., Smaldino, S., Spector, M., Sprague, D. and Thompson, A. (2010), Educational implications of the digital fabrication revolution. *Journal of Research on Technology in Education*, 42 (4), 331–338.

Burke, J. (2015), Making sense: can makerspaces work in academic libraries? *Paper Presented at ACRL 2015* [online]. Available at: http://www.ala.org/acrl/acrl/conferences/acrl2015/papers (accessed 30.03.17).

Chen, K. K. (2009), *Enabling Creative Chaos: The Organization Behind the Burning Man Event*. Chicago, IL: University of Chicago Press.

Criado, T. S. and Otárola, M. C. (2016). Urban accessibility issues: techno-scientific democratizations at the documentation interface. *City*, 20 (4), 619–636.

Davies, S. R. (2017), *Hackerspaces: Making the Maker Movement*. Cambridge: Polity Press.

Dewey, J. (1916), *Democracy and Education: An Introduction to the Philosophy of Education*. New York, NY: The MacMillan Company.

Dougherty, D. (2012), The maker movement. *Innovations*, 7 (3), 11–14.

Eaves, S. (2014a), Innovative approaches to knowledge transfer, experiential learning and SME application within business education. In Małgorzata Zięba, M and Zięba, K. (Eds.), *Innovative Approaches to Business Education-Selected Issues*. Denmark Central Region: VIA University College.

Eaves, S. (2014b), Hybrid enterprises in the creative sector: catalysing the co-opportunity of inclusion innovation in the quadruple helix. *British Academy of Management Conference 2014*, 9–11 September 2014, Belfast Waterfront, Belfast, UK.

Eaves, S. and Walton, J (2013), An introduction to STRIKE: STRuctured Interpretation of the Knowledge Environment. In B. Janiunaite, A. Pundziene and M. Petraite (Eds.). *Proceedings of the 14th European Conference on Knowledge Management*. Academic Conferences and Publishing International Limited, pp. 174–183.

Estrella, K. and Forinash, M. (2007), Narrative inquiry and arts-based inquiry: multinarrative perspectives. *Journal of Humanistic Psychology*, 47 (3), 376–383.

Finley, S. (2008), Arts-based research. In G. Knowles and A. Cole (Eds.), *Handbook of the Arts in Qualitative Research: Perspectives, Methodologies, Examples and Issues*. Los Angeles, CA: Sage, pp. 71–82.

Fox, S. (2014), Third Wave Do-It-Yourself (DIY): Potential for prosumption, innovation, and entrepreneurship by local populations in regions without industrial manufacturing infrastructure. *Technology in Society*, 39 (November), 18–30.

Gershenfeld, N. (2012), How to make almost anything: the digital fabrication revolution. *Foreign Affairs*, 91 (6), 43–57.

Halverson, E. R. and Sheridan, K. (2014), The maker movement in education. *Harvard Educational Review*, 84 (4), 495–504.

Hsu, Y. C., Baldwin, S. and Ching, Y. H. (2017), Learning through making and maker education. *TechTrends*, 1–6. doi:10.1007/s11528-017-0172-6

Irani, L. (2015), Hackathons and the making of entrepreneurial citizenship. *Science, Technology, & Human Values*, 40 (5), 799–824.

Johnson, P. and Robinson, P. (2014), Civic hackathons: innovation, procurement, or civic engagement? *Review of Policy Research*, 31 (4), 349–357.

Komssi, M., Pichlis, D., Raatikainen, M., Kindström, K. and Järvinen, J. (2015), What are hackathons for? *IEEE Software*, 32 (5), 60–67.

Küpers, W. (2011), Dancing on the limen – embodied and creative inter-places as thresholds of be(com)ing: phenomenological perspectives on liminality and transitional spaces in organisation and leadership. *Tamara: Journal for Critical Organization Inquiry*, 9 (3–4), 45–59.

Lande, M. and Jordan, S. (2014), Making It Together, Locally: A Making Community Learning Ecology in the Southwest USA. *Frontiers in Education Conference (FIE), 2014 IEEE*.

Lewis, J. (2015), *Barriers to Women's Involvement in Hackspaces and Makerspaces* [online]. Available at: http://access-space.org/wp-content/uploads/2015/10/Barriers-to-womens-involvemen (accessed 18.03.17).

Makerspaces.com (2014–2017), Available at: www.makerspaces.com/what-is-a-makerspace/ (accessed 19.03.17).

Maldini, I. (2016), Attachment, durability and the environmental impact of digital DIY. *The Design Journal*, 19 (1), 141–157.

Mao, Y., Yu, K., Isakov, M. S., Wu, J., Dunn, M. L. and Jerry Qi, H. (2015), Sequential self-folding structures by 3D printed digital shape memory polymers. *Scientific Report*, 5, Article number: 13616.

Mortara, L. and Parisot, N. G. (2016), Through entrepreneurs' eyes: the Fab-spaces constellation. *International Journal of Production Research*, 54 (23), 7158–7180.

Mortara, L. and Parisot, N. G. (2017), How Do fab-spaces enable entrepreneurship? Case Studies of 'Makers' – Entrepreneurs. *International Journal of Manufacturing Technology and Management*. (Special Issue: 3D Printing: The Next Industrial Revolution).

Naboni, R. and Paoletti, I. (2015), *Advanced Customization in Architectural Design and Construction*. Cham: Springer.

Nascimento, S., Pólvora, A., Paio, A., Oliveira, S., Rato, V., Oliveira, M. J., Varela, B. and Sousa, J. P. (2016), Sustainable technologies and transdisciplinary futures: from collaborative design to digital fabrication. *Science as Culture (London)*, 25 (4), 520–537.

Nesta (2015), *UK Makerspaces: The Data: Open Dataset of UK Makerspaces* [online]. Available at: http://www.nesta.org.uk/uk-makerspaces-data (accessed 18.03.17).

Neves, H. and Mazzilli, C. D. T. S. (2013), Open design – a map of contemporary Open Design structures and practices. *10th European Academy of Design Conference–Crafting the future* [online]. Available at: https://heloisaneves.com/2013/03/12/open-design-a-map-of-contemporary-open-design-structures-and-practices/ (accessed 18.03.17).

Paganelli, A., Cribbs, J. D., 'Silvie'Huang, X., Pereira, N., Huss, J., Chandler, W. and Paganelli, A. (2016), The makerspace experience and teacher professional development. *Professional Development in Education*, 1–4.

Richards, J. (2016), Shifting gender in electronic music: DIY and maker communities. *Contemporary Music Review*, 35 (1), 40–52.

Shapiro, S. D. (2016), Engaging a wider community: the academic library as a center for creativity, discovery, and collaboration. *New Review of Academic Librarianship*, 22 (1), 24–42.

Slatter, D. and Howard, Z. (2013), A place to make, hack, and learn: makerspaces in Australian public libraries. *The Australian Library Journal*, 62 (4), 272–284.

Sleigh, A., Stewart, H. and Stokes, K. (2015), Open Dataset of UK Makerspaces: A User's Guide. Nesta, London.

UNESCO (2017), *Improving Measurement of Gender Equality in STEM*. Available at: http://www.unesco.org/new/en/natural-sciences/priority-areas/gender-and-science/improving-measurement-of-gender-equality-in-stem/ (accessed 30.03.17).

Vossoughi, S. and Bevan, B. (2014), *Making and Tinkering: A Review of the Literature*. National Research Council Committee on Out of School Time. STEM, pp. 1–55.

Wong, A. and Partridge, H. (2016), Making as learning: makerspaces in universities. *Australian Academic & Research Libraries*, 47 (3), 143–159.

Chapter 3

Constructing Creative Democracy at School by Reading the Classics: A Dialogue between Martha Nussbaum and John Dewey

Gonzalo Jover, Rosario González Martín and Juan Luis Fuentes

Abstract

The year 2016 marked the 100th anniversary of *Democracy and Education*, one of John Dewey's most widely translated and published books around the world still in the author's lifetime. Nowadays, in a context in which pedagogy is bogged down in 'economicism' and suspicion towards any proposal that hints of value, Dewey's ideas once again provide a ray of hope for a possible future. One of the contemporary authors that has fostered this hopeful reading of Dewey is Martha C. Nussbaum, whose appeal to bringing the humanities back to schools motivated a project on approaching the classic texts with the Information and Communication Technologies (ICTs), which we have developed during the past years with secondary education students from three schools in Santiago de Chile, Madrid and London. The project is based on an open reading of Sophocles's *Antigone* through an online application that enables students from the participating schools to interact. This chapter delves deeper into the theoretical bases of the project. In the first two sections, we analyse the interpretation that Nussbaum and Dewey each made of *Antigone*. Then, in the third, we present the Antigone project as a learning experience promoting a creative democracy, as Dewey called it.

Keywords: Creative democracy; *Antigone*; digital humanities; international citizenship education; Dewey; Nussbaum

Introduction

Last year marked the 100th anniversary of *Democracy and Education*, one of John Dewey's most widely translated and published books around the world even in the author's lifetime. After years of being eclipsed, pragmatism re-emerged in the 1980s, sparking new interest in the American pedagogue and his work. However, readings of Dewey today differ greatly from those a hundred years ago, when many regarded pragmatism as a risk. Nowadays, in a context in which pedagogy is bogged down in 'economicism' and suspicion towards any proposal that hints of value, pragmatism once again provides a ray of hope for a possible future (Jover, 2016a).

One of the contemporary authors who has fostered this hopeful reading of Dewey is Martha Nussbaum. In *Not for Profit: Why Democracy Needs the Humanities*, Nussbaum recounts the following scene that took place at the same school Dewey had headed a hundred years earlier:

> In November 2005, a teachers' retreat was held at the Laboratory School in Chicago – the school, on the campus of my own university, where John Dewey conducted his pathbreaking experiments in democratic education reform, the school where President Barack Obama's daughters spent their early formative years. The teachers had gathered to discuss the topic of education for democratic citizenship, and they considered a wide range of educational experiments, studying figures ranging from Socrates to Dewey in the Western tradition to the closely related ideas of Tagore in India. But something was clearly amiss. The teachers – who take pride in stimulating children to question, criticize, and imagine – expressed anxiety about the pressures they face from wealthy parents who send their kids to this elite school. Impatient with allegedly superfluous skills, and intent on getting their

children filled with testable skills that seem likely to produce financial success, these parents are trying to change the school's guiding vision. They seem poised to succeed. (Nussbaum, 2010, p. 4)

Nussbaum invokes Dewey in her defence of a liberal education based on cultivating the humanities, which runs against the priority of economic objectives made manifest in this scene, and prizes critical thinking, creative imagination and empathy. In her view, recovering that form of education constitutes a requirement 'in keeping democracies alive and wide awake' (ibid., p. 10), that is to uphold the type of democracy as an ethical ideal as Dewey proposed in chapter 7 of *Democracy and Education*, where he defined it as 'a mode of associated living' (Dewey, 1930 [1916], pp. 94–116).

Nussbaum's appeal to bringing the humanities back to schools motivated the venture 'Rereading the classic texts with the ICTs: a citizenship and intercultural project based on Dewey's democratic concept of education', which we have developed over the past three years with secondary education students from three schools in Santiago de Chile, Madrid and London (Jover et al., 2015). The project is based on an open reading of Sophocles's *Antigone* through an online application that enables students from the participating schools to interact. For researchers, the project also offers a glimpse into how students construct their civic values in the purest Dewey tradition of democracy as 'conjoint communicated experience' (Dewey, 1930 [1916], p. 101). Nevertheless, this alliance between Nussbaum and Dewey harbours a paradox. The rise of pragmatism has often been seen as a factor responsible for the decline of the humanities in the curriculum, and many of the controversies sparked by the directions education is taking in our so-called knowledge society, hearken back to the dispute between John Dewey and Robert Maynard Hutchins in the 1930s regarding what the latter deemed the nefarious influence of pragmatism on higher education (Jover, 2016b). In fact, as Nussbaum herself acknowledges (Nussbaum, 2010, pp. 121–122), Dewey was as opposed to a professional education stripped of its scientific and social underpinnings as he was to a liberal education devoid of the conditions of life of the time.

Our aim in this chapter is to delve deeper into the theoretical basis of the above-mentioned project. In the first two sections, we analyse the reading that Nussbaum and Dewey each made of *Antigone*. In the third section, we present the project as a learning experience promoting a creative democracy, as Dewey called it.

On *Antigone* and Nussbaum

Antigone takes place at the end of the siege of *Seven against Thebes*. Polynices, son of Oedipus, has fought against the city to seize power from his brother Etheocles. In the struggle, Oedipus's sons mortally wound each other. Creon declares that Polynices's body must remain unburied, exposed to degeneration and left as fodder for the carrion animals. Antigone, who is sister of the two fighters, refuses to obey the order and is captured while trying to honour her brother's body. At the moment of her arrest, she implores Creon in her defence:

> Yes. Zeus did not announce those laws to me. And Justice living with the gods below sent no such laws for men. I did not think anything which you proclaimed strong enough to let a mortal override the gods and their unwritten and unchanging laws. They're not just for today or yesterday, but exist forever, and no one knows where they first appeared. So I did not mean to let a fear of any human will lead to my punishment among the gods. I know all too well I'm going to die – how could I not? – it makes no difference what you decree. (Sophocles, *Antigone*, pp. 450–462)

The play has been the object of attention of numerous philosophers, especially since the nineteenth century, as George Steiner pointed out in his now classic treatise on the matter (Steiner, 1996). Among the different readings of the play, the centreline around which all others are placed, by affirmation or negation, is Hegel's, who considered it 'one of the most sublime, and in every respect most consummate work of art human effort ever produced' (Hegel, 1920 [1835], vol. II, p. 215). In Hegel's interpretation, the two sides at the heart of the contention embody a relation based on separate unilateral truths. In his *Lectures on Aesthetics* he wrote:

> The public law of the State and the instinctive family-love and duty towards a brother are here set in conflict. Antigone, the woman, is pathetically possessed by the interest of family; Creon, the man, by the welfare of the community. Polynices, in war with his own father-city, had fallen before the gates of Thebes, and Creon, the lord thereof, had by means of a public proclamation threatened

> everyone with death who should give this enemy of the city the right of burial. Antigone, however, refused to accept this command, which merely concerned the public weal, and, constrained by her pious devotion for her brother, carried out as sister the sacred duty of interment. In doing this she relied on the law of the gods. The gods, however, whom she thus revered, are the *Dei inferi* of Hades, the instinctive Powers of feeling, Love and kinship, not the daylight gods of free and self-conscious, social, and political life. (ibid.)

In Hegel's dialectic, moral progress requires conflict between both perspectives, such that Antigone cannot be a heroine and Creon cannot be a tyrant. Nevertheless, not all readings share this vision, and Hegel's acquittal of Creon is sometimes seen as a justification of statism (Steiner, 1996, pp. 37–42). Nussbaum is among those who distance themselves from this reading.

Nussbaum analyses Sophocles's play in *The Fragility of Goodness: Luck and Ethics in Greek Tragedy and Philosophy*, originally published in 1986 and revised in 2001. The author rereads and interprets the Greeks to understand their proposals on articulating goods in favour of building a more harmonious society. In this text, she reflects on *Antigone*, and contrasts her view with those of Hegel's. To Nussbaum, Creon and Antigone represent a simplification of the structure of value commitments by stepping back from values that may come into conflict. Nussbaum states that this perspective 'has become firmly entrenched in modern thought' (Nussbaum, 2001, p. 51). Unlike with Hegel, she finds the content of Antigone's decision much more acceptable than Creon's. In a deep analysis of the characters, Nussbaum shows us how Creon reduces good to the 'good of the city' without acknowledging the individual demands, desires and purposes of the citizens, thereby ignoring any conflict that may arise in their articulation.

> Antigone, however, shows a deeper understanding of the community and its values than Creon does when she argues that the obligation to bury the dead is an unwritten law, which cannot be set aside by the decree of a particular ruler. The belief that not all values are utility-relative, that there are certain claims whose neglect will prove deeply destructive of communal attunement and individual character, is a part of Antigone's position left untouched by

the play's implicit criticism of her single-mindedness ...
There is a complexity in Antigone's virtue that permits
genuine sacrifice *within* the defence of piety (ibid.,
pp. 66–67, emphasis in the original).

Even so, Antigone does not acknowledge all the claims stemming from her appeal to the law of the gods: 'Justice is up here in the city, as well as below the earth' (ibid., p. 65).

Both characters hold a narrow view of 'good', a reduction aimed at removing any tension or conflict in deliberating on their action. To Nussbaum, *Antigone* is precisely a tale on deliberation and prudence. The main characters avoid conflict and simplify their arguments, but this leads them to tragedy. At the end of the play they find themselves facing the tragic outcomes of their stances. Creon acknowledges his mistake, referring to his son Haemon, stating 'I, I killed you, unhappy that I am – I, I say it truly' (*Antigone*, 1318–19). Antigone becomes afraid of death, which she had not feared before, thinking of the children she would never bear, torn at the conflict between her brother's interment and the good of the city. She reproaches the gods for this conflict.

To Hegel, Sophocles's play shows us 'the annulment of *contradictions* viewed as such, in the reconciliation of the forces of human action, which alternately strive to negate each other in their conflict' (Hegel, 1920 [1835], vol. IV, p. 321, cited in Nussbaum, 2001, p. 67, emphasis in Hegel's original). However, for Nussbaum, Sophocles's intention goes much further than that. An analysis of the words, the imagery offered, the incidents and their constant reinterpretation lead her to state that deliberation and prudence are more complicated than the harmonization and reconciliation of tensions. The play not only shows Antigone's and Creon's clear line of reasoning, but it also shows the sentinel's hesitation, the sensitivity to the particular, in which 'correct choice (or: good interpretation) is, first and foremost, a matter of keenness and flexibility of perception, rather than of conformity to a set of simplifying principles' (ibid., p. 69). The correct choice cannot be separated from the appraisal made in the emotional reaction. We can only carry out suitable deliberation if we go beyond a purely intellectual deliberation and also attend to the values underlying passion, tenderness or grief. 'The Sophoclean soul is more like Heraclitus's image of *psuche*: a spider sitting in the middle of its web, able to feel and respond to any tug in any part of the complicated structure' (ibid.). This form of deliberation and prudence, sensitivity and response to values and the conflict that arises from them, places us on a different plane from Hegel's.

To Nussbaum, conflicts cannot be settled by appealing to 'any harmonizing view of the state' (ibid., p. 74). The Hegelian city is obliged to make a choice to achieve harmony, and if 'it makes a serious attempt to honour all the gods, it must house uneasily those who do not honour one another and delight in facing mortals with conflicts; in which case, again, it ceases to be Hegelian' (ibid., p. 75).

Nussbaum makes no attempt to achieve that harmony. To her, the key of the play is in the appearance of the blind man led by a child. 'In this way, two see from one' (*Antigone*, p. 989), as they travel a 'common road' (*Antigone*, p. 988; ibid., p. 79). As Tiresias urges Creon, walking together requires curing an ill common to all humans: the passion to dominate. Good deliberation, prudence, is related to concession, letting go of stubbornness, and to flexibility. Nussbaum turns to Haemon to point out that in the quest and achievement of the ends, it is important to be receptive to the exterior demands, to cultivate a way of responding flexibly rather than clinging to a rigid position. She writes:

> Haemon's advice is that the true way of being humanly civilized requires the preservation of the mystery and specialness of the external, the preservation, in oneself, of the passions that take one to these mysteries. Such a life has room for love; and it also has room, as Tiresias's life shows, for genuine community and cooperation. Only the person who balances self-protection with yielding in this way can be either a lover or a friend: for the completely passive victim cannot act to help another, and the Creonic agent cannot see otherness. The 'razor's edge of luck' requires in this way the most delicate balance between order and disorder, control and vulnerability. (ibid., p. 81)

In short, Nussbaum understands Sophocles's play as not advocating the elimination of conflict, which she sees as part of progress and enrichment. From this perspective, flexibility is the condition of prudence and deliberation, and of what becomes possible by integrating the values in conflict.

On *Antigone*, Dewey and Democracy

Antigone did not go unnoticed by Dewey, whose links with the classics and Greek philosophy have once again come to the attention of current researchers (Kirby, 2014). Dewey was familiar with the Greek tragic poets, including Sophocles, whom he cites several times, especially in his works on moral philosophy. In his book *Ethics*, Dewey refers to *Antigone* in relation to the significance of Greece in the evolution of ethics. The book published with James Hayden Tufts in 1908 and reissued in 1932 develops ideas previously sketched out by Dewey in *Outlines of a Critical Theory of Ethics*, from 1891, and *The Study of Ethics: A Syllabus*, from 1894. In the latter, Dewey writes:

> The origin of reflective morality was in Greece. Other ethical codes were either customary or else conceived to be absolute emanations from a divine will. The Greek was in the habit of discussing questions regarding ends and means of life. This strengthened by growth of democracy. Also by methods of education, which (in Athens) relied upon appeal to individuals' own intelligence rather than upon conformity to fixed rule. (Dewey, 1894, p. 2)

The main contribution of the Greek world to ethics is the 'opposition between the authority of the group, embodied in custom and institutions, on the one hand, and the urging claims of developing personality, manifest in both intelligence and desire, on the other' (Dewey and Tufts, 2013 [1908], p. 159). Aeschylus, Sophocles and Euripides depicted this conflict in their plays.

Social conditions, commerce, conscience of individual interest, liberation of work, the scientific spirit and dedication to knowledge all unleashed the intellectual forces of individualism, thereby questioning the instituted forms of religious and political authority. This process of breaking away from the conventional forms of authority takes place in two different directions. The first is the direction of a higher reality, which is not the reality given, condemned, as in Plato, to being a world of shadows. This higher reality, the original source of duty, is 'nature' (*physis*), which the sophists confronted with 'custom' or 'convention' (*nomos*). This is the clash Dewey and Tufts find depicted in *Antigone*:

> In the *Antigone* of Sophocles, the command of the ruler is opposed to the 'higher law' of kinship and nature. The law of man is not the law of nature or of God. To disobey this conventional law of man is to be guilty of 'holiest crime'.

> The old standards, both of religion and of political life, crumbled before the analysis of the developing intelligence, and the demand for some standard could be met only by the intelligence itself. (ibid., p. 168)

Dewey in this sense had already referenced the playwrights and Sophocles in *The Study of Ethics: A Syllabus* (Dewey, 1894, p. 3) and in the entry for 'Nature' in the *Dictionary of Philosophy and Psychology*, from 1902, with an explicit allusion to *Antigone*. The play represents the conception of a universal, eternal law of nature whose philosophical underpinnings based on reflection and intellectual investigation would be taken up by Socrates (Dewey, 1902, p. 140).

The second sense of that distancing from the conventional is 'the growing consciousness of the self' (Dewey and Tufts, 2013 [1908], p. 194), a consciousness that would take hold in the pride and self-sufficient endurance of the stoics. The consciousness of the ancients was to a large extent composed of *Nemesis*, the messenger of divine justice and punishment, and *Aidos*, the feeling of shame from public opinion and the higher authority of the gods. And yet in the tragic poets there were already inklings of a more intimate, personal conception. In *Ethics*, Dewey once again turns to Antigone and the line she speaks in the first dialogue with her sister Ismene:

> The whole Antigone of Sophocles is the struggle between obedience to the political rulers and obedience to the higher laws which as 'laws of reverence' become virtually inner laws of duty: 'I know I please the souls I ought to please'. (ibid., p. 195)

All in all, for Dewey and Tufts, Sophocles remains in this process of intimate consciousness, halfway between Aeschylus and Euripides:

> Aeschylus set man over against the gods, subject to their divine laws, but gave little play to human character or conscious self-direction. With Sophocles, the tragic situation was brought more directly into the field of human character, although the conception of destiny and the limitations marked thereby were still the dominant note. With Euripides, human emotions and character are brought into the foreground. (ibid., pp. 193–194)

In the tragedy of Sophocles, convention finally wins out over the laws of nature. Of Antigone, the character, it may be said that like Socrates, she perished 'as the victim of the tragedy of moral progress, of the change from the established to the new' (ibid., p. 168). Dewey cites Hegel's *History of Philosophy* as one of the sources for studying Greek ethics (Dewey, 1894, p. 3) but distances himself from the Hegelian interpretation, which sees Antigone's final submission to the will of the gods as an act of nobility (Hegel, 1995 [1842], vol. 2, p. 93). In Dewey, this submission means that 'the new' is still in the coming. As Karavakou points out, the exception that Hegel found in Socrates and Antigone regarding dissolving the individual ego into the collective 'we' was not enough for Dewey:

> Even in the case of Antigone and Socrates, their protest was expressed in the name of a right given to them by the gods, not a right of personal choice and conscience ... In as much as Dewey was critical of modern abstract individualism and classical liberalism, he was equally critical of the old Hellenic tradition that left no space for individual expressions and social diversity. (Karavakou, 2014, p. 89)

The specialized literature disagrees on the extent to which the initial tie with Hegel and idealism influenced Dewey's pragmatism (Garrison, 2006; Good, 2006; Fairfield, 2010). In his 1930 autobiography *From absolutism to experimentalism*, he recognized the 'permanent deposit' of Hegelianism on his philosophy and his appreciation of Plato. It is worth quoting extensively:

> Acquaintance with Hegel has left a permanent deposit in my thinking. The form, the schematism, of his system now seems to me artificial to the last degree. But in the content of his ideas there is often an extraordinary depth; in many of his analyses, taken out of their mechanical dialectical setting, an extraordinary acuteness. Were it possible for me to be a devotee of any system, I still should believe that there is greater richness and greater variety of insight in Hegel than in any other single systematic philosopher – though when I say this I exclude Plato, who still provides my favourite philosophic reading ... Nothing could be more helpful to present philosophizing than a 'Back to Plato' movement; but it would have to be back to the

dramatic, restless, cooperatively inquiring Plato of the *Dialogues*, trying one mode of attack after another to see what it might yield; back to the Plato whose highest flight of metaphysics always terminated with a social and practical turn, and not to the artificial Plato constructed by unimaginative commentators who treat him as the original university professor. (Dewey, 2008 [1930], pp. 154–155)

Dewey naturalized Hegel, made him more Darwinian (Kloppenberg, 1986; Rorty 1995) and pragmatized Plato. In chapter 7 of *Democracy and Education*, dedicated to 'the democratic conception in education', he made clear what he liked and disliked about the Greek philosopher:

No one could better express than he the fact that a society is stably organized when each individual is doing that for which he has aptitude by nature in such a way as to be useful to others (or to contribute to the whole to which he belongs); and that it is the business of education to discover these aptitudes and progressively to train them for social use. Much which has been said so far is borrowed from what Plato first consciously taught the world. But conditions which he could not intellectually control led him to restrict these ideas in their application. He never got any conception of the indefinite plurality of activities which may characterize an individual and a social group, and consequently limited his view to a limited number of *classes* of capacities and of social arrangements. (Dewey, 1930 [1916], p. 102, emphasis in the original)

Plato has been defined as a moral monist by current political philosophers such as Parekh (2006) for positing that there only exists one good life, relegating the rest to a second level of validity, which situates him as an unsuitable theoretical basis for organizing a multicultural society. Dewey went beyond this analysis. As a philosopher of education, he was interested in the role education played in the Platonic utopia and the consequences this way of thinking has on democracy. To Dewey, the value of pluralism lies not only in the enrichment it lends to social interaction, to which he concedes great importance throughout his pedagogical work, and especially in his proposal for a *common school* (Pring, 2016). Along with this effect, the value of pluralism also lies in the space it gives for personal initiative. Despite the strong social bond among citizens created through education, to Dewey's mind, the Platonic society is not a very democratic one. The social function of education is not merely social; it must also be democratic, preventing the former from absorbing and eliminating the latter, and fully assimilating the individual and his uniqueness by the force of the majority and its needs. Despite their orientation to social contribution, platonic classes are vastly inferior to the diversity that individuals display and have a clear 'subordination of individuality' (Dewey, 1930 [1916], p. 105).

Dewey contrasts Plato's view with Rousseau's, for whom the diversity of human nature is prized and supported in its unfettered development, especially before the coercions and constraints placed by political organizations and the state. 'The emancipated individual was to become the organ and agent of a comprehensive and progressive society' (ibid., p. 107). Even though this formulation places greater value on individuality and its free, unique expression, Dewey warns of its insufficient precision and its mistake in not including the state in its articulation and orientation to the common good. This negation eventually led to mistaking nationalist education for the social function of education, the former being constrained to the national borders, limiting the possibilities of a democratic education understood 'as a freeing of individual capacity in a progressive growth directed to social aims' (ibid., p. 115).

An Educational Experience of Creative Democracy with *Antigone*

Nussbaum and Dewey both drew back from the Hegelian reading of *Antigone*, but for different reasons. As Mougan (2013) notes, Nussbaum's approach to Greek culture has always highlighted the theme of the vulnerability of human beings. To her, the trouble with much of philosophy has been the lack of recognition of the fragile, vulnerable nature of human existence and the attempts to deny it by appealing to grandiose ideas of omnipotence. The Hegelian solution to Antigone's problem strikes her as inappropriate because it involves denying that vulnerability. The same attitude explains her rejection of the forms of social control and of the contractualist theories based on the idea of the self-sufficient individual. In contrast, Nussbaum proposed the need to teach a sense of community aimed at cooperation and reciprocity. For both Nussbaum and Dewey, the essence of democracy is 'the possibility of cooperative and constructive resolution' (ibid.,

p. 85). Unlike Nussbaum, however, Dewey advocated forms of control that would ensure the bases of that construction. That control does not come from the force of any good or ultimate end, of any design, whether human or divine, but from the common interests and associated activity. For Dewey, it is in this lack of design that democracy has its deepest root.

As Bernstein points out, 'democracy was never simply one topic among others for Dewey. All of his thinking – whether concerning education, experience, aesthetics, philosophy, politics, or inquiry – sprang from and led back to reflections on democracy' (Bernstein, 2006, p. 191). Among the texts the American pragmatist dedicated to democracy, there is one that Bernstein considers especially relevant, the short conference called 'Creative Democracy: The Tasks before Us', written by Dewey in 1939 on the occasion of his 80th birthday. Behind his words was the rise of Nazism and the events that set off World War II. At the conference, Dewey developed the notion of democracy as a way of life. As much as this formulation of democracy seemed to him more suitable than others that simply take it as an instrument of governance, he clarified that it may still be taken as a purely external mechanism if one loses sight of the fact that it involves 'a *personal* way of individual life' (Dewey, 2008 [1939], p. 226, emphasis in the original), in other words, a personal way of being that is expressed in everyday attitudes and behaviours. Democracy conceived that way is based on two conditions: (1) faith in the common person's abilities to think and act intelligently and (2) freedom of communication and dialogue as found 'in free gatherings of neighbours on the street corner to discuss back and forth what is read in uncensored news of the day, and in gatherings of friends in the living rooms of houses and apartments to converse freely with one another' (ibid., p. 227).

To characterize this type of democracy, Dewey used the adjective 'creative'. Creative here means there is no predefined end to be achieved, that the fate of human beings is in their hands, that democracy must be reinvented every day, because it constitutes more a way of walking than a finish line to reach. To Bernstein, this is where the radicalness of the concept comes in. 'Situated creativity is one of the most basic categories in Dewey's thinking. The democratic personality is one that is flexible, fallible, experimental, and imaginative' (Bernstein, 2006, p. 203). Dewey's creative democracy implies daring to experiment with ideas, to change them as a result of experience, and a deep respect for and openness to the ideas of others (ibid.). It thus embodies a kind of teaching methodology built upon what he called the *habit of amicable cooperation*, which, as occurs in sports, does not exclude rivalry but does involve deep trust in the capacity for dialogue and in the possibility of being changed by it. In the lead-up to World War II, Dewey turned this habit into the condition of a genuinely democratic faith in peace:

> A genuinely democratic faith in peace is faith in the possibility of conducting disputes, controversies and conflicts as cooperative undertakings in which both parties learn by giving the other a chance to express itself, instead of having one party conquer by forceful suppression of the other – a suppression which is none the less one of violence when it takes place by psychological means of ridicule, abuse, intimidation, instead of by overt imprisonment or in concentration camps. To cooperate by giving differences a chance to show themselves because of the belief that the expression of difference is not only a right of the other persons but is a means of enriching one's own life-experience, is inherent in the democratic personal way of life. (Dewey, 2008 [1939], p. 228)

Dewey's notion of democracy inspired our project 'Rereading the classic texts with ICTs'. One of the main objectives of having our secondary education students at the three schools – in Santiago de Chile, London and Madrid – read *Antigone* is to foster the sort of dialogue that creative democracy needs, and thereby interact with each other. If Sophocles' play captivated the great philosophers, including Dewey and Nussbaum, it can also captivate our students and make them reflect on the great questions and conflicts regarding the city and individual rights, and the complexity of weaving a healthy and sustainable democratic social harmony, creative and capable of including everyone's unique and diverse contribution. Let us therefore take the discussion sparked by *Antigone* to our students' virtual spaces and turn them into the 'living rooms' of which Dewey spoke (ibid., p. 227). We did this by taking Sophocles' text to make an online application with a number of multimedia activities that let students read selected excerpts, mainly ones that reflect the opposing roles of Antigone and Creon, as well as other main characters in the plot, such as Ismene. They also put themselves in the shoes of the main characters by writing a blog telling the story from their point of view which they could then share. The application encouraged them to connect the tale to current events similar to the one in the Greek tragedy by making use of online news, YouTube videos, pictures, audio clips and the like. Finally, they were given the chance to take the author's place and propose an alternative ending that would lead to a more satisfactory solution. They could even intervene by adding a character whom they felt would reflect the possibility of finding a better solution to the conflict.

The students' writings subsequently revealed a significant integration of Sophocles' narrative. This integration is worthwhile pedagogically in terms of literary and historic content. Moreover, it also included the cooperative work of writing up the stories, which were done in groups rather than individually. This obliged the students to take on each character's role and then work with rational argument and emotions in order to understand the different other, as Nussbaum wished. The following excerpt exemplifies how some of the students integrated their story into Sophocles' play in order to provide a new creative and conciliatory vision:

> Suddenly, out of the chorus stood Martinus, one of the elders.
>
> — Martinus: My Lord Creon, we all know that treason must be punished, but what worse punishment than death itself? Polynices confronted his brother and his people, and has already received his punishment.
>
> — Creon: If I do not carry through with my role as King, who will ever respect me? Punishment must be given for offenses against the people of Thebes, the laws must be enforced.
>
> — Martinus: You are right, my liege, treason must be punished by exile. Very well, I propose Polynices be buried in another city and thereby finish out his sentence during his death.

The students recognize the conflict, for example, when they state that 'both uncle and niece want justice to be done from the ethical point of view, but their ethical reasons clash and that leads them to confrontation'. However, often only partial visions of the problem are found, in which one character's perspective is taken and the other's is vilified.

In this regard, it is meaningful to see greater attention received by Antigone or Creon to the detriment of other characters such as Ismene, whose more conciliatory attitude is somewhere between the two stances. For example, the students in this example value Creon's stubbornness in upholding legality and not allowing any rebelliousness, 'so that Thebes can be a well respect and honourable city'. Still, the one who draws more empathetic attitudes from the students is Antigone. In her, they see duty to the sacred, customs, religion and family above the laws. They have her say things such as 'I cannot remain indifferent to the injustices of my uncle'; 'I will go with a calm heart from doing the right thing'; 'I will die happy, defending my blood'.

The students detected several current problems that can be analysed in light of the reflections inspired by Sophocles' play. They made allusions to the situation of the Mapuches in Chile, who some students assimilated with the character of Antigone, putting the state on their side in theory but not in practice. Opposite them they put the upper-class landowners, identifying them with Creon. Moreover, they compared the Greek tragedy to today's labour conflicts in which companies pry into the private life of their workers. They differentiated between workers who accept that reality and those who rebel against it much as Antigone herself behaved. The precarious working conditions of young researchers in the United Kingdom, the refugee situation in Turkey, arrests due to political reasons in Venezuela, the rights of Islamic girls, were other news items cited. In each of them, the students responded to affirming the other, the underdog, the oppressed. They recognized the responsibility of engaging in action to defend the rights of all from a more communitarian perspective. Indeed, they became aware of the immorality of simply ignoring injustices. One student wrote:

> In seeing the number of examples of stories that relate to Antigone that people have come up with I have realised that there are so many things in the world that we need to change and that unfortunately, a lot of the time, we do not realise this or do anything about it. Furthermore, I have learnt more about the relationships between characters in Sophocles' play *Antigone* and I have also come to see that ancient literature, and indeed all literature can teach us things about ourselves and the way we interact with other people.

The students also came up with different solutions to Antigone's death. Some of them advocated exile rather than the inherent evil of the death penalty. Others appealed to Haemon to mediate with his father, or to Teiresias with his ruler, to beg for Antigone's life, sometimes successfully, by using emotional pleas. Yet others suggested Antigone and Haemon to flee, with Creon's permission rather than his having to kill his own son.

Indeed, the students became aware of the need for civic commitment, and not 'just sit there like a lump' in the face of today's injustices. They clearly differentiate between public and private, morality and law, the sacred and the secular, *filia* and *civitas*. They understand that conflict resolution goes through stages: recognizing the rights of all, understanding the importance of hearing the different sides to a problem, widening the focus away from the confrontation of two antagonistic positions. In contrast, when discussing current events, the students characteristically focused only on the underdog, which makes us think about the need to have a more encompassing view of reality that does not reject conflict, as Nussbaum postulated.

Aside from the customary motivation that ensues from using technology, the interaction with students from other places turned out to be one of the most appealing aspects of the experience as it enabled them to find out about social problems in situations and contexts different from their own, from the point of view of adolescents. Moreover, the teachers positively noted the students' opportunity to take on the role of creators of history, which we think is an exercise in that creative democracy as a form of moral attitude as Dewey conceived it:

> So stated, democracy is belief in the ability of human experience to generate the aims and methods by which further experience will grow in ordered richness. Every other form of moral and social faith rests upon the idea that experience must be subjected at some point or other to some form of external control; to some 'authority' alleged to exist outside the processes of experience. Democracy is the faith that the process of experience is more important than any special result attained, so that special results achieved are of ultimate value only as they are used to enrich and order the ongoing process. Since the process of experience is capable of being educative, faith in democracy is all one with faith in experience and education. All ends and values that are cut off from the ongoing process become arrests,

fixations. They strive to fixate what has been gained instead of using it to open the road and point the way to new and better experiences. (Dewey, 2008 [1939], p. 229)

In Dewey, the concepts of democracy and education are intimately related in a pragmatic sense. Just as in Dewey's pragmatic notion of education as 'continuous reconstruction of experience' (Dewey, 1930 [1916], p. 93), there is no outside purpose to guide the process, there is none in his notion of democracy. There is no *telos* to guide human growth, individually or socially. For that reason, just as the only criterion for distinguishing the educational quality of an experience is 'to promote the enriched growth of further experience' (Dewey, 1997 [1938], p. 73), it may also be said that 'the cure for the ills of democracy is more democracy'. Dewey adopts this old adage, clarifying that it does not mean 'introducing more machinery' into the democracy, but 'returning to the idea itself' (Dewey, 1954 [1927], p. 144). With our project on rereading *Antigone*, we have hoped to trigger that return by immersing our students in the context in which democracy itself was born.

References

Bernstein, R. (2006), Creative democracy. The task still before us. In S. G. Davaney and W. G. Frisina (Eds.), *The Pragmatic Century. Conversations with Richard J. Bernstein*. Albany, NY: SUNY Press, pp. 191–203.
Dewey, J. (1894), *The Study of Ethics: A Syllabus*. Ann Arbor, MI: Inland Press.
Dewey, J. (1902), Nature. In J. M. Baldwin (Ed.), *Dictionary of Philosophy and Psychology*, vol. 2. New York, NY: Macmillan, pp. 138–141.
Dewey, J. (1930 [1916]), *Democracy and Education. An Introduction to the Philosophy of Education*. New York, NY: The Macmillan Company.
Dewey, J. (1954 [1927]), *The Public and Its Problems*. Denver, CO: Alan Swallow.
Dewey, J. (2008 [1930]), From absolutism to experimentalism. In J. A. Boydston (Ed.), *John Dewey. The Later Works, 1925-1953. Volume 5: 1929-1930*. Carbondaleb, IL: Southern Illinois University Press, pp. 147–162.
Dewey, J. (1997 [1938]), *Experience and Education*. New York, NY: Touchstone.
Dewey, J. (2008 [1939]), Creative democracy. The task before us. In J. A. Boydston (Ed.), *John Dewey. The Later Works, 1925-1953. Volume 14: 1939-1941*. Carbondale, IL: Southern Illinois University Press, pp. 224–230.
Dewey, J. y and Tufts, J. H. (2013 [1908]), *Ethics*. Redditch: Read Books Ltd.
Fairfield, P. (Ed.) (2010), *John Dewey and Continental Philosophy*. Carbondale, IL: Southern Illinois University Press.

Garrison, J. (2006), The 'Permanent Deposit' of Hegelian thought in Dewey's theory of inquiry. *Educational Theory*, 56 (1), 1–37.
Good, J. A. (2006), *A Search for Unity in Diversity: The 'Permanent Hegelian Deposit' in the Philosophy of John Dewey*. Lanham: Lexington Books.
Hegel, G. W. F. (1920 [1835]), *The Philosophy of Fine Art*. London: G. Bell and Sons, Ltd.
Hegel, G. W. F. (1995 [1842]), *Lecciones sobre la Historia de la Filosofía*. México: FCE.
Jover, G. (2016a), Democracy and education then and now: 'De-pragmatizing' and 'ultra-pragmatizing' readings of John Dewey's pedagogy. In P. Cunningham and R. Heilbronn (Eds.), *Dewey in Our Time. Learning from John Dewey for Transcultural Practice*. London: UCL IOE Press, pp. 40–55.
Jover, G. (2016b), Aprendizaje y pragmatismo universitario en la sociedad del conocimiento. In M. A. Santos (Ed.), *Sociedad del conocimiento. Aprendizaje e innovación en la universidad*. Madrid: Biblioteca Nueva, pp. 23–40.
Jover, G., González Martín, M. R. and Fuentes, J. L. (2015), Exploración de nuevas vías de construcción mediática de la ciudadanía en la escuela: de Antígona a la narrativa transmedia. *Teoría de la Educación. Revista Interuniversitaria*, 27 (1), 69–84.
Karavakou, V. (2014), Let education in the cave: reclaiming a progressive political role for the individual in a modern democracy. In C. C. Kirby (Ed.), *Dewey and the Ancients. Essays on Hellenic and the Hellenistic Themes in the Philosophy of John Dewey*. London: Bloomsbury, pp. 79–99.
Kirby, C. C. (Ed.) (2014), *Dewey and the Ancients. Essays on Hellenic and the Hellenistic Themes in the Philosophy of John Dewey*. London: Bloomsbury.
Kloppenberg, J. T. (1986), *Uncertain Victory: Social Democracy and Progressivism in European and American Thought, 1870-1920*. Oxford: Oxford University Press.
Mougan, J. C. (2013), M. Nussbaum, J. Dewey and education for democratic citizenship. *Pragmatism Today*, 4 (2), 84–90.
Nussbaum, M. C. (2001), *The Fragility of Goodness. Luck and Ethics in Greek Tragedy and Philosophy*. Cambridge, MA: Cambridge University Press.
Nussbaum, M. C. (2010), *Not for Profit. Why Democracy Needs the Humanities*. Princeton, NJ: Princeton University Press.
Parekh, B. (2006), *Rethinking Multiculturalism: Cultural Diversity and Political Theory*. Basingstoke: Palgrave.
Pring, R. (2016), *Una filosofía de la educación políticamente incómoda*. Madrid: Narcea.
Rorty, R. (1995), Dewey between Hegel and Darwin. In H. J. Saatkamp (Ed.), *Rorty & Pragmatism: The Philosopher Responds to His Critics*. London: Vanderbilt University Press, pp. 1–15.
Sophocles (440 B.C. [2007]), *Antigone* (I. Johnston, Trans.), Arlington: Richer Resources Publications.
Steiner, G. (1996), *Antigones. How the Antigone Legend Has Endured in Western Literature, Art, and Thought*. New Haven, CT: Yale University Press.

PART 2
DEWEY, EXPERIENCE AND BODIES

Chapter 4

Dewey and the Alexander Technique: Lessons in Mind−Body Learning

Charlotte Woods, Malcolm Williamson and Jenny Fox Eades

Abstract

Drawing on Dewey's accounts of learning the Alexander Technique (AT), this chapter explores why he found the process so powerful. As AT teachers, we explain how the technique enables practitioners to become aware of fixed, unconscious habits and to bring them under conscious control. With a new student, work begins with physical habits. However, because physical, cognitive, emotional and social functionings are interdependent, AT lessons typically enable flexibility in each of these spheres. Dewey's writings show his strong theoretical commitment to the idea of learning as practical and experiential. His AT lessons were truly revelatory in providing him with both direct, embodied experience of the power of habit to drive human behaviour and a practical means of becoming aware of, and resisting, his own habits of thought and action.

Perceptions are shaped by habit in such a way that the senses can be unreliable in working out how to respond in a given situation. Dewey's practice of the AT revealed to him the dissonance between his habitual self in activity and his conscious view of himself. Dewey was challenged by his AT lessons, which required an open, enquiring attitude and sense of humility. In the AT, Dewey found a means of pursuing an active, critical, self-directed process of discovery and adaptation akin to childhood learning. AT begins with the self, our 'tool of tools'. Through fundamentally modifying the self, the AT supports the openness and flexible response to the physical and social world that characterize productive experiential learning.

Keywords: Mind—body unity; Alexander Technique; habit and learning; experiential learning; learning as enquiry; potential

Introduction

Among education scholars it is well known that mind and body are inseparable in Dewey's proposals for education. His deep ideological conviction of the important role of bodily experience in learning was reinforced by his practice of the disciplined psycho-physical method for self-awareness known as the Alexander Technique (AT). Dewey called this approach 'thinking in activity' (Alexander, 1985, p. 42), drawing a distinction between conceptual learning and 'learning to do' (Alexander, 2004, p. 9). The influence of the AT on Dewey's thinking is apparent to anyone who has had similar experiences, but he was often frustrated by his inability to convey verbally what he had understood through practice. As educators and AT teachers, we can appreciate why most Dewey scholars might feel bemused about the high regard in which Dewey held the 'weirdo' F. Matthias Alexander (Cunningham et al., 2007, p. 49) and the long association of the two men. Our aim is to shed light on this conundrum.

We draw on Dewey's own accounts of learning and applying the AT by which he gained insights that were revelatory and transformative. We consider how awareness and control of maladaptive physical habits by 'intentional inhibition' (Filevich et al., 2012) and how the consequent restoring of an integrated psycho-physical functioning cultivated via the AT can affect habits of mind, and thus the educational process, in ways that can be profound. In enabling the practitioner to bring habit under conscious control, Dewey experienced the AT as a means of developing individuals' capacity to engage with, and learn from, their physical and social environment in an open and flexible way. It provided him with meta-awareness to engage critically with the process through which he was developing his own potentialities and which he saw as an invaluable tool for others in becoming the agents of their own learning.

This chapter is timely in a number of ways. Intellectually, over the past three decades, a rekindling of interest in corporeality across the social sciences has given birth to the new interdisciplinary field of 'body studies' (Shilling, 2012). Within education scholarship specifically, bodies have increasingly become the focus of attention (Cunningham et al., 2012). It has been argued that, as attempts are made to move away from the dominance of the standards agenda, opportunities are being sought to 'pre-empt the educational neglect of the body and its dissociation from the mind' (Doddington, 2015, p. 65). Given Dewey's own commitment to mind–body unity in education, as a counterweight to academic focus on the philosophical, historical and political in his work, we offer this consideration of his ideas on the relevance of his regular AT practice to his own capacity to learn. Finally, the chapter contributes to recent work on the influence of academic outsiders, such as Alexander, in shaping Dewey's philosophical development through his willingness to be cast in the role of learner (Cunningham et al., 2007).

We see our principal contribution in terms of offering a practitioner perspective and do not claim to provide significant new theoretical insights. Nonetheless, our ideas have evolved through long engagement with a wide range of theoretical and historical sources. Of particular relevance in developing our understanding are selected published works of Dewey (Dewey, 1938, 1957, 2007); contemporary work in body studies (Shilling, 2012) and, particularly, the works of pragmatist philosopher and Dewey scholar, Richard Shusterman (2006, 2008); insights gained from neuroscience (Eagleman, 2015) and the ideas around developing individual potential in Beauvais and Higham (2016). Our knowledge of Dewey's experience of learning the AT and the long-standing relationship between Dewey and Alexander (Murray, 1982) is derived from a detailed analysis of Dewey's introduction to Alexander's works, Alexander's own writings and those by expert commentators on their professional relationship (Eastman, 1942; Lamont, 1959; Mixon, 1980; Boydston, 1986; Martin, 2002; Dalton, 2002; McCormack, 2014). Finally, we draw on our own insights gained as practitioners and teachers of the AT and via correspondence with leading thinkers in our discipline.

This chapter briefly introduces theories relevant to the part played by the body in conscious thought. It then provides background on the relationship between Dewey and Alexander, proposing reasons why the significance of Alexander's work for Dewey's philosophical development has not been more widely recognized. We then attempt to provide a sufficient explanation of the AT, and its connection with habits of mind, for a non-expert audience to begin to appreciate its relevance for Dewey's ideas on education. These connections are illustrated by drawing on Dewey's own account of developing his own potential via the Technique, and our experience as long-term practitioners.

Body, Mind and Thinking

Mind–body unity in the process of learning, and ultimately in the cultivation of wisdom and virtue, underpins various non-Western and ancient philosophical traditions (e.g. martial arts, yoga, ancient Greek philosophy). Yet the idea is problematic for mainstream education scholarship in the contemporary Western world, where traditionally the mind is privileged and the body is marginalized or, at best, viewed as subservient in the learning process.

Dewey was categorical about the 'evil' impacts of the separation of mind and body in educational policy and practice. In *Democracy and Education*, he wrote: 'It would be impossible to state adequately the evil results which have flowed from this dualism of mind and body, much less to exaggerate them' (Dewey, 2007, p. 108). Shilling (2012, p. 30) notes that this aversion to the body in Western scholarship is evidenced in the way the thinking of pragmatists such as Dewey, G.H. Mead, William James and C.S. Peirce was roundly rejected by classical European sociology. We find persuasive Shilling's own theoretical approach, which rejects both the wholesale adoption of either naturalistic or sociocultural approaches to thinking about the body. While we recognize that some physiological and neurological research can be criticized for excluding the powerful role of the social environment in shaping human capacity, it is our conviction that, as Shilling (2012) has pointed out, the body constitutes a foundation of the conscious mind.

Shusterman makes a powerful case against the 'anti-somatic bias' among humanities intellectuals, arguing that the body is the basic instrument in all human activity, 'our tool of tools, a necessity for all our perception, action and even thought' (2006, p. 2). He proposes an interdisciplinary field that he calls 'Somaesthetics' concerning 'the body as a locus of sensory-aesthetic appreciation and creative self-fashioning' (ibid.). The framework has three branches: *Analytic* somaesthetics, which is the realm of theory and description; *pragmatic* somaesthetics, which has a normative and prescriptive character and proposes specific methods for cultivating and comparing somatic improvements and *practical* somaesthetics, which is about actually pursuing self-care through 'intelligently disciplined practice aimed at somatic self-improvement'

(Shusterman, 2008, p. 29) and includes a range of movement-based reflective practices that include the AT.

It is this practical element that is the most neglected by academic philosophers, with Dewey being an exception. Consistent with Dewey's philosophy, practical somaesthetics has a strong social dimension: the growth and development of individuals, each committed to the construction of a society in search of its own improvement. According to Shusterman, Dewey provides 'probably the most balanced and comprehensive vision among 20th-century somatic philosophies' (Shusterman, 2008, p.12). He attributes Dewey's advocacy for 'self-conscious somatic reflection in the realm of concrete practice' (ibid., p. 11) in large part to his long-standing work and friendship with Alexander, founder of the AT, of whom he wrote: 'He [F.M. Alexander] has made one of the most important discoveries that has been made in practical application of the unity of the mind-body principle' (Letter 1946 to Joseph Ratner, cited in Boydston, 1986).

Without direct experience of them, it is difficult to appreciate the fundamental associations between somaesthetic disciplines, intellectual growth and social relations. Shusterman (2006) explains how such practices 'refuse to divide body from mind penetrating beneath the skin surfaces and muscle fibre to realign our bones and better organize our neural pathways through which we move, feel and think' (p. 14). Enhanced bodily awareness can enable practitioners to recognize when they are in the grip of deep-seated feelings that they would otherwise not be conscious of. Awareness of one's own fear, excitement, anger or prejudice, for example, allows for active choices about how to respond. In this way, efforts at self-cultivation with a bodily dimension also have an important social dimension.

Through his personal experience, the unity of mind and body had become central to Alexander's understanding of human functioning and, through his Technique, he had developed a practice to restore their effective integration.

John Dewey and F. Matthias Alexander

The 36-year friendship and intellectual association of John Dewey and F. Matthias Alexander began with their meeting in the winter of 1916 shortly after the completion of *Democracy and Education* (Murray, 1982; Alexander, 2004, p. 124; McCormack, 2014). Dewey had already developed his major themes along with fellow Pragmatists, William

James and C.S. Peirce (Cunningham et al., 2007, p. 51). What is being claimed is that Dewey's lessons with Alexander provided a powerful *practical* demonstration and instancing of the theoretical notion of mind–body unity that Dewey held so dear. He was able to witness first-hand how functional integrity can be restored by self-preventing (inhibiting) maladaptive habits.

Education in its broadest sense lay at the heart of what fascinated both men and where they found common ground. Both were committed to a vision of education where individuals are granted autonomy to shape their own learning. An important point of synergy was the recognition that, beyond the structures and processes imposed by formal education systems, to achieve greater control over their learning, individuals also need to resist the considerable constraints posed by their own unconscious habits. The sense of excitement that characterized their discussions is palpable in this quotation from Alexander:

> I have gone on with Professor Dewey, and we have spent night after night discussing these matters. We speak ... of giving children freedom in schools, but no one has ever thought of the lack of freedom within the self. (Fischer, 1995, p. 158)

Dewey saw the AT as a way of retaining, or regaining, the innate habit of productive, flexible learning that is the hallmark of effective growth and of avoiding enslavement to fixed habits of thought and action. The Technique offered Dewey a practical means to achieve a greater sense of agency through bringing unconscious habit under conscious control, a process Alexander refers to as attending to the 'means whereby' (i.e. process-oriented learning versus 'end-gaining' or goal-oriented learning).

In academic circles, it might seem surprising that Dewey took notice of someone like Alexander with little scientific respectability. However, a number of authors have commented on Dewey's intellectual modesty and openness to alternative ideas. He gave time to individuals outside established academia, which at the time would have included Dewey's female students, and who were often regarded as 'weirdos' with eccentric views (Boydston, 1986; Cunningham et al., 2007, p. 28). As has been argued, Dewey realized that his own thinking was enriched when taking the role of learner 'undergoing the kind of questioning in the face of trouble or doubt or desire that he himself so famously claims is the starting point of thinking' (Cunningham et al., 2007, p. 29).

That Dewey's and Alexander's ways of thinking were mutually influential is well documented (Murray, 1982; Boydston, 1986; Jones, 1997; Dalton, 2002; Martin, 2002; Shusterman, 2008; McCormack, 2014). From his world of academia, Dewey was able to help Alexander frame his practical discoveries into the contemporary language of science (Dalton, 2002, p. 119). Dewey's influence is clearly evident in the second edition of Alexander's first book, *Man's Supreme Inheritance*, published in 1918, and he made numerous recommendations on the draft of Alexander's definitive *Constructive Conscious Control of the Individual* (1923).

For his part, Alexander can be seen as an important influence on Dewey. McCormack (2014) identifies Alexander as a significant but 'neglected influence' in his doctoral thesis on the subject. McCormack demonstrates that Alexander's influence is found in all Dewey's subsequent writing, which he describes as a continuing theme sometimes rising to the surface, sometimes woven into the context of meaning like a theme in musical counterpoint (McCormack, 2014, p. 57). In particular, there is the 'Alexander chapter', 'Habit and Will' of *Human Nature and Conduct* (Dewey, 1922), based on his 1918 Stamford lectures (see McCormack, 2014, p. 56, note 55). His lessons with Alexander were fresh in his mind and Irene Tasker, Alexander's teaching assistant, accompanied the Deweys on their train journey across America (Tasker, 1978).

In light of the evident importance of practice in the AT to Dewey's thinking, it is perhaps surprising that it has been given little attention by most educators and academics, a point made by various champions of Alexander's work, including Aldous Huxley:

> It is a most curious fact that of the literally millions of educators who, for two generations, have so constantly appealed to Dewey's authority, only an infinitesimal handful has ever bothered to look into the method which Dewey himself regarded as absolutely fundamental to any effective system of education. (Huxley, 1956, p. 21)

It is possible to identify a number of reasons why Alexander's influence on Dewey has been neglected. First, there is the 'anti-somatic bias' in Western scholarship referred to in the previous section (Shusterman, 2006, 2008; Shilling, 2012): Dewey explored the historical significance and implications for education of this bias in *Democracy and Education*. This aversion to the corporeal has systematically marginalized the practical and experiential — and therefore all practical, embodied disciplines — in favour of the theoretical and intellectual in academic discourse.

A second reason for this neglect of Alexander's influence flows from the first. In his writing, Dewey rarely makes explicit reference to Alexander's contribution for fear of misunderstanding and ridicule by his Columbia colleagues. As the following quotation shows, taken from a letter to Joseph Ratner, Dewey's official biographer in 1946, Dewey was concerned that his interest in the AT might appear to them like a passing fad. This may explain why, though he wrote introductions to three of Alexander's books, Dewey only made specific references to Alexander in two of his main works — *Human Nature and Conduct* (pp. 28, 35) and *Experience and Nature* (p. 296n, 302n) (see also McCormack, 2014, pp. 4–5 note 6). Boydston (1986) also cites a letter that Dewey wrote to Joseph Ratner on this point, in which he says 'I don't talk about it [the AT] very much because unless one has had personal experience it sounds to others just like another one of those enthusiasms for some pet panacea'.

The above quotation also suggests a third reason why Alexander's influence on Dewey's philosophical development might have been deliberately understated: Dewey was frustrated by his inability to explain AT to his colleagues. It is the classical dilemma of how to convey an experience verbally, and one that caused him some frustration: 'I have always been baffled and held back by my sense of inability to convey the method to anyone who had not been through a personal experience of it' (Dewey, cited in McCormack, 2014, p. 112).

Additionally, there was Alexander's reported quick temper and difficult character (Mott, 1972, p. 27; Dalton, 2002, pp. 100–101). From his upbringing and lack of formal education, Alexander had learned to place great importance on self-reliance. He was not a natural collaborator and was fiercely proprietorial of his teaching as providing his means of livelihood. Dewey set up several initiatives to have claims scientifically investigated (Dalton, 2002, p. 233) and was exasperated by Alexander's unwillingness to cooperate (McCormack, 2014, p. 111; Dalton, 2002, p. 233).

Embodied Learning via the AT

In this section, we provide a brief background on the Technique and why and how it is typically learnt in the initial stages. In the interests of brevity and accessibility, our approach is necessarily selective and non-technical. For additional information about the Technique and how it is taught, accounts are provided in Little et al. (2008) and MacPherson et al. (2015).

The Technique can be considered as a form of embodied contemplative practice in which the practitioners learn to say 'no' or to 'inhibit' their 'too quick and unthinking response[s] to stimuli' (Alexander, 2000, p. 80). In a nutshell, the Technique enables the practitioners to become aware of their own fixed, unconscious habits and to 'unlearn' them in order that optimal physiological habits may be cultivated. People take lessons in the AT for a wide range of reasons. For example, actors, musicians and dancers use it as part of their professional practice to enhance the quality of their performance. Those diagnosed with 'musculoskeletal' or 'psychological' conditions that have a functional component to the cause or continuance of their problem may take lessons.

Over time, students of the Technique develop a more acute awareness of the body as lived-in, moving and relating to the outside world, with an emphasis on *sensing* and being 'present'. In considering how the Technique changes the practitioner, we find the idea of the 'body schema' helpful. This concept was developed to 'address the problem of how we are able to coordinate our bodies to perform actions without having complete sight of them and without being able to monitor consciously our every movement' (Shilling, 2012, p. 233). Our body schema develops from both our physical and social environment. General awareness of our bodily appearance, size and capacities, and of the position of our bodies in space, develops slowly from infancy. It is essential in the coordination of our sensory and motor facilities and is also a 'prerequisite of our capacity to construct a coherent self-identity and exercise social action' (ibid., pp. 233–234). Through manipulation of, and interaction with, things in our physical world, our body schema is enlarged. As Dewey notes (ibid., p. 234), our senses are a means of connecting with what lies beyond our bodily frame. The body schema can be 'stretched by social norms, values and technologies, but remains in conversation with bones, flesh, blood and senses' (ibid., p. 235).

Throughout Alexander's working life (c.1894–1955), he developed subtle, non-verbal 'hands-on' guidance in his teaching that re-educates the body-sense and provides the individual with more reliable impressions of movement and effort in carrying out everyday activities. The students' commitment and their ability to inhibit their usual behaviour is fundamental. A teacher is normally considered essential in the early stages to help the student become aware of, and learn how to self-prevent, previously unconscious, maladaptive habits (i.e. rushing ahead without giving sufficient time and thought to *how* something is done). These habits typically involve extra muscular tension and fixation, especially in the dynamic relationship of the head, neck and back. Breaking long-standing habits of posture and movement can be challenging. Therefore, in addition to lessons, to derive significant benefits from the AT requires regular individual practice and application in daily life. Once learned, the method can be applied in any situation. As Mixon points out: 'Dewey can hardly have considered habit the key to social psychology if the limited capacity characteristic of bodily habits (habits that can be seen) fails to generalize to other sorts of habits' (Mixon, 1980, pp. 176–177).

Alexander recognized that our physical, cognitive, emotional and social functions are interdependent and that good coordination involves the effective integration of all of them (Alexander, 1985, p. 21). Poor functioning in any of these will adversely influence the others. For example, tension experienced after long hours hunched over a computer resembles the physical markers of the 'startle' response (Jones, 1997, pp. 30–33), a largely unconscious defensive reaction to threat. Over time, this cowering, hunched posture, and its emotional correlates, can become habitual, seriously limiting our repertoire of postures, shaping our prevailing mood, thought processes, social and emotional experience and our ability to comprehend situations and respond appropriately.

Individuals who come for lessons may initially be surprised that what drew them to lessons, for example, a bad back or performance anxiety, is not directly addressed. This is because the aim of the AT is to enable the individuals to work on their overall coordination. The benefits derived will always be indirect and arise from the better integration of the different areas of functioning (physical, cognitive, social and emotional). Once initiated, study of the Technique represents a journey of discovery. Typically the person studying the Technique will notice changes in different areas of functioning in ways that are entirely individual and often unexpected. Beneficial side effects might include, for example, becoming less quick to anger, or less inclined to hasty judgement, less anxious, improved peripheral vision, or suddenly discovering new and better ways of tackling familiar tasks in the home or workplace.

There is ample evidence in interviews, personal correspondence and writing not destined for his academic peers that Dewey was profoundly affected by his experience of the AT, calling it fundamental and describing it as bearing 'the same relation to education that education itself bears to all other human activities' (Dewey, 1932). This is no small claim for the potential power of the Technique to support learning. In the remainder of the chapter, we will endeavour to bring our understanding of the Technique to bear, in providing an interpretation of this claim. In so doing, we hope to provide an inkling of why Dewey's experience of becoming aware of, and inhibiting, habitual responses (via the AT) might have been so significant for him.

Habit and Learning

Dewey's version of education is one in which individuals have a degree of control over what and how they learn: interest and enquiry of the world around them leads to learning. Dewey recognized the power that habit exercises over individuals' freedom to perceive their social and physical world and to think, feel and act within it, following William James' lead (1950). Habit is fundamental and determines what the senses identify, select and perceive as significant, the path of enquiry and the concepts and meanings that are formed.

In *Democracy and Education*, Dewey argues that habits possess us when they become routine ways of acting, disconnected from conscious deliberation. They put an end to plasticity of behaviour and the individuals' power to vary or adapt their thoughts and actions appropriately to different circumstances. He draws a distinction between blind routine that enslaves us and habits that a person is conscious of and can take responsibility for:

> In the merely blind response ... there may be training, but there is no education. Repeated responses to recurrent stimuli may fix a habit of acting in a certain way. All of us have many habits of whose import we are quite unaware. Consequently they possess us, rather than we them. They move us; they control us. Unless we become aware of what they accomplish, and pass judgment upon the worth of the result, we do not control them. (Dewey, 2007, p. 27)

As the above quotation shows, for Dewey, any education worthy of the name involves both conscious awareness of habits and a reliable means of passing judgement on them. This poses a problem in light of recent neuroscience research suggesting that, though 'the conscious mind excels at telling itself the narrative of being in control' (Eagleman, p. 2016, p. 104), even decisions perceived as spontaneous are influenced by a lifetime's experience. Crucially, in terms of understanding how work on the body via the AT might influence other areas of functioning, it is emotional signals from our *body* that provide a summary of our situation and enable us to make moment-to-moment, split-second decisions (Eagleman, 2015, p. 121). Though we are largely unaware of them, it is these physiological signatures that enable individuals not to be paralysed by the wealth of choices available in navigating through a highly complex world. Our experience as practitioners of the AT confirms for us that, by preventing (inhibiting) our habitual responses to stimuli and reducing unnecessary muscular bracing, new and unfamiliar options are able to come to consciousness and can be tested as to their potential usefulness.

We believe that Dewey found learning the AT so significant because it gave him first-person, embodied experience of the power of habit to drive human behaviour, and of the conscious mind's propensity for self-delusion in this respect. This realization is likely to have been profound for Dewey who prided himself on his ability for rational thinking. While his academic writing demonstrates his strong theoretical attachment to the idea of learning as practical and experiential, his own means of intellectual development in the academy could not have been further from his proposals for development of the immature intellect. His lessons in the AT offered Dewey a transformative experience in embodied learning. Further, they provided him with a practical means for achieving the two elusive elements of his educational vision, bringing habitual action under conscious control and providing a yardstick against which to measure success.

In order to convey how the AT allows the practitioners to become aware of and to better control their hitherto unconscious habits, it is necessary to introduce one of the cornerstones of F.M. Alexander's thinking, which he termed 'unreliable' or 'faulty sensory appreciation'.

Unreliable Sensory Appreciation

Perhaps the main impediment to changing habits is our strong tendency to rely on *sensory feelings*. Alexander was able to demonstrate that feelings (sense of position and movement, expenditure of effort, etc.) are conditioned by established habit and so are an unreliable guide to working out how best to respond in new or unfamiliar situations. He discovered that unconscious maladaptive habits in the way a person speaks, sits, stands, breathes or walks will, in time, be familiarized and feel 'right' and normal. For this reason, someone can feel comfortable even though they are sitting or lying in inappropriate positions that are constraining or damaging to health.

This reliance of the brain on proprioceptive information that is often inaccurate poses a significant problem for the notion of education proposed by Dewey. First, accurate perceptions of habit are not readily accessible to conscious awareness. Second, how is it possible to use judgement wisely in evaluating habits when 'our habitual judgements of ourselves are warped because they are based on vitiated sense material'? (Dewey, 1932). Through 'hands-on' feedback from the teacher, together with verbal explanation and instructions, the students come to appreciate the difference between their habitual way of being and how it feels to inhabit their bodies and interact with their environment more 'naturally'; 'how to be otherwise' (Wilson, 1998, p. 253).

With practice and sometimes, as in Dewey's case, 'the tremendous mental difficulty found in not "doing" something as soon as an habitual act is suggested' (Dewey, 1932), students learn to stop and think before acting in habitual ways. They are enabled to pass judgement on whether to proceed with their habitual response or to choose a more appropriate alternative instead. They develop the capacity to 'stop and think', one of Dewey's hallmarks of intelligence. In *Democracy and Education*, he writes '[t]o be intelligent we must "stop, look, listen" in making the plan of our activity' (p. 80). In *Experience and Education*, he encapsulated it as, 'stop and think' (Dewey, 1963, p. 64). In describing his experience of the AT, Dewey explains that through acquiring the ability to have control over habits, the students are also given greater control in determining their behaviour. He contrasts this with the Pavlovian conditioned reflex that renders the individual 'a passive puppet to be played upon by external manipulations' (Dewey, 1932).

We find clear parallels between Dewey's idea of learning through experience in childhood as set out in *Democracy and Education*, and his own accounts of working with the Technique. For Dewey, the AT allows practitioners to use their embodied experience as a tool in exploring their own potential. In the next section, we explore this territory.

The Technique as a Process of Self-Development

In *Democracy and Education*, Dewey makes plain that in childhood learning, emphasis is to be placed on experience, interacting with the environment in ways that progressively modify both the activities and the environment. Here, 'immature' is seen as a positive attribute, characterized by openness and inquisitiveness in exploring the physical and social world. Dewey contrasts this conception of education with formal education, employing the presentation of 'cultural products'. Dewey sees such products, when isolated from their connections with the present environment in which individuals have to act, as 'a kind of rival and distracting environment' (Dewey, 2007, p. 63). In describing his own experiential learning about the functioning of the living body via the AT, Dewey states: 'I found the things which I had known – in the sense of theoretical belief – in philosophy and psychology, changed into vital experiences which gave a new meaning to knowledge of them' (Dewey, 1932). He compares this experience with the kind of knowledge gained through accessing 'cultural products' in the formal study of anatomy:

> The anatomist may 'know' the exact function of each muscle ... But if he is himself unable to co-ordinate all the muscular structures involved in, say, sitting down ... how can he be said to *know* in the full and vital sense of the word? (Ibid., p. 9)

In considering why Dewey found the experience of practising the Technique so significant in validating his theoretical beliefs, we find appealing the discussion of 'potential' put forward in Beauvais and Higham (2016). Their article critiques the highly problematic ways in which the term is used in the discourses of politicians, the education community and popular media. In their conceptualization, a child's potential is a 'negotiated, situated, ever-changing creation' (ibid., p. 573), a process involving conflicts and challenge. The conflicts in this understanding arise principally through interactions between children acting ethically as agential subjects with one another, though Beauvais and Higham acknowledge that encounters offering valuable learning experiences may also be introspective, as with the AT, or with non-humans.

Arising from this idea of potential, Beauvais and Higham advocate a pedagogy of challenge, in which students are unsettled, given freedom to act, to be faced with conflict and to be allowed to fail as a result.

Higham cites evidence that teenagers can find interpersonal conflict, especially in encounters with difference, to result in significant learning. He hypothesizes that a sense of dissonance between who an individual would like to be and who they are in practice during the moment of challenge can act as a catalyst for change. This is entirely in keeping with the pragmatists' perspective, in which 'the embodied, intentional subject acts in and upon the social and material contexts in which they live through cycles of action informed by overlapping portions of habit, crisis and creativity' (Shilling, 2012, p. 247).

As, in fact anyone experiences in applying the AT, what Dewey experienced during his lessons was a strong sense of dissonance between his habitual self in activity and his conscious view of himself. His work with Alexander revealed to him that his idea of his appearance and how he moved was wholly inaccurate. For a person to accept that their sense of self is incorrect, and to be willing to explore this dissonance, requires an open, enquiring attitude and a sense of humility, to embody the qualities of the 'immature' learner in Dewey's sense. Undertaking the most basic activities without falling into habit can be immensely difficult, as this quotation from Dewey illustrates:

> For to find that one is unable to execute directions, including inhibitory ones, in doing such a seemingly simple act as to sit down, when one is using all the mental capacity which one prides oneself upon possessing, is not an experience congenial to one's vanity. (Dewey, 1932, p 10)

Despite its challenges, Dewey persevered with the Technique and came to appreciate the far-reaching benefits for other areas of functioning in bringing physical habits under conscious control. He said of his own journey in studying the Technique: 'as one goes on, new areas are opened, new possibilities are seen and then realized; one finds himself continually growing and realizes that there is an endless process of growth initiated' (Alexander, 1932, p. 10). Dewey told his close friend Max Eastman: 'I used to shuffle and sag, now I hold myself up. A person gets old because he bends over' (McCormack, 2014, p. 50). He also makes reference to the 'the great change in moral and mental attitude that takes place as proper co-ordinations are established' (Dewey, 1932).

The direction of travel for each student of the Technique will be different. The role of the teachers is to provide feedback to their students to help them identify barriers to their own freedom to progress and to identify points of dissonance between their habitual use of themselves and that of a version of themselves with better coordination. In bringing habit under conscious control, as Dewey experienced it, the individual is enabled 'through his own co-ordinated activities to take possession of his own potentialities' (ibid., p. 11). In negotiating this sometimes hostile territory between the actual and potential self, it is the student who takes the responsibility.

Students need to learn how to think for themselves, find practical solutions to daily challenges and feel at home in their surroundings. It is not surprising then that these capacities are encouraged in institutions that focus on practical learning – centres for music and the performing arts, for example. But practical intelligence is desirable for all students in a changing world: to adapt old skills and to learn new ones, to cope in different environments and cultures and to be aware of one's changing needs for health and well-being.

In Dewey's words, AT provides both a 'standard of psycho-physical health' (i.e. optimal integrated functioning) and a method by which 'this standard may be progressively and endlessly achieved' (i.e. a lifelong process of enquiry and discovery), bearing 'the same relation to education that education itself bears to all other human activities' (Dewey in Alexander, 1985, p. 12). We take this to mean that Dewey saw the technique as providing the individual with the possibility of reliably learning how to learn: a means of pursuing an active, critical, self-directed process of discovery and successful adaptation. This begins with the self but, through fundamentally modifying this, our 'tool of tools', this active process can result in the openness and flexible response to our physical and social world that characterize productive learning from experience.

References

Alexander, F. M. (1985 [1932]), *The Use of the Self*. London: Gollancz.
Alexander, F. M. (2000 [1942]), *The Universal Constant in Living*. London: Mouritz.
Alexander, F. M. (2004 [1923]), *Constructive Conscious Control of the Individual*. London: Mouritz.
Beauvais, C., Higham, R. (2016), A reappraisal of children's potential. *Studies in the Philosophy of Education*, 35 (6), 573–587.
Boydston, J. A. (1986), John Dewey and the Alexander Technique. Keynote address. *First International Congress of Teachers of the Alexander Technique*, Stony Brook University, New York, NY. Available at: http://www.alexandercenter.com/jd/deweyalexanderboydston.html (accessed 12.12.15).

Cunningham, C. A., Granger, D., Fowler-Morse, J., Stengel, B, Wilson, T. (2007), Dewey, women, and weirdos: or, the potential rewards for scholars who dialogue across difference. *Education and Culture*, 23 (2), 27–62.

Cunningham, R. B., Telford, R. D., Fitzgerald, R., Olive, L., Prosser, L., Jiang, X. and Telford, R. M. (2012), Physical education, obesity, and academic achievement: A 2-year longitudinal investigation of Australian elementary school children, *American Journal of Public Health*, 102 (2), 368–374.

Dalton, J. C. (2002), *Becoming John Dewey*. Bloomington, IN: Indiana University Press.

Dewey, J. (1932), Introduction to F. Matthias Alexander. *The Use of the Self*. New York, NY: E. P. Dutton and Co. Available at: http://www.alexandercenter.com/jd/johndeweyus.html (accessed 10.10.17).

Dewey, J. (1957 [1922]), *Human Nature and Conduct*. New York, NY: Random House Inc. (The Modern Library). First published by Henry Holt and Company, New York.

Dewey, J. (1963 [1938]), *Experience and Education*. New York, NY: Collier Books.

Dewey, J. (2007 [2016]), *Democracy and Education*. Teddington: The Echo Library.

Doddington, C. (2015), Embodied arts experience: the educational value of somaesthetics. In M. Fleming, L. Bresler and J. O'Toole (Eds.), *The Routledge International Handbook of the Arts and Education*. New York, NY: Routledge, pp. 60–67.

Eagleman, D. (2015), *The Brain: The Story of You*. Edinburgh: Canongate Books Ltd.

Eastman, M. (1942), Heroes I have known, Chapter 12. *The Hero as Teacher*. New York, NY: Simon and Schuster.

Filevich, E, Kühn, S and Haggard, P. (2012), Intentional inhibition in human action: the power of 'no'. *Neuroscience and Biobehavioral Reviews*, 36 (2012), 1107–1118.

Fischer, J. M. O. (Ed.) (1995), *F M Alexander: Articles and Lectures*. London: Mouritz.

Huxley, A. (1956), *Adonis and the Alphabet and Other Essays*. London: Chatto & Windus.

James, W. (1950 [1890]), *The Principles of Psychology, Volume I, Chapter IV 'Habit'*. New York, NY: Dover Publications Inc. First Published by Henry Holt and Company.

Jones, F. P. (1997), *Freedom to Change*. London: Mouritz.

Lamont, C. (Ed.) (1959), *Dialogue on John Dewey*. New York, NY: Horizon Press.

Little, P., Lewith G., Webley, F., Evans, M. and Beattie, A. (2008), Randomized controlled trial of Alexander Technique lessons, exercise and massage for chronic and recurrent back pain. *British Medical Journal*, 337, a884.

MacPherson, H., Tilbrook, H. and Richmond, S. (2015), Alexander Technique lessons or acupuncture sessions for persons with chronic neck pain: a randomized trial. *Annuals of Internal Medicine*, 169 (9), 653–662.

McCormack, E. D. (2014), *A Neglected Influence – Frederick Matthias Alexander and John Dewey*. London: Mouritz. Originally published as PhD thesis, Toronto University, 1958.

Martin, J. (2002), *The Education of John Dewey*. New York, NY: Columbia University Press.

Mixon, D. (1980), The place of habit in the control of action. *Journal of Theory of the Sociology of Behaviour*, 10 (3), 169–186.

Mott, F. J. (1972), *The Little History*, vol. 2. Edenbridge: Mark Beech Publishers. Available at: http://www.mouritz.co.uk/Mouritzpdfs/mottlittlehistory1972.pdf (accessed 26.03.17).

Murray, A. (1982), *John Dewey and F. M. Alexander: 36 years of friendship*. Published privately, Urbana Centre for the Alexander Technique (School of Music, University of Urbana IL).

Shilling, C. (2012), *The Body & Social Theory* (3rd Ed.). London: Sage.

Shusterman, R. (2006), Thinking through the body, educating for the humanities: a plea for somaesthetics. *Journal of Aesthetic Education*, 40 (1), 1–21.

Shusterman, R. (2008), *Body Consciousness: A Practical Philosophy of Mindfulness and Somaesthetics*. Cambridge: Cambridge University Press.

Tasker, I. (1978), *Connecting Links [An informal talk, 9th October 1967]*. London: The Sheildrake Press.

Wilson, F. R. (1998), *The Hand*. New York, NY: Vintage Books.

Chapter 5

Black Bodies in Schools: Dewey's Democratic Provision for Participation Confronts the Challenges of 'Fundamental Plunder'

Sue Ellen Henry and Kathleen Knight Abowitz

Abstract

In this chapter, we read Ta-Nehisi Coates' *Between the World and Me* (2015) against Dewey's *Democracy and Education* (1916) to glean insight into how Deweyan transactionalism can help theorize greater democratic participation for the corporeally disenfranchised, that is, those persons who experience sociocultural and/or political marginalization due to the racialized status of their bodies. We argue that transactionalism carries promise to help interrupt current, systemic practice that negatively reifies Black bodies and reasserts Black bodies as central, full participants in democratic action. An analysis of transactionalism as interpreted from *Democracy and Education* and other Deweyan writings is followed by an analysis of Coates' memoir, *Between the World and Me*, focusing on his experiential understanding of how Black bodies exist in educational institutions. We conclude the chapter with possibilities for an embodied ideal of democracy, and some educational practices that can follow from it.

Keywords: Transactionalism; habits; race in education; democratic participation; embodiment; racial privilege

Introduction

In this chapter, we read Ta-Nehisi Coates' *Between the World and Me* against Dewey's *Democracy and Education* to glean insight into how Deweyan transactionalism might help theorize greater democratic participation for the corporeally disenfranchised, that is, those persons who experience sociocultural and/or political marginalization due to the racialized status of their bodies.

Coates' memoir of an African American man living in twenty-first-century United States of America is cast in the style of James Baldwin's *The Fire Next Time* and has become a touchstone text in a time of intense racial tensions in US society. While there is perhaps no time in American history in which racial tensions were absent, the Black Lives Matter movement and other new movements for racial justice in the face of ongoing police brutality of the modern era have made Coates' memoir extraordinarily timely. It has been lauded by critics, well-received by American readers, was a finalist for the Pulitzer Prize and won the National Book Award. Critic James Hamilton calls the book, written in the form of a letter from Coates to his 15-year-old son, 'a love letter written in a moral emergency' (Hamilton, 2015).

Coates tells us how contemporary US democracy looks from the body of a Black man. The democratic ideal – described so reverently in relation to education in *Democracy and Education* – is analysed by Coates with frank disappointment. This juxtaposition presents a unique opportunity for some fresh analysis of Deweyan democratic education. Coates narrates the story of his life, telling of his growing up in urban Baltimore, his college experience at Howard University (a historically Black university in Washington, D.C.) and coming to consciousness as a Black man growing up in a family of Black nationalists, living in context of the so-called American Dream. Coates wrestles openly with democracy's promise, in prose beautifully rendered with equal parts of anger and despair, providing a moving contraposition to Dewey's staid, and largely race-blind analysis.

In this treatment, we will not revisit Dewey's broader scholarly or personal record on race, racial analysis or racism as a corrosive social reality among democratic communities. This analysis has been commendably done by others. Thomas Fallace, most notably, demonstrates that Dewey's views on race around the time he wrote *Democracy and Education* can be best characterized as ethnocentric (2011). Revealing the deeply Darwinian hold over intellectuals like Dewey during the late nineteenth and early twentieth centuries, Fallace has shown that

Dewey's thinking reflected the view that other races were deemed socially deficient and not yet evolved. While his later work demonstrated a much more thoroughgoing cultural pluralism, in *Democracy and Education*, Dewey's ideas were less sophisticated. We take Fallace's analysis as a given and a starting point.

In this chapter, we are most interested in bringing Deweyan transactionalism to bear upon Coates' contemporary analysis of racism in the United States. Building on insights from philosophers Shannon Sullivan and Sarah Stitzlein, this chapter argues that transactionalism carries promise in interrupting current, systemic practice that negatively reifies Black bodies and reasserts Black bodies as central, full participants in democratic action. We begin with an analysis of transactionalism as revealed (in an early rendering relative to Dewey's later works on the topic) in *Democracy and Education*, laying out the relevant concepts and perspectives it contains for understanding racism and racialized bodies in US society. We then turn to Coates' text to understand what it means to carry a Black body in a society organized as a nominally democratic state wherein racialized violence thrives. We focus especially on Coates' discussions as they touch upon educational environments, and conclude the chapter with possibilities for an embodied ideal of democracy, and some educational practices that can follow from it.

Using Dewey's Transactionalism as a Lens for Interpreting Racial Embodiment

The concept of transactionalism in Dewey's philosophy is not fully realized in *Democracy of Education*; it would be over 30 years after that text that his most complete thinking on the subject would be published with Arthur Bentley in *Knowing and the Known* (Dewey & Bentley, 1949). Yet Dewey's notions of both democracy and education in the 1916 text are laden with transactional foundations: with Dewey's naturalistic philosophical assumptions, with his broad and social views of education, with his anti-dualistic philosophical method, in his notion of habits, and with his vision of democracy as associational, social and moral. These foundations, described more fully below, set the stage for bringing *Democracy and Education* into conversation with Coates' analysis of his experiences of racial embodiment in US society.

Dewey's naturalism takes many forms in *Democracy and Education*, starting on the very first page in his description of education as a necessity of life itself – that every living thing uses energy to convert matter in their environment into means for growth. The organism physically exists in and through its environments in continuous processes of change, growth, conversion of energies and transformation of forms. The human organism exists physically in a larger context of experience: 'customs, institutions, beliefs, victories and defeats, recreations and occupations' (Dewey, 1916, p. 2). One of these human contexts is the custom, institutions and beliefs about race, racialized identities and racial power.

Dewey's naturalist account of education rejects strong notions of individualism and the atomistic views that have shaped notions of personhood in philosophy and in education (Fesmire, 2015; Garrison et al., 2016). This naturalism enables the text to express racial understandings. As living organisms, persons are fully connected to, act upon and are derived from their environments and social contexts, including the environments which produce 'race' as a powerful construct. This naturalist foundation provides the context for Dewey's broad view of education as a social function, the main component of *Democracy and Education*'s argument in the first third of the text. Because educators working in formal education often neglect education's social function by disconnecting subject matter from students' life experiences, in the text Dewey stresses the importance of a proper balance between the formal and informal, incidental and intentional aspects of education in schools. It is through this balance that the three functions of schooling, all social in nature, can be realized: simplifying and ordering the factors of disposition educators wish to develop; purifying and idealizing existing social customs; and creating a wider, better balanced environment through which young people will develop (ibid., p. 22). Too often, schools will reproduce our current social relations rather than purify or idealize social customs. This point is particularly salient with regard to racial relations and customs. Racist constructs, which tend to be narrowed, restrictive views on human possibility, are often simply unreflectively reproduced in schools; Deweyan naturalist notions of the environment as the educational medium can help remind us that racialized habits and dispositions might be intentionally reshaped by educators in schools.

Dewey's naturalist account of growth relies on experiential inquiry, which Dewey develops through disabusing his readers of classic dualisms in epistemological and moral thinking: body versus mind, individual versus community, physical versus emotional and spiritual. In particular, Dewey's notion of mind as a social, embodied concept is particularly useful for thinking through racial identity, power and agency.

In the chapter 'Aims in Education', he says that mind is 'purposeful activity controlled by perception of facts and their relationship to one another' (ibid., p. 103). This concept of mind is active and transactional in its weighing of present conditions to ends in view and present relationships to probable consequences. It has a body, whose experiences in the world propel reflection which can bring intelligence to our actions. Notions of embodied experience, linkages between learning and environments, the importance of formal and informal educational settings and the social functions of schooling towards a wider and better balanced world will all be useful, as we look at Coates' commentary on his schooling years in Baltimore public schools and later at Howard University.

In naturalist accounts of racial learning and social growth, the idea of habit is important. Our racialized performances and relationships are often the product of habit, that is patterns of routinized and often unreflective action. The idea of habits receives focused treatment from Dewey in *Democracy and Education* in chapter 4, 'Education as Growth'. As living organisms, our growth is hinged upon our plasticity, which is our power to 'modify actions on the basis of the results of prior experiences'; we 'learn to learn' and to adapt to constant changes in circumstance and environment (ibid., pp. 44–45). But we also acquire habits, or efficiencies of doing, which brings 'economic and effective control of the environment' (ibid., p. 46). Habits are embodied intelligences that typically harden into unconscious action and thought, but can be brought to the light of reflective consciousness through the use of mind. In such light, a new habit can become a new site of agency. Drawing from Dewey's analysis of habit, Stitzlein's excellent treatment of racial and gendered performances in schools shows how our performances around racial identities are strongly habituated (Stitzlein, 2008). Racist ideology does indeed exist, but often, for US educators, racism is a product of not so much a set of conscious beliefs but below the level of consciousness; 'this includes shaping the ways in which we habitually enact our own races ... and interact with those who are different from ourselves' (Stitzlein, 2008, p. 3). Race is 'defined and inculcated by habit', requiring educators to carefully consider the unconscious patterns of thinking and acting racially, and creating new conditions for reflecting on and changing the conditions of these school transactions (Stitzlein, 2008, p. 5).

Dewey's naturalism in *Democracy and Education* helps him attack dualisms and develop more embodied-mind concepts like that of habit. This naturalism also provides building blocks for his democratic ideal, one which envisions democracy not as a formal system but as certain types of human associations meeting two criteria: awareness of 'how numerous and varied are the interests which are consciously shared' and 'how full and free is the interplay with other forms of association' (Dewey, 1916, p. 89). These criteria point to Dewey's conjoining of social, political and moral aspects of his democratic ideal, and also to his sense that democracy is an experiential process of balancing multiple interests and overlapping social groups – including groups with explicitly or implicitly racial meanings – in constant interplay. The associational and moral meanings of democracy for Dewey are the key contention as we bring Coates' condemnations of US historical foundations of racist plunder to interplay with Dewey's ideas.

What It Means to Carry a Black Body

Dewey's transactionalist theory provides a useful lens for reflection on persistent challenges of racism and its structural legacies in contemporary society. *Between the World and Me* provides the contemporary student of democracy and education with a narrative account of the Black male body in modern institutions, exposing the ways in which habits surround racial acts to perpetuate legitimized violence against Black bodies. Black Americans are killed at 12 times the rate of people in other developed nations (Silver, 2015). US police officers killed 102 unarmed Black people in 2015, five times the rate of unarmed Whites (*Mapping Police Violence*). The consequence of this violence, in all its overt and symbolic forms, shapes our collective experience of race and democracy. Without full acknowledgement of these enduring structural factors in our democratic practice, there is little chance for social justice. Coates' text serves as a powerful, clear narrative of the current situation and paints in stark relief the stakes we face at this moment.

Ta-Nehisi Coates' account of the Black male body as performed and acted upon in the street and school interprets the experience of Black bodies in public spaces and institutions. Starting from the nested corporeal experience of living with a Black body in the American physical and historical context, Coates' challenge for African Americans is to find authentic ways to live that acknowledge this fraught ontological situation.

Written as a letter from father to son, Coates recounts his experience as a young Black man navigating the streets and public schools of Baltimore, Maryland (USA) in his youth, and later, finding an intellectual and corporeal home at Howard University. Later chapters explore the case of Coates' friend Prince Carmen Jones, the child of a Black family who rose up from poverty to achieve middle-class comforts, who was killed by police officers in Prince Georges County, Maryland.

Coates challenges the post-racial giddiness of an Obama era with a distinct message about the US mythos. Coates' rich narrative drives his message: that the American 'Dream' mythology papers over the grim reality of the 'fundamental plunder' (Coates, 2015, p. 109) of the White classes over Black citizens, starting with slavery and continuing through state-supported and -sponsored violence on the streets and in schools. This habit of plunder has enormous consequences for Black bodies, as Coates attempts to warn his only son of the hazards that accrue. This history and its contemporary reality for the somatic experience of African Americans echo the literary trope of haunting and displacement, a defining feature of the much modern African American literature penned by figures such as Toni Morrison, James Baldwin and Jean Toomer (Parham, 2009). As such, Coates reinforces the contextualized nature of Black and White relations resulting in the construction of race, but maintains that Blacks 'made ourselves into a people' (Coates, 2015, p. 149) largely through the use of Black bodies to write, educate, dance and love in their own way. Coates explores four particular environments central in shaping his experience of carrying a Black body: his family, the streets of Baltimore, the Baltimore public schools and Howard University.

Growing up in Baltimore was, for Coates,

> to be naked before the elements of the world, before all the guns, fists, knives, crack, rape, and disease. The nakedness is not an error, nor pathology. The nakedness is the correct and intended result of policy, the predictable upshot of people forced for centuries to live under fear. (Ibid., p. 17)

As such, in his formative years on Baltimore streets, there was a 'constant jeopardy' (ibid., p. 18) that resulted in living with/in a Black body. Indeed, a similar but qualitatively different type of violence was present in his own household, which he maintains was ruled by the belt. Yet his home also gave him the rich world of the written word as a tool for education and liberation. His father was a librarian at Howard University. His mother frequently turned a school punishment into a writing assignment — a moment he remembers as spurring critical thought about his interactions with others.

> When I was in trouble at school (which was quite often) [my mother] would make me write about it. The writing had to answer a series of questions: Why did I feel the need to talk at the same time as my teacher? Why did I not believe that my teacher was entitled to respect? (Ibid., p. 29)

The balance of violent streets and school constraints on the body, with the flights of exploration brought by the written words encouraged in his home, posed a significant contradiction and source of development for Coates' self-concept as a Black man.

Writing in the 1960s, Frantz Fanon makes the same case for how he came to self-understanding as a raced person. While Coates tracks his racial and gender identity development from the point of view of the body, Fanon works from the position of the mind and body. Describing the consequences of racism for his mind, Fanon writes,

> ... the white man explained to me that, genetically, I represented a stage of development: 'Your properties have been exhausted by us. ...Study our history and you will see how far this fusion has gone.' Then I had the feeling that I was repeating a cycle. My originality had been torn out of me. I wept a long time... (Fanon, 1967, p. 129)

Central to both these experiences is a deep sense of personal isolation, loneliness, fear, separation and seclusion. Rejecting other traditional communities such as the church, Coates' family taught him to turn to careful observation and writing as a way of knowing and coping, both of which serve as foundational practices of 'interrogation, of drawing myself into consciousness' (Coates, 2015, p. 29). This commitment to 'ruthless interrogation', coupled with wide reading of Black writers, led to a central lesson: 'I was not an innocent. ...And feeling that I was as human as anyone, this must be true for other humans' (ibid., pp. 29–30).

Coping physically for Coates required a different use of his body. 'To survive the neighbourhoods and shield my body, I learned another language consisting of a basic complement of head nods and handshakes' (ibid., p. 23). But these tactics failed him in both the streets and school.

As Coates acknowledges, he was trapped by his body: not violent enough for the streets and too violent for school. What was he to do? He used language, at the encouragement of his family, to 'ruthlessly interrogate' his condition. His family's influence as committed readers and thinkers also drew him to the works of Malcolm X and writings of the Black Panther Party. These writings strongly shaped his racial context and helped to restore the Black body he carried with him as a source of power and capacity, rather than a harbinger of fear and loathing. It also called into question the validity of the treatment of the Black body as it had been historically coordinated into the habits of White privilege.

Coates explains how the schools he attended as a boy did not work in the same way as his family's Black pride. The schools were about further curtailing the work of his Black body. 'Fail to comprehend the streets and you gave up your body now. But fail to comprehend the schools and you gave up your body later. I suffered at the hands of both, but I resent the schools more' (ibid., p. 25). Because the schools had the legitimacy of compulsory attendance and societal support for what it meant to 'grow up and be somebody' (ibid., p. 25), its damning power was both concealed and validated. The results for Black bodies is severe: 'To be educated in my Baltimore mostly meant always packing an extra number 2 pencil and working quietly. Educated children walked in single file on the right side of the hallway, raised their hands to use the lavatory, and carried the lavatory pass when en route' (ibid., p. 25). This state-mandated focus on corporeal self-control is particularly instituted today in 'no excuses' charter schools working with large populations of poor and students of colour (Henry, 2014). Such systems work, in Deweyan terms, by separating mind from body and emphasizing corporeal self-control to repress the mind in coordination with the body. Under these circumstances, Black bodies are flagged a priori as problematic, requiring surveillance, heavy control and discipline, thus furthering their corporeal disenfranchisement.

Fortunately, his family's encouragement to read and write about his experience as a means of understanding his Black body led to Coates' matriculation to Howard University. For Coates and many others, Howard is an African American Mecca. Beyond the institutional aspects of Howard which are concerned about all the typical issues in higher education, there is the Mecca quality that Howard cultivates both in its own history and in its Washington, D.C. location (known as a vibrant, historically dominant African American city) for African American citizens. 'The Mecca – the vastness of Black people across space and time – could be experienced in a twenty-minute walk across campus' (Coates, 2015, p. 41). At Howard, Coates was able to strongly critique the notion that Black history was inferior because Black bodies were inferior, a notion made real through the history of enslavement and violence against the Black body (ibid., p. 44). Being at Howard provided Coates opportunities to see the trajectories of power that had been part of his own history, resulting in a recalibration of the notion of the Black body.

> Contrary to this theory [of inferiority of the Black body and thus Black people], I had Malcolm. I had my mother and father. I had my readings of every issue of *The Source* and *Vibe*. ...Writers Greg Tate, Chairman Mao, dream hampton – barely older than me – were out there creating a new language... This was ... an argument for the weight and beauty of our culture and thus of our bodies. And now each day, out on the Yard, I felt this weight and saw this beauty, not just as a matter of theory but also as a demonstrable fact. And I wanted desperately to communicate this evidence to the world, because I felt ... that the larger culture's erasure of black beauty was intimately connected to the destruction of black bodies. (Ibid., p. 44)

In pursuit of this claim of Black beauty, Coates follows his family legacy strategy of constructing his own 'trophy case' of Black achievers to whom he looked up and wanted to emulate. This approach was critiqued by many of his faculty at Howard; while the culture honoured a deep sense of reverence for the history lost in the 'amorphous residue of plunder' (ibid., p. 49), which characterizes Black history and the Black body, through his education, Coates was challenged to recognize the conflicts between his trophy authors around questions of race. For example, what was better, Douglass's call for integration or Martin Delany's nationalism?

Such questions bring to the fore the notion of the American 'Dream' and its need for continual interrogation. Coates maintains that the 'Dream' is a fantasy perpetuated by the habits of White privilege, ensnaring marginalized people into its contradictory message of value through personal achievement and the ignorance of structures that impede individual capacity to gain 'value' through these means. In order to cope with these contradictory messages, the Dream traps Black bodies into internalizing and perpetuating bigotry towards others as a means to personal power in this corrupt system. By building distinct boundaries between the interests of marginalized populations rather than alliances, 'hate gives identity' (ibid., p. 60).

In response, Coates advises his son to aim towards allegiance and alliance-building, standing together with others and supporting 'their' causes, with the aim to interrupt the corruption by seeing the mutuality of interests among those who share in their marginal corporeal experience. Coates emphasizes that it's not worth it to wait on 'Dreamers' – those advantaged by White privilege – to awaken to the recognition of their Whiteness and all that this White privilege has 'done to the world' (ibid., p. 146). Instead, it is essential to focus on the collective inherent in the Black body, through the shared experience of living with a marginalized, victimized body, and to see this position from the power it offers. Reminiscing about a homecoming weekend at Howard, Coates describes the effect of seeing this collective power in the participants, of seeing himself in a community:

> And I felt myself disappearing into all of their bodies. The birthmark of damnation faded and I could feel the weight of my arms and hear the heave in my breath... That was a moment, a joyous moment, beyond the Dream – a moment imbued by a power more gorgeous than any voting rights bill. ...Black power is the dungeon-side view of Monticello – which is to say, the view taken in struggle. (Ibid., pp. 148–149)

Coates reveals here how the collective body–mind becomes the means by which public, social change is made. It requires remembering the power of the past, and not reducing oneself to the present violence of the streets that rule that world.

All the while, Coates is, however, working with eyes wide open. While standing together – allegiance – may be a way forward, Coates is not naive to the threats such a call has for his son who moves in a Black body, viewed through the lens of White privilege as a collective Black body. Chief among the threats to the American 'Dream' is the criticism of the police and elected officials. 'The problem with the police is not that they are fascist pigs but that our country is ruled by majoritarian pigs' (ibid., p. 79).

Through this analysis, Coates raises our collective consciousness of the body–mind, the ways in which the transactions between bodies-minds in society work to limit or extend the opportunities for democratic practice. Of particular interest is the juxtaposition between body and mind, education and schooling, identities and interests, habits and artistry, to think and act differently as a democratic body of citizens with desperately unequal access to political, social and institutional power.

Working towards Democracy in Education in the Face of 'Plunder'

In this final section, we sum up how transactional philosophy can bring us insights into how racial embodiments in public spaces and schools can be better understood and engaged. Thus far we have provided Dewey's treatment of transactionalism as he introduces it in *Democracy and Education*: the embodied mind, the social aims of schooling, powerful notions of habit and the associational, moral understandings of the democratic ideal. Coates' memoir shows how his active mind makes sense of life in a Black body, first in the habits of racialized violence and corporeal containment learned in Baltimore streets and schools. Later, Coates reveals the powerful educational possibilities contained in the associational and moral community of diverse bodies at a place like Howard University, in which shared interests and a body/mind working in sync towards chosen ends can yield significant growth. As such, Coates illuminates the tensions those who move with Black bodies face in managing sets of incompatible habits of corporeal violence and corporeal collaboration.

Societies are formed of bodies; bodies populate and bring social forms of consciousness into action. One essential lesson to emerge from the overlay of Coates's description of the lived reality of Black bodies and Dewey's transactionalism is the emerging co-constitutive nature of bodies and societies. Dewey's work describes this fundamental transaction in the early chapters of *Democracy and Education*, and Coates' book thoroughly explores the contemporary realities of raced bodies in social relations. Viewing experience from this position illuminates the body–mind continuum, and offers a critical understanding of the 'fundamental plunder' experienced by Black bodies.

A transactionalist 'body–mind' framework takes aim at the racist critique held by many Whites: that Black bodies are under siege *because* they participate in activities that require social discipline, that is crime, poverty, drugs, resistance to education. Indeed, rather than questioning whether Coates is 'accurate', a transactional position starts from that the phenomenology of the statement as a given description of another's lived experience, and then goes further to wonder what happens to society and other lived experiences as a result. Transactional inquiry demands a holistic view of how lived experiences and resulting perspectives are intertwined and interrelated. It demands far more than examining our individual intentions as educators, as Coates points out:

> It does not matter that the 'intentions' of individual educators were noble. Forget about intentions. What any institution, or its agents, 'intend' for you is secondary. Our world is physical. Learn to play defense – ignore the head and keep your eyes on the body. Very few Americans will directly proclaim that they are in favor of black people being left to the streets. But a very large number of Americans will do all they can to preserve the Dream. No one directly proclaimed that schools were designed to sanctify failure and destruction. But a great number of educators spoke of 'personal responsibility' in a country authored and sustained by a criminal irresponsibility. (Coates, 2015, p. 33)

Further disabling the discourse of 'personal responsibility' and good intentions are transactionalist tools for understanding racialized power. Sullivan (2001) argues that a transactional position raises the important questions of resources and access to power, which then leads into querying habits that sustain barriers associated with these social features. The benefit here is not just that individuals are believed when describing the consequences of living 'across and through' various historically marginalized bodies, though that is certainly one improvement. A more critical benefit is that a transactional point of view has the notion of power at its core. Such an orienting beginning takes direct aim at those discriminatory social habits that serve to manufacture and maintain ingrained, yet unconscious, oppression. Sullivan explores this capacity to expose such a pattern of internalized, habitualized oppression when examining the category of 'disabled' from a transactional frame: 'It has become a question of what different resources do people with different physical conditions need to function effectively, why are resources distributed the way in which they currently are, and who has the authority to make decisions about the distribution of resources' (Sullivan, 2001, p. 24). The power of this example is that it illuminates the different questioning framework that a transactional position asserts: starting first with deep questioning of social thinking norms that corporeal differences linked with notions of power, which by extension then allows for their possible interruption.

One further advantage of this transactional frame is that it allows a more thoughtful investigation of the habits – corporeal and cognitive – of privilege, and the political, historical and social dynamics associated with these unearned advantages. Applied to racial phenomenology, Coates argues that what makes someone White or Black is their experience, the power dynamics and the associated social habits that influence their existence, not physiognomy:

> ... race is the child of racism, not the father. ...Difference in hue and hair is old. But the belief in the preeminence of hue and hair, the notion that these factors can correctly organize a society and that they signify deeper attributes, which are indelible – this is the new idea at the heart of these new people who have been brought up hopelessly, tragically, deceitfully, to believe that they are white. (Coates, 2015, p. 7)

Powerfully here, Coates charts the historical trajectory of the habits of White privilege, and how they are made and remade through the transaction of bodies and society.

It is this set of White privilege habits that creates conditions of 'fundamental plunder' for Black bodies. These collective habits endure in individuals as well as in social structures that constitute society. Such racialized habits become unconsciously internalized by individuals and institutionalized, hardened in rituals and routines, encased and then normalized. As Stitzlein analyses in her work, these racialized habits of discrimination and White privilege have deep historical roots and are embedded in corporeal habit. 'Many historians have studied race in terms of how the body *appears*, but few have studied race in terms of what the body *does*' (Stitzlein, 2008, p. 32). Instead, utilizing Dewey's idea of habits and transactionalism, Stitzlein sketches a picture of the making of race and the legitimizing of racial discrimination based, via corporeal habit, on actions and beliefs that become naturalized, the 'default and seemingly natural ways in which [racial discrimination] acts, moves, and communicates' (ibid., p. 32). Put simply, 'habits reproduce the historical meanings of race' (ibid., p. 32).

Given this analysis, many questions arise. Are we trapped forever in these systems? Are there reasonable ways to disrupt these habits of mind and body in order to interrupt cycles of oppression? Many authors advance means by which to 'unlearn' racism. Many of these approaches work at the individual level first, helping individuals see the embedded stereotypes operating in their mind. Yet working from Dewey's pragmatic, community focus takes aim at these cycles from a different angle, one that works on the individual mind—body, while insisting on the mind—body at the community level simultaneously. By highlighting the notion of organisms so characteristic of Dewey's work on democracy, the body is brought into view as a place of action — the verb 'bodying' — rather than 'body' as a noun. Different from 'embodying', 'bodying' exposes the views of others' bodies from the position of dominant bodies. Such a starting position honours Coates' description of the movement of the Black body and the impact of others' bodies of others on it, particularly the construction of 'fundamental plunder' both historically and corporeally. Utilizing transaction as a means towards understanding 'the way one interacts with the world and the way one comes into being' foregrounds the critical understanding of the consequences of racial oppression on Black bodies from the body—mind perspective (ibid., p. 13). As Sullivan writes, 'to posit a transactional relationship between the physical and mental is to grant the qualitative impact mental life makes upon human existence, but in such a way that understands mental life as an outgrowth of some of the physical world that is organic' (Sullivan, 2001, p. 27).

Philosophers in the pragmatist tradition continue to explore ways that transactionalism can shape the educational and scholarly work we do with race, racialized thinking and habits. Educators can enable all individuals to gain greater understanding of how their bodily comportment is sustained and sedimented into concealed habits of racialized action (ibid., p. 94). 'Keep your eyes on the body', Coates tells us. Ignore, at least for a while, what people will say about racial bodies and differential treatment and 'responsibility' or by extension, 'grit'. Pay attention to what they do to and with your body, he advises. Coates' narrative reminds us of the powerful ways that the full and free interests and associations of Dewey's democratic criteria are material and embodied. Critical as he was about unnatural dichotomies that drove thinking into ditches, Dewey reminds us of the contemporary status of the Black body in school understood as an 'intruder'.

> In part bodily activity becomes an intruder. Having nothing, so it is thought, to do with mental activity, it becomes a distraction, an evil to be contended with. For the pupil

has a body, and bring it to school along with his mind. And the body is, of necessity, a wellspring of energy; it has to do something. But its activities, not being utilized in occupation with things which yield significant results, have to be frowned upon. They lead the pupil away from the lesson with which his 'mind' ought to be occupied; they are sources of mischief. The chief source of the 'problem of discipline' in schools is that the teacher has often to spend the larger part of the time in suppressing the bodily activities which take the mind away from its material. A premium is put on physical quietude; on silence, on rigid uniformity of posture and movement; upon a machine-like simulation of the attitudes of intelligent interest. (Dewey, 1916, p. 141)

Should students resist this sort of treatment, especially Black student bodies, then both physical and mental violence will likely result. In such a system, the only way forward is disembodiment of the mind, so that the simulation of the 'attitudes of intelligent interest' is manifest in mental activity alone. Only the mind is valuable in this situation because the cultural habits, imbued in the Black body, are seen as generating distractions. In this situation, both the see-er and the seen are racialized, but the see-er gets to hide behind schooled notions of 'pro-social values' and 'positive behaviour', as defined by the school.

Embodied inquiry, and inquiry around the status of bodies in any system, however, reveals personal and cultural truths. In this learning, we might achieve more positive freedom, a required condition of working towards democracy as a form of associated action. Such a position on freedom requires a vision of freedom as capacity *to* act, rather than simply freedom from restraint, and as such requires structures that coordinate, facilitate action. Such is the requirement of democracy. Sullivan considers this work, borrowing from Richard Shusterman's 'somaesthetics', as that which integrates 'bodily practices into the discipline of philosophy itself such that trust and wisdom are pursued through somatic experience' (Sullivan, 2001, p. 112). Sullivan states that 'this is a radical task, one that involves a change in philosophy that deeply threatens its tidy distinctions between mind and body, as well as its sense of what counts as "real" philosophy' (ibid., p. 112). Deweyan democratic ideals continue to demand such radical thinking and practices from us, a century into the influence of *Democracy and Education*.

References

Coates, T. (2015), *Between the World and Me*. New York, NY: Spieget & Grau.
Dewey, J. (1916), *Democracy and Education*. New York, NY: Macmillan Company.
Dewey, J. and Bentley, A. (1949), *Knowing and the Known*. Boston, MA: Beacon Press.
Fallace, T. (2011), *Dewey and the Dilemma of Race: An Intellectual History, 1895-1922*. New York, NY: Teachers College Press.
Fanon, F. (1967), *Black Skin, White Masks*. New York, NY: Grove Press.
Fesmire, S. (2015), *Dewey*. New York, NY: Routledge.
Garrison, J., Neubert, S., Reich, K. (2016), *Democracy and Education, Reconsidered: Dewey After One Hundred Years*. New York, NY: Routledge.
Hamilton, J. (2015), Review, between the world and me. *Slate*, 9 July 2015.
Henry, S. E. (2014), *Children's Bodies in Schools: Corporeal Performances of Social Class*. New York, NY: Palgrave Pivot.
Mapping Police Violence (2017), Available at: https://mappingpoliceviolence.org (accessed 10.10.17).
Parham, M. (2009), *Haunting and Displacement in African American Literature and Culture*. New York, NY: Routledge.
Silver, N. (2015), Black Americans are killed at 12 times the rate of people in other developed countries. FiveThirtyEight, 18 June 2015. Available at: https://fivethirtyeight.com/features/black-americans-are-killed-at-12-times-the-rate-of-people-in-other-developed-countries/ (accessed 10.10.17).
Stitzlein, S. (2008). *Breaking Bad Habits of Race and Gender: Transforming Identity in Schools*. Lanham: Rowman & Littlefield Publishers.
Sullivan, S. (2001). *Living Across and Through Skins: Transactional Bodies, Pragmatism and Feminism*. Bloomington: Indiana University Press.

Chapter 6

Education in the Open: The Somaesthetic Value of Being Outside [*]

Christine Doddington

Abstract

Over the last few decades, the formal school curriculum in many countries has become increasingly prescribed and attainment orientated with an insistent pressure to measure progress in the name of 'raising standards'. This form of constraint on educational practice has provoked counter trends in a desire to enrich the curriculum. Situating learning activities in the open air have become increasingly popular as a counter to formalised schooling. The UK, for example, has seen legislated outside spaces for early years and a growing interest in Forest Schools. The long tradition of activity centres, outside school visits and field trips—offering a valuable way to augment formal learning—has survived in many school settings. The claims for the benefit of taking learning outside are extensive. They range across claiming value for both individual and societal well-being, improving mental and physical health, as well as a way of sustaining inclusion, social cohesion and democratic practice (Nichol, Higgins, Ross, & Mannion, 2007). This article explores how aesthetics and the body may be seen to feature in outside educational experience. By drawing on the work of Richard Shusterman and his extensive work on somaesthetics, the purpose

---

[*]This article appeared originally in *The Journal of Educational Alternatives* ISSN 2049-2162, Volume 3 (2014), Issue 1 pp. 41-59, available at http://www.othereducation.com/index.php/OE/article/view/41

of the article is to augment or ground claims for the worth of 'outside' learning in embodied aesthetic experience and therefore help illuminate what is distinctively educational about moving learning beyond the walls of the school.

Keywords: body; aesthetics; experience; outside; somaesthetics; experiential learning

> One's body (like one's mind) incorporates its surroundings, going beyond the (skin) .... we live...as much in processes across and 'through' skins as in processes 'within' skins' (Dewey, 1949, p. 119).

Introduction

The title 'Education in the Open' is designed to be an inclusive term covering the wide range of activities that take place in the name of education outside of the school-room. These activities might include fieldwork and adventure activities, as well as leisure and scouting activities, such as building shelters or dens. Moving education outside can also cover activities that normally take place in school buildings —it is obviously possible for classes and groups to read, sketch, write or even dance in the open air. The simplicity of the term is intended to be inclusive of current educational developments such as Forest Schools, as well as avoiding preconceptions that might come with the more traditional term of Outdoor Education. Education in the open is also meant to suggest that we need to be more open, and take a fresh look at how we conceptualise educational activity generally as against the more customary conception of academic, school-based learning. Generally, 'in educational institutions strongly influenced by Western rationality the focus of learning is on the universal' and as Bonnett goes on to point out, this conception is at fault because it 'valorizes the abstract over the particular and the cerebral over the tactile, and, for example, third person over first person understandings of the body and of bodily experience' (Bonnett, 2009, p. 7).

So, when education has 'left the building' in its broadest sense, what changes for the body?; and what is significant with the obvious change of 'place'?

The Body

Being outside offers the opportunity to move through space, and to move in qualitatively different ways. Being in the open air has a strong association with a feeling of less confinement and less control. Arguably, less physical constraint may also prompt psychological change. Any observer accompanying a group of children as they move outside for activities, will be struck by the quickening and changes in stance, gesture and talk that anticipation of this move outside provokes. It suggests that the outside context can immediately offer tangibly more freedom of movement and along with it, perhaps less constraint to habitual ways of behaving and thinking in school.

As well as spatial freedom, being outside offers demands or opportunities for increased levels of exertion and the emotional dynamics of physical challenge. Outside we may simply stand more than sit. Demands on the body, by being unconstrained in the ways I have described, suggest that we need to reflect on how the quality of bodily experience can change. At its most basic, a change of surroundings can incite an increased awareness of our bodies and how we use them. Shusterman's claim that the body is the 'organising core of experience' (Shusterman, 2004, p. 51) becomes pertinent here. The body's corporeal, emotional, kinaesthetic and sensual characteristics may have increased significance and feature as more integrated than when we sit in study mode, static and enclosed, with thought dominating our consciousness and separate from awareness of our bodies. Outside then, there is the possibility of increased body consciousness as the body quite naturally becomes more featured, more present and integral to action, to thought and therefore to learning. The question then arises: What value, if any, might this insight have for maximising the educational worth of being outside?

Place

Characteristics of a change in location also have the potential to be educationally significant. Many, but not all of the educational contexts associated with being outside assume closeness to natural aspects of environment and may extend from the patch of grass outside the classroom to an experience of wilderness and nature in the raw. The range is obviously broader than this though. Outside places can, for example, be urban too. In addition, the exchange from inside to outside is significant in terms of the meanings and expectations embedded in a location's design. Outside moves us away from strictly practical, pedagogical or economically determined educational spaces, into what we might call 'real world' contexts. Outside we are subject to the contingency of the elements and are in locations and landscapes that are either predominantly natural or constructed for multi-purpose usage. To the extent that any environment outside is shaped and determined by human purposes, these outside spaces, unlike schoolrooms, are frequently places that have multiple uses, and certainly may be subject to uses other than the educational. Where exactly is the educational value then, in this kind of change of place?

Justifying the Value of Activities Outdoors

There is already an extensive body of work dedicated to arguing for the value of the many different kinds of activities that comprise Outdoor Education. Overall, outdoor education places an emphasis on adventuring and physical activities that develop strength, vigour and skill. Alongside this description there are often claims concerning the value of freedom of movement, how activity promotes health and how being outside enhances appreciation of the natural world. In curriculum terms, these claims are often attached to aspects of PSHE (Personal, Social and Health Education) and Environmental Education. In journals and courses devoted to outdoor education benefits claimed might include: increased self-awareness; self-esteem; memory capacity; heightened motivation and the ability to collaborate. In addition, outside experiences are held up for their therapeutic powers or for the inculcation of desirable dispositions and virtues such as resilience, perseverance, and curiosity (see e.g. Richards et al., 2011).

Higgins and Nicol draw attention to this diversity of claims and explain that there are internationally, different accounts of the central elements of outside education because 'Outdoor education is a cultural construct which is thought about and applied in different ways within and between countries' (Higgins and Nicol, 2002, p. 1). It is clear that different conceptualisations bring different implications: '…behind the diversity of approaches lie different theoretical understandings and practical applications of outdoor education' (ibid., p. 2). In terms of theorising what constitutes outdoor education and its value, a number of writers cite constructivism as the main source of understanding and explanation for why outside activity is educationally valuable. The suggestion is that constructivism rests well with notions of 'experiential learning' and therefore draws on 'a constructivist pedagogy whereby the learners construct their own view of the world based on personal experience' (ibid.).

In terms of its philosophical roots, this theory was presaged in the work of John Dewey. My view is that the relevance of Dewey's philosophical work to theorising education in the open lies, in particular, in his two key, interconnected emphases on environment and experience and his elaboration of the notion of habit. It is worth revisiting and setting these out in more detail. They can begin to open fresh insights for an understanding of the worth of learning activity in the open air.

Experience

Much of Dewey's mainstream philosophical work rests on what might be called his philosophy of experience. By way of explanation, he cites mis-educative experience almost as much as describing what counts as educative experience. Despite claims from his many critics, he makes it clear that: 'It is not enough to insist upon the necessity of experience, nor even of activity in experience. Everything depends upon the quality of experience which is had' (Dewey, 1938/1997, p. 27).

Dewey gives extensive analysis and argument for 'experience' needing to be at the heart of education and the open nature of growth that, in turn, determines an experience as educational. For this reason, any form of enterprise, such as outside education claiming to centre around experiential learning in a Deweyan sense, needs to set out the qualities inherent in those learning experiences distinguishing it as educationally valuable. To help reveal the qualities of valuable experience, Dewey firstly separates two aspects to any experience: 'the immediate aspect of agreeableness or disagreeableness' and the 'influence' that experience has on future experiences. He suggests that, independent of desire or intent, whether we want it or not, 'every experience lives on in further experiences' (ibid.). Unlike educationalists who might see enjoyment, happiness or excitement in experiences as an intrinsic warrant for educative experience, Dewey argues that the agreeableness, enjoyment or otherwise of an experience is relatively straightforward and is not the root of educational worth. Instead, he points us decisively to the effect of an experience. What really counts is how experiences connect and achieve what he calls 'continuity'. This will happen 'if an experience arouses curiosity, strengthens initiative, and sets up desires and purposes that are sufficiently intense to carry a person over dead places in the future' (ibid., p. 38). Continuity of experience then, connects to our experiences in the past and presses us forward in anticipation and on towards greater receptivity and further enriching experience. Dewey argues 'Its (experience's) value can be judged only on the ground of what it moves toward and into' (ibid.).

The answer to the direction and ground of truly educative experiences is what Dewey calls 'growth'—the promotion of cumulative flourishing or enrichment. Growth cannot be pre-determined. For Dewey, we can evaluate whether an experience is educational by asking: 'Does this form of growth create conditions for further growth or does it set up conditions that shut off the person... from the occasions, stimuli and opportunities for continuing growth in new directions'. (ibid., p. 36). In terms of practice, it would be easy to distinguish times when individuals have experiences that turn them away from further pursuits outside, make them reluctant to bodily engage with activities, or in contrast, generate an openness, a desire to return or extend those experiences further in some way.

One can see something of the sense of Dewey's persistent adherence to open-endedness and continuity of experience. Understood properly, this idea avoids some of the traps and clichés often attributed, perhaps erroneously, to progressivism. Enjoyment still has value, but experiences that are merely enjoyable, that merely excite or make us happy may not be educative. In contrast, an experience that gives us an appetite for seeking out experience, that allows us to expand our powers, our understandings, our sensibilities and responsiveness to the world and to others—in other words—to grow, has more lasting value than merely agreeable experience. 'Every experience' (worthy of the title educative), he writes, 'should do something to prepare a person for later experiences of a deeper and more expansive quality. That is the very meaning of growth, continuity, reconstruction of experience' (ibid., p. 47).

It could be argued that Dewey's conception of growth is vague or too general to be of use, however I have tried to indicate that Dewey's view in its open-endedness is worth revisiting as it is both complex and significant. Prescription of the ends of a conception of on-going human flourishing is highly problematic—how would we go about pre-determining the sensibilities necessary for someone other than ourselves to engage, relish and pursue further experiences that deepen and expand their sense of their existence? If we did try to specify and steer for this in a heavy-handed way, would this not be to fall into a trap of actually narrowing the educational potential inherent in any transaction between an individual and environment? The trap would include making assumptions about what helps us to flourish personally and projecting these requirements onto others. Dewey goes on to argue that the main point of education is to intensify this desire for continuity in growth through experience, rather than weaken it: 'If impetus in this direction is weakened instead of being intensified, we don't just fail in preparing someone for the future—we actually rob them of natural capacities that, if strengthened, would enable someone to become self-sufficient and resilient to cope with the circumstances that person might meet in the course of their life' (ibid., p. 48).

Environment

In his writings on education, Dewey attaches significance to what he calls, collateral learning, which is the familiar idea that incidental learning frequently occurs for the learner over and above any subject-based, pre-ordained learning. This idea, together with his account of experience, takes us into the wider notions of education that are being explored here. However, we need to go further to do justice to Dewey and experience, by considering his analysis of environment. Dewey sees experience not just in relation to the individual and their perceptions. Experience is necessarily embedded within the environment in which an individual is always inevitably placed. It is the integration, or to use Dewey's own word, the *trans-action* between individual and environment that constitutes experience (Garrison, 1998).

An experience is always what it is because of a transaction taking place between an individual (their needs, desires, purposes and capacities) and what at that time constitutes his [sic] environment (persons, subject matter, physical location, equipment) that surrounds the individual. The environment... is whatever conditions interact with personal needs, desires, purposes, and capacities to create the experience which is had. (Dewey, 1938/1997, pp. 43–44)

This then constitutes the physical and intellectually situated sense of environment 'that is replete with social meaning and significance' (ibid.). Dewey elaborates this by offering three senses in which environment can be significant. Environment affects experience by giving us

- the concrete, physical environment in which we are placed;
- the intellectual stance and heritage of ideas that form the conditions of where we are at this time and in this place;
- the social, emotional and ethical environment, or, in other words—environment is always coloured by the way we relate to others and the world. Humans are never in isolation from their constituted social nature, even when they experience solitude.

On this view, it is clear that some of the features of environment lie within, as well as outside, the individual. In Dewey's account, humans are always situated in ways that include orientation, placement and communication. So while the move to the outside draws our attention to the first sense where the distinctive physical features will undoubtedly impinge on us, it is important to recognise the significance of Dewey's second and third dimensions of environment. The justification of Outdoor Education can be argued for in terms of the social, emotional and ethical value of group outdoor activity. Comradeship, teamwork, trust and cooperation can feature in collective activity involving, for example, white water rafting, outside play or building dens (Magnussen, 2012). The second sense of environment highlights our assumptions and ways of looking at the world as we step into the open air. It calls us to attend to our implicit stance towards nature, and for instance, the ecological environment.

However, the impact of this composite sense of environment becomes clearer when Dewey explains its significance for his view of experience: 'Interaction of environment and organism is the source, direct or indirect, of all experience' (Dewey, 1934/2005, p. 153), and later, 'Experience is the result, the sign, and the reward of that interaction of organism and environment which, when it is carried to the full, is a transformation of interaction in participation and communication' (ibid., p. 22). If educationalists are charged with the shaping of learning activity to encourage its full educational worth of 'transformation' and 'reconstruction' of experience, then all three senses of environment need consideration. Simply stepping outside has more to it than the initial phrase or action might imply.

Habit

Dewey suggests that whilst as individuals we 'transact' with environment to make meaning in our experiences, in this transaction, habit plays an essential role—our habitual approach is what allows us to perceive, to select and discriminate, to make sense of the experienced world. We might assume that one useful contrast here would be between mindless, habitual behaviour and conscious, thoughtful action. However, Dewey challenges this assumed separation of habit and consciousness by saying that reason and consciousness, our sense-making, depends upon, and actually emerges from, our human 'habits'. Habits provide the frame by which we are able to perceive, recognise, imagine, and recall, as well as make judgments and reason. He argues that his

conception of habit goes deeper than the ordinary conception of a habit as a more or less fixed way of doing things… It covers the formation of attitudes… that are emotional and intellectual; it covers our basic sensitivities and ways of meeting and responding to all the conditions that we meet in living. (Dewey, 1934/2005, p. 35)

In other words, habit indispensably forms the lens through which we make sense of the world.

This implies that habit is not opposed to reason and control, with mindless habitual acts on the one hand and rational decisive action on the other. Instead, the real contrast for educationalists is between an inferior way of viewing the world that is routinised and thus 'unintelligent' or unaware, and a more perceptive, 'intelligent or artistic' engagement that is 'fused with thought and feeling,' which Dewey argues should become the educated way of responding and making sense of the world. Thus, the choice is between experience relying on unperceptive habit and an orientation that adopts a more 'flexible, sensitive habit'. The claim would be that there is potential in outside experience to challenge and stimulate more flexible and sense-aware orientations to the experience undergone.

To pursue this quality of orientation further, it is helpful to look again at Dewey's conceptualisation of the body and in particular, how this has been developed in the work of Richard Shusterman.

Body Consciousness

Throughout his extensive philosophical writing, Dewey famously and consistently attacked what he suggested were false dualisms, in particular the mind/body distinction which he felt profoundly misleads us, causing us to overlook the part that the soma or body plays in emotion, thought and action. There are of course a number of philosophers, particularly in continental philosophy that have argued for greater understanding of the significance of the body—Foucault and Merleau-Ponty perhaps spring to mind before thought of the Pragmatists. Bonnett writes for example:

> Amongst others, Merleau-Ponty (1962), has developed the idea of the body as a site of perception, learning and knowledge, and it seems clear that its movements express myriad sensitivities and accommodations to a proximate environment in terms of which that body, its movement and its environment, are initially rendered intelligible and from which the sense of its own being—self—continuously springs, and in which it is continuously anchored. (Bonnett, 2009, p. 3)

But the argument for how the Descartian mind/body dualism has prevented adequate acknowledgement of the significance of the body, was an early part of pragmatist thinking, particularly in terms of our emotional lives. William James argued, 'A purely disembodied human emotion is a nonentity' (James, 1983, pp. 173–4). If we try to abstract from any strong emotion 'all the feelings of its characteristic bodily symptoms, we find we have nothing left behind' (ibid.). Shusterman adds: 'We cannot get away from the experienced body with its feelings and stimulations, its pleasures, pains and emotions...all affect is somatically grounded' (Shusterman, 2000, p. 153).

However, there is an important distinction between Dewey and what James wrote about in terms of bodily action. James, and indeed Merleau-Ponty, both stress the body's place in emotion and they argue that developed bodily action requires an unthinking spontaneity. So for them, reflection can inhibit effective action. In contrast, Dewey wants to retain a role for reflection and argues that it is conscious bodily self-awareness that is the key to both better thought and action. The idea is that rather than some general self-awareness, body consciousness enriches and allows a person to be more 'present'. And for Dewey, body consciousness is significant for enhancing continuity of experience, helping to give an appetite for further experience that actually expands or grows the consciousness we have of our body and our consciousness generally.

Shusterman similarly emphasises the importance of reflection, resolutely embedding a role for mindfulness in body consciousness and explaining how he wishes to 'emphasise the reflective and cognitive dimensions of somaesthetics' (Shusterman, 2012, p. 14). At the same time, Shusterman stresses the body's sentient subjectivity wherein we can 'improve our perceptual faculties through better use of the soma' (ibid., p. 141). One of Shusterman's main interests is in using somaesthetics as a critique of the current obsessions that are attached to the appearance and care of the body and he therefore challenges the triviality of how these obsessions manifest themselves in modern life. Shusterman attempts to channel the idea of our understanding and care of the body/mind into a form of philosophy, seeing somaesthetics as 'a discipline devoted to the critical, ameliorative study of the experience and use of the body as a locus of sensory-aesthetic appreciation (aesthesis) and creative self-fashioning' (Shusterman, 2004, p. 51). For those unfamiliar with his work it may be helpful to very briefly explain where Shusterman's notion of pragmatic somaesthetics sits within his broader theory of somaesthetics.

Somaesthetics

Shusterman distinguishes different dimensions to the discipline of somaesthetics. Analytical somaesthetics is the study of the basic nature of our bodily perceptions and practices, their particular function in our knowledge and construction of reality. So, Merleau-Ponty and Foucault, for example, both raise socio-political issues; they explain how notions of health, beauty, and gender are all socially constructed and how the body is shaped and employed as an instrument to maintain power. For Shusterman, all these aspects fall within analytical somaesthetics. He goes on to argue that pragmatic somaesthetics is an approach that presupposes, but transcends, analytical somaesthetics. Pragmatic somaesthetics focuses on the various activities and disciplines advocated to 'improve' us bodily and mindfully. Apart from representational or appearance issues of the body and performative aspects of the body (he cites martial arts and dance as examples), Shusterman suggests improvement can occur with practices that focus on the aesthetic quality of the body's experience, a strand which he calls the 'experiential.'

There is little opportunity to do full justice to Shusterman's work here but with an emphasis on the body and aesthetic experience, I wish to focus on three features that I have identified as growing out of Shusterman's 'experiential' strand of pragmatic somaesthetics which can be further illuminated by revisiting aspects of Dewey's notion of the aesthetic. My belief is that the following are directly pertinent to education in the open. The three aspects I raise are: the aesthetic nature of immediacy within experience; the aesthetic challenge inherent in bodily-conceived engagement in the environment and the significance of flexible, sensitised habit to generate growth and desire for experience.

Experiential Somaesthetic Practice—Immediacy

In *Art as Experience* (1934/2005) Dewey integrates his notion of aesthetic into the heart of his conceptualisation of experience, whilst Shusterman's overall stress on body consciousness, necessary to our flourishing, suggests a strong aesthetic quality of immediacy—the here and now; the felt, aliveness of being.

The felt immediacy in our experience is palpable, but it is also momentary. Yet, despite being elusive and difficult to describe, this felt immediacy is indispensable as a motivating factor in striving for the continuity of experience so prized in Dewey's account. We should not approach life in ways that turn the flow of experience leaden—Dewey works towards identifying an intuitive, fluidity of action when he writes 'if each act has to be consciously searched for at the moment and intentionally performed, execution is painful and the product is clumsy' (Dewey, 1938/1997, p. 43). Shusterman points out that for Dewey, the immediacy of qualitative feeling is essential glue holding and shaping experience and thus is highly desirable. But if we acknowledge it is elusive, remains indescribable and reflectively ungraspable, how can we make use of it?

It may help here to remind ourselves of early childhood experience, which can arguably be seen as naturally, aesthetically charged. Peter Abbs for example, argues that life is first experienced sensually and kinesthetically—the tactile, rhythmic, the vocal, the imagined, are all experienced bodily as a child, much more so than later in life. He argues these aesthetic qualities retain their significance for experience later in the arts.

Nearly all the early shaping responses of human life are aesthetic in character, bringing through pleasure, pain or a diffuse sense of well-being, intimations of the nature of our common world. Long before we are rational beings, we are aesthetic beings; and we remain so, though often undeveloped and unsubtle, till ultimate insensibility defines the end of individual life. For death, in the precise words of Philip Larkin, administers 'the anaesthetic from which none come round'. (Abbs, 1989, p. 4). The question that follows is whether this sensibility can be developed further and become sufficient for an experience to be educational in its ability to drive us toward greater receptivity and thus encourage 'growth'. While immediacy may be present in an early childhood awareness of the world, can it also feature in maturity? Michael Bonnett seems to echo the significance of immediacy with his notion of anticipation. He suggests that dislocation from a familiar situation can be threatening. A change of place or moving outside for example, may be daunting. On the other hand, change can also be liberating. Bonnett draws our attention to this 'anticipation,' when unfamiliar territory can provoke a readiness and an openness to what is forthcoming. He writes, might 'such anticipation be emancipatory through provoking new kinds of receptiveness, sensitivity?' (Bonnett, 2009, p. 7). He gives some graphic examples of how anticipation might sit well with and even capture something of the immediacy that I believe Shusterman wishes to stress. Bonnett writes:

> The anticipation experienced on a fine spring morning by the walker as she sets off, or of the fisherman as he approaches the riverbank at dawn, or that of the trysting lover, is of a very different calibre... Here anticipation is experienced as an openness to and embracing of the unknown that is to come—the challenges and the sights, the smells, the textures, the ambiences and surprises of, say, different spots and times of day. It speaks of a keen attentiveness. Such anticipation quickens life, gives a heightened sense of being. It is a form of futurity, and of ecstasis. (Bonnett, 2009, p. 7)

Thomas Alexander's insight into Dewey's aesthetics is also helpful here—he too suggests that we begin with 'raw' aesthetic experience—'those experiences that call forth attention and compel us, making experience 'come alive' as it were' (Alexander, 1998, p. 14). But he adds that for something to qualify as an experience, it has to run its course to fulfilment; it will thus have a beginning and an end. Alexander explains:

> The beginning is initiated by a tensive excitement that compels us to focus on the unfolding experience... Dewey calls this 'impulsion' ... while the field of experience is rendered focused and kept within limits by what Dewey terms 'closure' or 'fusion'... the sense of bringing the experience to an end. (ibid.)

Dewey speaks of the pervasive, qualitative 'feel' of a situation which is consciously manifest throughout the course of the experience and gives it a sense of unity, and in Alexander's words, is completed by: 'a bounding horizon... within which all our conscious awareness of meaning... occurs... As experience becomes aesthetic... this pervasive quality that marks out an experience as whole, continuous and meaningful is vividly present'. (ibid., p. 15). This creates what Alexander has called 'an aesthetically consummated experience' (ibid., p. 13). To qualify as an experience in the sense Dewey claimed, there needs to be a transforming consummation or completion, 'in which the world opens itself to us and reveals a felt or sensed meaning and embodied value (in a non-verbal way)' (ibid., p. 14).

Perhaps stepping outside to engage bodily with the world has a natural shape and ending as we step back indoors. But for this engagement to qualify more surely as education, the experience needs in part to change us and, significantly, to provoke a desire to return to the open, to re-engage, relish openness to feelings and what is around us; to savour and extend that form of engagement. Alexander speaks of an aesthetically consummated experience largely in terms of art, but I think the transfer to open air activity and experience is clear, for it is the consummation of the aesthetic nature of that experience that becomes crucial if there is to be a change in the way the world is seen and felt.

While stepping onto an urban street or walking through grass can be experienced as mundane activity, approaching such steps in ways that increase sensibility to both body and world strengthens the educational potential (see Shusterman, 2008). To shape this sensibility through expressions that bring the experience to consciousness, strengthens it even more. To then round the experience in some sense, to reflect back and share what was noticed, experienced and thought, offers the possibility of completing and consummating the aesthetic worth and transforming effect of experience itself. It is these dimensions that pick up Shusterman's own emphasis on 'the reflective and cognitive dimensions of somaesthetics, its concern with acutely discriminating bodily perceptions and with meditative experiences of beautiful inner feelings' (Shusterman, 2012, p. 14).

If this argument stands, there is a subtle distinction emerging with Shusterman's own advocacy of experiential somaesthetics for improvement of body consciousness. He is both convinced and convincing about the need to directly train adults' proprioception (the self-sense of strength, effort and relation of different parts of the body), to cultivate somatic discipline and enhance bodily introspection by minute adjustment of bodily positioning. But the young, particularly children, already have some instinctive awareness and are disposed to move through space. This suggests there are already advantages that can be maximised in their education, particularly when it takes place in the open air. That said, it is important that we do not lose sight of the overall, ambitious aim of somaesthetics. It is to improve the body physically and the body as the site of 'subjectively lived experience' by 'rendering external physical form and inner perceptual experience more aesthetically satisfying while adding grace and efficacy to our somatic performance' (Shusterman, 2012, p. 17).

The Challenge in Bodily-Led Engagement with the World

The clear focus on quality of experience and the importance of 'felt immediacy,' challenges the assumption that outdoor activity should focus on control of the body. Instead, the need is to become bodily attentive in environmental trans-actions. Shusterman mentions a notable shift from ideas of commanding the body, to the development of an ability to listen to the body in its everyday situatedness in the methods he cites, such as the Alexander Technique or Feldenkrais method. However, it could be said that to listen to our bodies, for example, in the throes of demanding active pursuits, may be difficult or counter-productive, if not impossible or dangerous. Furthermore, there must be limits to explicit consciousness during such experiences.

Nevertheless, developing immediate body consciousness through being bodily attentive may well be an important feature of gaining skill in these situations. To bodily sense the need to adjust one's position on a wind board may eventually become more crucial than the beginner's laborious control of body placement in response to instruction. This is not an argument against developing careful somatic adjustment or 'cultivating somatic discipline' (Shusterman, 2012, p. 141). The point is that there is clearly an argument for both aspects. In terms of educating the young, there may be the need to keep momentary awareness of their natural somatic and aesthetic sensibility alive, alongside or even prior to increased control of the body.

The idea of developing body consciousness in the moment, suggests the cultivation of a specific form of aesthetic awareness. Literature and the arts have long tried to convey the sensual quality of experiencing certain activities—sailing in stormy waters or trudging along riverbanks in the rain, for example. If there is a need to maximise the educational potential of being outside, appreciating the need for an aesthetic response in this situation may help. There are many forms of expression that can make explicit, cherish, and lead to sharing the felt immediacy of experience in ways that heighten sensibility both in attending to the environment and the felt body. In particular, images, movement, words and sounds, clearly have the power to help form what might be otherwise ungraspable. Here then is the link to why Shusterman draws in a Deweyan understanding of aesthetics. Pragmatic somaesthetics places a particular stress on mindfulness as a significant feature. In education, the expression of feelings and experience can occur through a variety of imagery and media, as well as simply talk.

To licence an experience outside as educational, there needs to be opportunities for communication, for sharing meaning and felt experience. The forming of felt experience into consciousness and shape, requires the individual to re-present their experience for themselves and in relation to others. My suggestion is that the pragmatist emphasis on puzzlement as a spur to learning is experienced here as more of an aesthetic challenge—an ongoing provocation to be attentively situated, to relate, to feel, then to re-present; all as part of becoming bodily conscious and mindful when outside.

Flexibility in Habit and Environment

David Granger is another writer who attempts to revision aesthetic education with reference to Dewey. In his work, Granger speaks of 'situations that have an array of components' and says that situations 'are in the main organised and purposive and 'stable' thanks to the continual work of habits—so they have a tendency to evoke certain pre-set or 'scripted' behaviours' (Granger, 2006, p. 36). This suggests a tendency then, towards the routinised form of habit mentioned earlier which, it can be argued, is a particularly dominant characteristic of learned behaviour within the schoolroom.

In contrast, Granger describes situations that stimulate, that 'can change in (overt or) subtle ways from moment to moment—situations can go from routine, to problematic in what seems a blink of an eye' and he stresses that, in these cases, there will be an 'elaborate array of components' which mean every situation has its own qualitative sense of being unique (Granger, 2006, p. 36). Education in the open, with its ensemble of natural and sociocultural components, has rich potential to provoke somaesthetic reflection and expression and inspire more flexible habit. The immediacy of experience, where thought and feeling is bodily fused, is more likely to occur in transactions with situations and places where there is a likelihood for the environment to be felt as fresh and changing, and unroutinised. So the 'open' can offer expanded opportunities for provoking experience that will challenge or jolt us into more flexibility of what we might call integrated body/mindfulness. Sense-ful with conscious sensibility.

Conclusion

This chapter is concerned with the theorising that can underpin the practice of education taking place in the open. There are numerous sound and extensive arguments which can be mounted to support this form of educational activity, as well as many different accounts of what that practice might look like. However, this chapter has sought to find space for 'body consciousness' as part of outdoor education. Shusterman argues that foregrounding the body serves to 'improve our understanding of the body's background functioning so we can also improve its effective performance through the reconstruction of poor habits' (Shusterman, 2012, p. 17). Yet this, together with the aesthetic potential I have outlined, may be easily overlooked in more cognitive justifications or straightforward physical accounts of educating outside.

In the search for worthwhile characteristics of educational experience in the open, two themes have emerged. The first is the often unappreciated primacy of the body as a source of sensibility and intelligibility. The traditional neglect of children's bodies in favour of their minds in education has a long history. Outdoor education is frequently seen in terms of physical activity but there is the potential for conceptualising an even richer educational experience. This is one that includes physicality but acknowledges the aesthetic dimension of soma. Taking children outside to learn immediately offers the potential for developing body consciousness. However, without educationalists having a full understanding of the place and value of body consciousness and the aesthetic in outside learning, much of that potential for educational experience and growth may remain unrealised.

Secondly, the aesthetic nature of experience, its features of immediacy, compulsion and potential for consummation, are all aspects that can be richly heightened in outside experience. Being outside can become naturally distinctive for urging the body into conscious awareness—we feel cold, stretched, discomfort, we immerse ourselves in water, get stung, feel the rush of adrenalin, feel exhilarated, or creep and crunch our way through leaves. We exert ourselves, become tired, conscious of our breath, and our muscles as they ache. But we can also meditate—contemplate the night sky—sit close to one another, rest, touch, support one another and talk about our experiences.

Drawing from the richness of Dewey's extensive thought, Shusterman has developed a complex view of somaesthetics which I have argued has relevance for education in the open. He mainly directs his work at ongoing adult cultivation of body consciousness and there is little reference to what this might mean in terms of the young, immature learner. However, I believe these ideas offer clear potential across the ages. To the notion of experience in its transactional corporeality I have tried to echo Shusterman and bring into play a distinctive Deweyan conception of aesthetics, which can have resonance for all ages. It captures something of why placing education in the open may be worthwhile. At the same time, I am conscious that there are clear, significant implications in all of this for education inside too—hence my ambiguous title, education in the open. The trend to take learning outside, to extend children's physical experiences through activities, adventure and pursuits is simply one of the best opportunities currently available in education for attending to mindful body consciousness and the pragmatic, aesthetic nature of being.

When learners step outside they may each notice different things. What they see in the location, their feelings, their appreciation of the elements and their perception of themselves and their place in the urban or natural landscape, are all aspects that may be individually different. Yet all these aspects are ripe for education. The question is how teachers can enhance their student's experience, that is, increase their sensibility and aid their capacity to express, re-present and relate to others through these aspects of their experience. If being out of doors does urge aesthetic sense-awareness and consciousness of both environment, the self and the body, it is the gradual developing of sensibility and discernment, through reflection, through 'expression' and 'sharing' that helps move that experience into having lasting effect, being influential and ultimately being somatically and educationally worthwhile.

Acknowledgement

I would like to thank the participants of the *Philosophical Perspectives on Outdoor Education International Conference* held at the University of

Edinburgh in April 2012, for their insightful discussions on an earlier version of this chapter and, in particular, Professor Morwenna Griffiths and Dr Helen E. Lees for their encouragement and support before, and during, the writing of the article.

References

Abbs, P. (1989), *'A is for aesthetic': Essays on Creative and Aesthetic Education.* New York, NY: Falmer.
Alexander, T. M. (1998), The art of life: Dewey's aesthetics. In L. Hickman (Ed.), *Reading Dewey: Interpretations for a Postmodern Generation.* Bloomington, IN: Indiana University Press, pp. 1–22.
Bonnett, M. (2009), Schools as places of unselving: An educational pathology? In Dall'Alba, G. (Ed.), *Exploring Education through Phenomenology: Diverse Approaches.* Oxford: Wiley-Blackwell.
Dewey, J. (1934/2005), *Art as Experience.* New York, NY: Perigree Books.
Dewey, J. (1938/1997), *Experience and Education.* New York, NY: Touchstone.
Dewey, J. (1949), Knowing and the known. In Boydston, J. A. (Ed.), *John Dewey: The Later Works: 1925–1953*, vol. 16. Carbondale & Edwardsville: Southern Illinois University Press.
Garrison, J. (1998), John Dewey's philosophy as education. In L. Hickman (Ed.), *Reading Dewey: Interpretations for a Postmodern Generation.* Bloomington, IN: Indiana University Press, pp. 63–81.
Granger, D. (2006), *John Dewey, Robert Pirsig, and the Art of Living: Revisioning Aesthetic Education.* New York, NY: Palgrave Macmillan.
Higgins, P. and Nicol, R. (2002), Outdoor Education: Authentic Learning in the Context of Landscapes: Vol. 2. Kinda Education Centre, Sweden.
James, W. (1983), What is an Emotion? In *Essays in Psychology.* Cambridge: Harvard University Press.
Magnussen, L. I. (2012), Play—the making of deep outdoor experiences. *Journal of Adventure Education and Outdoor Learning*, 12 (1), 25–39.
Merleau-Ponty, M. (1962), The body in its sexual being. In *The Phenomenology of Perception* (C. Smith, Trans.). Boston, MA: Routledge and Kegan Paul.
Nichol, R., Higgins, P., Ross, H. and Mannion, G. (2007), Outdoor education in Scotland: a summary of recent research. *Scottish Natural Heritage.* Available at: http://www.snh.org.uk/pdfs/publications/education/ocreportwithendnotes.pdf (accessed 30.01.14).
Richards, K., Carpenter, C. and Harper, N. (Eds.) (2011), Special issue: outdoor and adventure therapy. *Journal of Adventure Education and Outdoor Learning*, 11 (2).
Shusterman, R. (2000), *Performing Live: Aesthetic Alternatives for the Ends of Art.* Cornell: Cornell University Press.

Shusterman, R. (2004), Somaesthetics and education: exploring the terrain. In L. Bresler (Ed.), *Knowing Bodies, Moving Minds: Towards Embodied Teaching and Learning*. London: Kluwer Academic.

Shusterman, R. (2008), *Body Consciousness: A Philosophy of Mindfulness and Somaesthetics*. Cambridge: Cambridge University Press.

Shusterman, R. (2012), *Thinking through the Body: Essays in Somaesthetics*. Cambridge: Cambridge University Press.

PART 3
DEWEY, EXPERIENCE, DEMOCRACY AND EDUCATION

Chapter 7

Dewey and the Democratic Curriculum

Neil Hopkins

Abstract

This chapter uses Dewey's seminal *Democracy and Education* (1916) as a key text to investigate the concept of the democratic curriculum. I argue that a democratic curriculum is one where a series of educational innovations or procedures are followed. These are as follows: a removal of the existing division between 'academic' and 'vocational' education; pedagogy in the form of discussion and dialogue; negotiation of curriculum aims and objectives with students and other local stakeholders. The focus of attention will be on the English school curriculum (both primary and secondary), especially concerning the National Curriculum, and the debate over 'standards' and testing. A tentative link between the democratic curriculum and increased student motivation and participation is made.

Keywords: Dewey; democracy; curriculum; stakeholders; standards

Introduction

The issue of what constitutes the appropriate forms of study in any given curriculum is inevitably a political decision. Who makes that decision will determine the sources of power in the education system, be they local, regional or national. The idea of a democratic curriculum, where stakeholders other than local or national government have a significant say in what makes up the curriculum, has a long heritage. Educational thinkers of the stature of John Dewey have asked questions and sought answers on the subject of who should control what is learnt by students and when. The purpose of this chapter is to discuss the idea of the democratic curriculum in terms of recent developments in the control and management of the English school curriculum. I will be defining the democratic curriculum on two broad fronts: as a means of challenging the traditional dichotomy of 'academic' and 'vocational' education that has persisted in English education for several centuries and advocating the negotiation of key learning objectives and curriculum content among students, teachers and other stakeholders.

The chapter takes a series of themes to structure the discussion. Dewey's *Democracy and Education* (1916) is a key text with regard to the democratic curriculum. Dewey's concept of the democratic curriculum will be explored by comparing his ideas with the German educationalist, Georg Kerschensteiner (a contemporary of Dewey less well known in the English-speaking world, whose ideas on democracy and education were often close to Dewey's). Dewey and Kerschensteiner were both highly influential in advocating forms of education that encompassed the theoretical and the practical. Indeed, Dewey's epistemology gave equal weight to applied and theoretical knowledge (Dewey, 2007, pp. 194–204).

The issue of 'standards' has been an ongoing debate in education for at least 40 years in England (from the publication of the first 'Black Papers' in the early 1970s). The increasing adoption of a neoliberal philosophy within many national school systems has blended discussion of 'standards' with talk of standardized testing, competitive league tables and cost efficiencies. I will discuss the impact this debate has had on the development of the school curriculum and how the concept and practice of the democratic curriculum has managed to survive and adapt as part of this debate. Particular mention will be made here of England's National Strategies in literacy and numeracy (1998 onwards) and the recent developments in academies and free schools in England.

By its very nature, the democratic curriculum is a highly politicized concept. Who owns the curriculum, and the aims and objectives associated with it, is about power and control within education itself. If the definition of a democratic curriculum is one where the content, structure and assessment of subjects (or other modes of inquiry) is a matter of negotiation between the various stakeholders that have a vested interest, then carrying this out is itself a political act. As a project, it remains a radical proposal (often too radical for many administrations to implement, even in diluted form). The example of Participatory Budgeting and the Citizen School in Porto Alegre is the exception rather than the rule (Gandin and Apple, 2002).

One hundred years since its first publication, Dewey's *Democracy and Education* still resonates in the debate over how or whether any curriculum should be democratic. For Dewey, the school was a place where students were introduced to the skills and attitudes associated with democratic citizenship, especially regarding learning as a collaborative activity. Part of Dewey's project in the Laboratory School in Chicago was also to try and break down the traditional hierarchy over the 'academic' and the 'vocational'. I will show that Dewey was highly sceptical of this division, seeing knowledge as a constant push-and-pull between theory and application. In this sense, Dewey was close in thought with his direct contemporary, Georg Kerschensteiner. Kerschensteiner was the Munich Director of Schools who instituted a policy where all students studied a range of 'academic' and 'vocational' subjects and was one of the pioneers of the modern German apprenticeship. Both thinkers challenged the current notion that activities of the mind took pre-eminence over activities of the hand, seeing this as a crippling and dangerously false dichotomy.

Dewey's Laboratory School could not possibly live up to all its ideals, and Schultz (2001) has identified how the institution could be removed, at times, from the political action around it rather than being at the heart of it. Dewey's advocacy of collaborative learning and the integration of the academic and the practical into the curriculum has also drawn criticism from those commentators who are concerned that a movement away from sharply defined subject areas would lead to a drop in 'quality' and 'standards', especially politicians, commentators and educationalists espousing neo-liberal credentials.

The democratic curriculum has, at its core, the idea that learning is a negotiation among those with a vested interest in such learning. Stakeholders are likely to include government, educational administrators, teachers, students, employers and the local community. There are practical implications in terms of the ability, confidence and age of the students involved, as well as the potential difficulty in consulting the various stakeholders over individual programmes. However, the principal key of negotiation is that no one agent or agency should own the curriculum to the extent of determining aims and objectives without the agreement of other stakeholders.

Democratic Education and the Academic/Vocational Divide

The academic/vocational divide has been a perennial issue within English education. Dewey saw implications for such a divide on both an educational level and epistemological level. He stated in *Democracy and Education*, 'the separation of "mind" from direct occupation with things throws emphasis on things at the expense of relations or connections' (Dewey, 2007, p. 109). Dewey believed education (and by implication, knowledge) was, essentially, a combination of both the practical and the theoretical. To view education as 'academic' or 'vocational' is in large part false dichotomy. This will be discussed in more detail below in relation to what constitutes a democratic curriculum.

Dewey, in *Democracy and Education*, famously referred to democracy as being 'more than a form of government; it is primarily a form of associated living, of conjoint communicated experience' (ibid., p. 68). For Dewey, democracy was a way of life (rather than merely a system of voting) and the school curriculum should reflect this: 'things gain meaning by being used in a shared experience or joint action' (ibid., p. 17). It is clear from these extracts that a fundamental aspect of a democratic curriculum, according to Dewey, is for students to discover knowledge and new learning in a collaborative way rather than being taught as individuals in near isolation (intellectually if not physically). Learning is a collective enterprise, something students do together, just as democratic governance should, ideally, involve all citizens.

If this is how the pedagogy within a democratic curriculum might look, what of the content of the curriculum itself? What would be studied in such a curriculum? Dewey argued for a curriculum that blended knowledge and experience and challenged 'the feeling that knowledge is high and worthy in the degree in which it deals with ideal symbols instead of with the concrete' (Dewey, 2007, p. 196). As Carr and Hartnett have observed:

> Dewey recognised that ... democratic education could only be realistically achieved if the existing separation of a 'liberal education' for an elite few from a 'vocational education' for the mass of ordinary people was abolished. (Carr and Hartnett, 1996, p. 63)

This echoes the thoughts of the nineteenth-century German educationalist Georg Kerschensteiner who argued for a curriculum that encompassed both general and vocational education, a blend of the 'traditional' academic subjects with subjects that are craft-based to ensure both the mind and the hand are trained in parallel (see Gonon, 2009 and Winch, 2006). By incorporating skills and disciplines not normally associated with the academic curriculum, Dewey and Kerschensteiner were attempting to break down some of the social barriers and divisions that occur between the 'academic' and 'vocational' disciplines that students were often 'pigeon-holed' into. For both thinkers, a school curriculum needed to reflect and build upon the wider interpretation of knowledge and understanding held by citizens in society at large (as workers, voters, family members, community activists). Any narrowing of focus (in terms of study) would potentially privilege or diminish aspects of education seen as important by Dewey and Kerschensteiner (particularly concerning the status of vocational education) (Gonon, 2009, pp. 83, 134, 169). Granted, any school curriculum is inevitably constrained by time and must always, to some extent, prioritize certain elements of knowledge over others at certain periods of a school term or year. What Dewey and Kerschensteiner were challenging was the constant privileging of theoretical knowledge over practical knowledge. For Dewey, particularly, this was not only socially divisive but a flawed understanding of the theory of knowledge. He was deeply suspicious of 'the separation of "mind" from direct occupation with things' as this 'throws emphasis on things at the expense of relations or connections' (Dewey, 2007, p. 109). It is the constant interaction between thought and application that enables such relations or connections to remain live and relevant.

A democratic curriculum, as understood by Dewey and Kerschensteiner,[1] is a curriculum that embodies, from a pedagogical point of view, the social interaction and collective enterprise necessary for active citizenship in a democratic society. It encourages and facilitates equality because 'a society to which stratification into separate classes would be fatal, must see to it that intellectual opportunities are accessible to all' (Dewey, 2007, p. 68). Also, such a curriculum does not overvalue the study of abstract ideas to the detriment of practical skills

---

[1] While Dewey and Kerschensteiner shared a great deal in common on education and the curriculum, it is important to note here that there were also fundamental differences between them. An example is Kerschensteiner's concept of educating a community into a 'moral collective personality', which finds no equivalence in any of Dewey's writings (Gonon, 2009, p. 181; Hopkins, 2013, p. 80).

and application. During Kershensteiner's time as director of schools in Munich, he devised a series of reforms the upshot of which

> was to increase the practical elements in ... the *Volkschule* or elementary school (up to the age of 14) and to develop a mandatory element of college education for apprentices. (Winch and Hyland, 2007, p. 34)

Such developments ensured that students in the *Volkschule* or on apprenticeships received an education that was not biased towards either the 'academic' or the 'vocational'. It is not, perhaps, a coincidence that vocational education has historically been held in higher regard in Germany than in England (Pring, 1995) due to the emphasis placed on all students towards maintaining a balanced and rounded education.

There have been criticisms of Dewey's ideas on democracy and curriculum design, not least by Dewey himself. According to Aaron Schultz,

> as he grew older Dewey himself increasingly lost faith in the ability of democratic schooling, alone, to equip citizens with the collective practices that would allow them to make their society a better place. (Schultz, 2001, p. 267)

One criticism Schultz has noted is the apparent lack of connection, at times, between Dewey's democratic school and the wider society in which it operated. For instance, Schultz has noted that while the 'violent and largely unsuccessful Pullman strike' was happening in Chicago, 'the relatively free and flexible structure of daily activity within the Laboratory School [founded by Dewey as an experiment in democratic schooling linked to the University of Chicago] was largely *unrepresentative* of daily life beyond the school, especially in the work environment' (Schultz, 2001, p. 274, emphasis in the original). I have already noted how Dewey saw the democratic school as preparation for (and a continuation of) citizenship in a democratic society, so this criticism can be taken one of two ways – it can be seen either as an indication that Dewey's model of a democratic curriculum was often out of touch with the political and social realities of the period, or as an example of how democratic society could and should be (as an 'ideal') during moments of social strife and political breakdown. The apparent disconnect, however, between the Laboratory School and political events in contemporary Chicago does appear to contradict Dewey's own emphasis on the need for interaction to draw out the relations between ideas and things.[2]

Whether Dewey should be criticized for the apparent disconnect between his views and the practical environment within the Laboratory School and the wider society is open to question. Dewey viewed the School (and education more generally) as a laboratory for democratic educational practices and pedagogies – the relationship between these and the challenges and conflicts within Chicago or elsewhere was not one of strict correlation or transfer. In some senses, it could be argued that Dewey's Laboratory School was a model on how democratic societies could develop and evolve rather than simply mirroring what was occurring within the host communities.

Standards and the Curriculum

There is a consensus among many academics and commentators that education in most Western countries has followed the neo-liberal economic agenda of the past 30 years (in terms of the language used and the practices adopted). In the words of Michael Apple, this has created a state of affairs in education where '[e]fficiency and an "ethic" of cost-benefit analysis are the dominant norms ... not only are schools transformed into market commodities, but so too now are our children' (Apple, 2006, pp. 31, 35). The emphasis on state-devised national curricula, often linked to assessment focused on tests that level or grade, has often restricted the room schools have for innovative and developmental approaches to the curriculum. The increasing practice of measuring schools and colleges by a system of league tables (in the name of public accountability and transparency) has reinforced the pressure on educational institutions to 'teach to the test' and avoid experimentation (as league tables are frequently based on national test results and related data) (Lingard, 2013).

For secondary schools in England, the use of General Certificate of Secondary Education (GCSE) results as a significant aspect of national

---

[2] A recent example of the democratic school in action in Dewey's home city of Chicago is the project carried out by Brian Schultz with his students in the Cabrini Green district (Schultz, 2006).

league tables has meant that teachers and students focus on gaining as many Grade A*-Cs[3] as possible to boost a particular school's score and position. This is at the potential expense of exploring the wider themes or issues within the curriculum that go beyond the narrow parameters of exam syllabuses and set texts. The proposed reform of GCSEs towards final exams and less coursework is likely to exacerbate such trends with negative consequences for less confident students (BBC, 2013). The increasing emphasis by the Conservative/Liberal Democrat coalition government (2010–2015) on the OECD's Programme for International Student Assessment (PISA) tests can be seen as an extension of this process — the assessment (by examination) of 15-year-old students on a narrow set of skills in reading, mathematics and science. The present administration is explicit in the links it makes between curriculum reforms and performance in international educational tests such as PISA (Department for Education, 2010b, pp. 8, 46–47).

The pressure to improve and maintain 'standards' and 'quality' (through the influence of PISA and other international educational rankings and comparisons) is becoming global in its reach. Robin Alexander, in his critique of UNESCO's Global Monitoring Reports (GMRs), has questioned the pervasive use of metrics to establish international definitions of what constitutes 'quality' in education. There is a danger that the focus becomes driven by 'inputs/outputs' rather than investigating the specific educational processes in any given jurisdiction:

> the quest for indicators and measures of quality produce ... an understandable preoccupation with *input and output* — pupil/teacher ratio, balance of male and female teachers, balance of trained and untrained teachers, expenditure per pupil as percentage of GDP, net enrolment ratio, adult literacy rate ... at the expense of indicators of *process*. (Alexander, 2015, p. 251, emphasis in the original)

It is this quest for the quantifiable that also prevents, in Alexander's view, a genuine engagement with the study of pedagogy in the international context (including the GMRs). Alexander acknowledges that pedagogy, in any educational jurisdiction, is intimately embedded within

---

[3]The GCSE now has a numerical grading system from 9 (highest) to 1 (lowest). Rather than attention being given to grades A*-C, the focus has moved to getting students to achieve grade 4 ('standard pass') and above.

local cultures, languages and practices and these do not lend themselves easily to measurable data that can be analysed and compared across borders. However, as Alexander reminds us, '[h]ard data is not necessarily useful data' (Alexander, 2015, p. 252) and he makes a strong case that research into pedagogy can have uses and implications for the international context (his own *Culture and Pedagogy* (2001) is an elegant example). These concerns directly affect any attempts to conceptualize and interpret the curriculum in a given region or country when the quantitative aspects of quality and standards become the dominant international discourse. There is a tendency to squeeze local contexts out of programmes of study in order to meet global targets and benchmarks. In England, these concerns were raised by the *Cambridge Primary Review* and this is why the editors advocated that at least 30 per cent of the school curriculum should be devised locally (Alexander, 2010). While it would be anachronistic to explicitly link Dewey to these contemporary global trends in education, he did identify situations not dissimilar to the ones some critics of neo-liberal education are currently stating:

> Natural instincts are either disregarded or treated as nuisances ... to be brought into conformity with external standards. Since conformity is the aim, what is distinctively individual in a young person is brushed aside, or regarded as a source of mischief or anarchy. Conformity is made equivalent to uniformity. (Dewey, 2007, p. 42)

Paul Carr has noted the following trends in terms of neo-liberal educational theory and practice:

> The shifting of focus in the neo-liberal educational agenda towards a constrained curriculum, supposedly high standards, greater focus on employability, and a proliferation of standards. (Carr, 2008, p. 119)

In England, this emphasis in employability was felt even in primary schools. With the development of the National Literacy and National Numeracy Strategies for primary schools in 1998 and 1999, the government involved itself with matters of classroom pedagogy as never before, requiring primary school teachers to follow a set teaching pattern with children in literacy and numeracy for up to two hours each day. This was based on the belief in government circles that England needed to 'raise standards' in these subjects to ultimately improve the country's educational and economic performance. This policy came at the expense of other areas of the primary school curriculum at Key Stages 1 and 2 (Alexander, 2001, p. 143).

While this structure did produce some improvements in literacy and numeracy (an increase in the number of children achieving the government's benchmark in these subjects in 2002, although not as many as the government had targeted), the Cambridge Primary Review, in its collection of evidence from key stakeholders, noted that many witnesses were concerned with a curriculum that 'was excessively prescriptive and needlessly detailed ... and that it had undermined teachers' professionalism' (Alexander, 2010, p. 215). Clearly, a curriculum where prescription and the undermining of professionalism are prevalent is not a democratic curriculum in the way I have defined it (where negotiation and consultation over curriculum objectives and content between stakeholders is central). A democratic curriculum, in Dewey's terms, is a participatory and experimental one:

> knowledge is a mode of participation, valuable in the degree in which it is effective. It cannot be the idle view of an unconcerned spectator ... The development of the experimental method as the method of getting knowledge and of making sure it is knowledge ... is the remaining great force in bringing about a transformation in the theory of knowledge. (Dewey, 2007, p. 247)

It is the prescription and over-attention to detail in government education policy that militates against a democratic curriculum. One cannot deny that many of the lessons planned and facilitated under England's National Literacy and Numeracy Strategies (and the Primary Strategy which followed them) encouraged, in the hands of creative teachers and students, examples of genuine participation and engagement. The problem lies in who has control over the curriculum aims and objectives that govern such participation. While it can be argued that firm government control over the curriculum has a semblance of democratic accountability (in societies where the government is elected by the people), this is not the same as schools having a democratic curriculum. Michael Reiss and John White have proposed (as a means of lessening government control of the school curriculum) the idea of a 'Commission' that would oversee curriculum aims every five years and would be independent of the government of the time. Reiss and White also suggest that the

National Curriculum should be non-statutory (as it is in Scotland) but schools would be expected to justify any deviation from the broad-based aims outlined by the Commission (Reiss and White, 2013, pp. 70–74). It is important to state here that any proposal to allow greater freedom for schools in the curriculum should be balanced by schools consulting with stakeholders (e.g. staff, students, community groups) to ensure that changes or experiments have a degree of democratic accountability.

A fundamental aspect of any curriculum describing itself as democratic is one where students are frequently encouraged to emancipate themselves

> from ... institutional authorities by promoting their right to exercise their own intelligence in all of their activities ... This emancipation is to be fostered by teachers. (Webster, 2009, p. 625)

Student emancipation from the over-reliance on institutional authority is unlikely to occur where curriculum objectives are laid down centrally (or locally) without any room for negotiation with those at the school level (be they staff, students or citizens in the local community). Equally, a fixation with 'standards' (in the guise of National Curriculum attainment levels or exam grades at GSCE and A Level) often runs counter to the need for students to challenge existing knowledge and habits of thinking. This is not to say that planning is not an essential part of any programme of learning (something that will be discussed in a later section of this chapter) – but there is a fundamental difference between planning and prescription.

Dewey was himself concerned with overt state control of the school system and the curriculum. He says in *Democracy and Education* that '[o]ne of the fundamental problems of education and for a democratic society is set by conflict of a nationalistic and wider social aim' (Dewey, 2007, p. 75). Dewey himself asks the question:

> Is it possible for an educational system to be conducted by a national state and yet the full social ends of the educative process not to be restricted, constrained or corrupted? (Ibid.)

The issue of a national curriculum with benchmarks and standards against which individual schools, teachers and pupils are matched could be seen as restricting or constraining. Dewey (like Mill before him) worried over whether state control of education would lead to a focus on what the state itself wanted from education rather than allowing children to develop a sense of autonomy and creativity that might be at odds with government requirements for efficiency or adherence to certain national beliefs and values.

It will be interesting to observe the current developments for academies and free schools in England as they are no longer under statutory requirement to implement the National Curriculum (Department for Education, 2010a).[4] Will this lead to examples of schools adopting or devising curricula akin to the democratic models discussed in this chapter? If so, they will be followed with genuine interest by those in education (academics, teachers, parents and commentators alike).

Stakeholders and the Curriculum

There is a responsibility on teaching staff as well as on government if curriculum aims and objectives are to be shared with students in a way that facilitates the democratic curriculum (as I have defined it). Chris Jane Brough argues: 'Committing to living democratically requires teachers to act democratically, like involving children in classroom decision-making and collaboratively co-constructing [the] curriculum' (Brough, 2012, p. 345). As Brough acknowledges, the idea of involving students in the creation of the curriculum can be problematic on several fronts. In terms of teachers themselves, '[some] ... perceive collaborative planning and shared decision-making in negative terms as a loss of control' (Brough, 2012, p. 349). Allied to this is the contention (explored in the section above) that

> In the UK ... national standards and testing have stifled creativity, narrowed school and classroom curricula, diminished children's engagement and sacrificed in-depth learning. (Ibid.)

---

[4]Although academies are not required to follow the National Curriculum, they are required to satisfy the requirements of a 'balanced and broadly based curriculum' (Academies Act 2010, Paper 32, 6 (a)).

If there are already these difficulties in trying to create a curriculum that is more participatory and inclusive of different voices and perspectives, why persist? What are the benefits of pursuing such a path? To return to Dewey's main point about the democratic school being part of a wider project for a democratic society, Gandin and Apple point to the experiment of the Citizen School in Porto Alegre, south-eastern Brazil, which is linked to the larger process of *Orçamento Participativo* (OP or Participatory Budgeting) in the city (Gandin and Apple, 2002, pp. 261–262). Participatory Budgeting is a deliberate attempt on the part of the city government to create forums, processes and mechanisms to enable the citizens of Porto Alegre to have a more active role in how services and institutions are run. 'In essence, the OP [Participatory Budgeting] can be considered a "school of democracy"' (ibid., p. 262). The Citizen School, according to Gandin and Apple,

> is organically linked to and considered part of the larger process of transforming the whole city ... The normative goals that guide practice in the schools are collectively created through a participatory process. (Ibid., pp. 263–264)

One of the ways participation is demonstrated within the Citizen School is through the local negotiation of curriculum aims and objectives. The curriculum is seen, at a fundamental level, as a construct of the local community, something the local population play an active role in discussing and creating (in terms of both the content and the perspective). According to Gandin and Apple, 'The starting point for the construction of curricular knowledge is the culture(s) of the communities themselves' (ibid., p. 367).

It is important to state that the creation of Citizen Schools in Porto Alegre is part of a very specific attempt at local democracy in an individual city. The application of such practices away from the original context is a problematic one – south-east Brazil has a range of cultural, educational and socio-economic priorities that are very different from those in England (Hopkins, 2013, p. 143). However, the example of the Citizen School and Participatory Budgeting shows what can be achieved in terms of the links between school and the community regarding democratic representation and active citizenship. The idea of community involvement in the curriculum was taken up by the Cambridge Primary Review in *Children, Their World, Their Education* (2010) where it argued that '[a] local element ... is appropriate, essential and therefore required' (Alexander, 2010, p. 262).

The important point, in terms of the democratic curriculum, with local influence and input over curriculum planning is the issue of consultation and accountability. The local elements of any curriculum need to be drawn up as part of an ongoing discussion with stakeholders in the community to ensure that points of view are raised and listened to from different perspectives. As Dewey stated, 'the school must itself be a community life' (Dewey, 2007, p. 261) and community involvement within the school and as part of the school is integral to such a view.

Another significant benefit a democratic curriculum potentially brings is in the area of student motivation and commitment. Brough, in a research project in three New Zealand schools, focused on student-centred curriculum integration (CI), which the author defines as 'a curriculum design theory where democratic education is reified and the curriculum is collaboratively planned' (Brough, 2012, p. 346). Brough describes democratic pedagogy (within the wider framework of student-centred CI) as requiring

> themes and planning to be collaboratively constructed with students. Subject-area lines are blurred, as discipline knowledge is repositioned within the context of enquiry. (Brough, 2012, p. 347)

This connects back to Dewey's proposals regarding the curriculum. Dewey was not against the idea of studying discrete subjects within a curriculum but emphasized the importance of applying knowledge to practical activities and experiments (as a means of discovery). Such views lend themselves to seeing potential in the crossing of subject boundaries, especially when investigations are a collaboration between students:

> Active connections with others are such an intimate and vital part of our own concerns that it is impossible to draw sharp lines ... In so far as we are partners in common undertakings, the things which others communicate to us as the consequences of their particular share in the enterprise blend at once into the experience resulting from our own special doings. (Dewey, 2007, p. 141)

This appears to run counter to the Department for Education's emphasis on the importance of a traditional curriculum where 'academic' subjects are to be studied in a discrete, compartmentalized way. John White, for instance, has been critical of the government's approach, describing it as a 'rigid ... [and] uncompromising opposition to ... interdisciplinary collaboration, themes and projects' (White, 2010, p. 8).

There is a focus, in student-centred CI, for curriculum aims and objectives to be devised (where possible) by means of negotiation between teacher and students. The sense of inclusion that the students gain from this method of course-planning has tangible consequences based on Brough's study:

> The findings showed that by including negotiation where possible, student ownership over learning was enhanced, motivation increased and the ability to self-manage was evident ... learning was retained and applied in new contexts. (Brough, 2012, p. 361)

This is only a relatively small study (as Brough points out) so care needs to be applied when drawing conclusions from the results. Nevertheless, the research produced a range of practical activities and processes that could well inform other researchers and practitioners interested in the democratic curriculum. The issue of questioning, for instance, was linked to the concept of democracy, 'since the way teachers asked questions either empowered or disempowered students' (Brough, 2012, p. 364). This passage conflates 'democracy' with 'empowerment' – while the concepts are often linked, they are not the same thing and this needed to be explored by Brough in more detail to ensure clarity in the use of different terms. Students and citizens can be empowered in ways that are not necessarily democratic (e.g. a student might feel empowered answering questions in such a way that he or she dominates the class discussion). That said, the point Brough is making here is close to Alexander on Bakhtin's discussion of dialogue and conversation:

> For him [Bakhtin], dialogue is 'inquiry and conversation' (that is to say, it combines questioning with the social ease of conversation) and 'if an answer does not give rise to a new question from itself, it falls out of the dialogue'. (Bakhtin cited in Alexander, 2001, p. 520)

The idea of pedagogy as dialogue here is critical. Alexander's description of questions leading on to other questions makes explicit the shared element in any worthwhile educational encounter. A democratic curriculum should have, at its core, the idea of knowledge as a shared pursuit between all those involved in a given learning environment. Julia Flutter (2007), for instance, makes a strong case for the use of 'pupil voice' as a means of developing teachers' own practice by eliciting ongoing feedback from students that will, in time, develop into a dialogue on what is effective teaching and learning. Flutter acknowledges that such negotiations need to be gradual and dealt with sensitively (to ensure teacher authority is not undermined and that all students in a given class, and not just the most articulate, are heard).

A conversation, to return to the Bakhtin quote above, implies a communication between peers (to a greater or lesser extent) – this is what differentiates it from an interview. If one or more agents control that conversation, then it becomes unequal and the communication itself is jeopardized. If education is a dialogue, then, by extension, the learning objectives and the structure of the curriculum should form part of that conversation. For a wider sense of dialogical education, Dewey offers this in *Democracy and Education*:

> since democracy stands in principle for free interchange, for social continuity, it must develop a theory of knowledge which sees in knowledge the method by which one experience is made available in giving direction and meaning to another. (Dewey, 2007, p. 252)

Conclusion

By its very nature, the democratic curriculum is a highly politicized concept. Who owns the curriculum, and the aims and objectives associated with it, is about power and control within education itself. If the definition of a democratic curriculum is one where the content, structure and assessment of subjects (or other modes of inquiry) is a matter of negotiation between the various stakeholders that have a vested interest, then carrying this out is itself a political act. As a project, it remains a radical proposal (often too radical for many administrations to implement, even in diluted form). The example of Participatory Budgeting and the Citizen School in Porto Alegre is the exception rather than the rule.

Almost 100 years since its first publication, Dewey's *Democracy and Education* still resonates in the debate over how or whether any curriculum should be democratic. For Dewey, the school was a place where students were introduced to the skills and attitudes associated with democratic citizenship, especially regarding learning as a collaborative activity. Part of Dewey's project in the Laboratory School in Chicago was also to try and break down the traditional hierarchy over the 'academic' and the 'vocational' (some learning might fit into neither category). I have shown that Dewey was highly sceptical of this division, seeing knowledge as a constant push-and-pull between theory and application. In this sense, Dewey was close in thought with his direct contemporary, Georg Kerschensteiner. Kerschensteiner was the Munich Director of Schools who instituted a policy where all students studied a range of 'academic' and 'vocational' subjects and was one of the pioneers of the modern German apprenticeship. Both thinkers challenged the current notion that activities of the mind took pre-eminence over activities of the hand, seeing this as a crippling and dangerously false dichotomy.

There has been criticism of Dewey's Laboratory School, notably by Shultz, with regards to how it could sometimes appear removed from the political action surrounding it (in the Pullman strike, for instance). Critics have also pointed to Dewey's use of collaborative learning and the integration of academic and practical learning within the Laboratory School curriculum. A major concern amongst such commentators is that a movement away from sharply-defined subject areas could lead to a drop in 'quality' and 'standards'.

Advocates of the democratic curriculum, such as Henry Giroux, argue for

> pedagogical relationships marked by dialogue, questioning and communication ... This view of knowledge stresses structuring classroom encounters that synthesize and demonstrate the relationships among meaning, critical thinking, and democratized classroom encounters. (Giroux, 2011, p. 38)

The democratic curriculum, as conceptualized in this chapter, advocates negotiation between those with a vested interest in a given programme of learning. It is acknowledged that the ability, age and confidence of the students could be challenging when consulting them alongside other stakeholders. However, the principal key of negotiation is that no one agent should own the curriculum to the extent of determining aims and objectives without thoughtful discussion with other stakeholders.

References

Alexander, R. (2001), *Culture and Pedagogy*. Oxford: Blackwell.
Alexander, R. (Ed.) (2010), *Children, Their World, Their Education: Final Report and Recommendations of the Cambridge Primary Review*. Abingdon: Routledge.
Alexander, R. (2015), Teaching and learning for all? The quality imperative revisited. *International Journal of Educational Development*, 40, 250–258.
Apple, M. (2006), *Educating the Right Way: Markets, Standards, God, and Inequality* (2nd Ed.). New York, NY: Routledge.
BBC (2013), *GCSE Overhaul in England Made Final by Ofqual* [online]. Available at: http://www.bbc.co.uk/news/education-24759476 (accessed 08.11.13).
Brough, C. J. (2012), Implementing the democratic principles and practices of student-centred curriculum integration in primary schools. *The Curriculum Journal*, 23 (2), 345–369.
Carr, P. (2008), Educating for democracy: with or without social justice. *Teacher Education Quarterly*, 35 (4), 117–136.
Carr, W. and Hartnett, A. (1996), *Education and the Struggle for Democracy*. Milton Keynes: Open University Press.
Department for Education (2010a). *Academies Act 2010*. Available at: www.legislation.gov (accessed 08.10.13).
Department for Education (2010b). *The Importance of Teaching*. London: DfE.
Dewey, J (2007 [1916]). *Democracy and Education*. Teddington: Echo Library.
Flutter, J. (2007), Teacher development and pupil voice. *The Curriculum Journal*, 18 (2), 343–354.
Gandin, L. A. and Apple, M. (2002), Challenging neo-liberalism, building democracy: creating the Citizens School in Porto Alegre, Brazil. *Journal of Educational Policy*, 17 (2), 259–279.
Giroux, H. A. (2011), *On Critical Pedagogy*. London: Continuum.
Gonon, P. (2009), *The Quest for Modern Vocational Education – Georg Kerschensteiner between Dewey, Weber and Simmel*. Bern: Peter Lang.
Hopkins, N. (2013), *Citizenship and Democracy in Further and Adult Education*. Dordrecht: Springer.
Lingard, B. (2013), Reshaping the message systems of schooling in the UK. In Wyse, D., Baumfield, V. M., Egan, D., Gallagher, C., Hayward, L., Hulme, M., Leitch, R., Livingston, K., Menter, I. and Lingard, B. (Eds.), *Creating the Curriculum*. Abingdon: Routledge, pp. 1–13.
Pring, R. (1995), *Closing the Gap: Liberal Education and Vocational Preparation*. London: Hodder & Stoughton.

Reiss, M. J. and White, J. (2013), *An Aims-Based Curriculum: The Significance of Human Flourishing for Schools*. Available at: http://eprints.ioe.ac.uk/16408/ (accessed 12.12.13).

Schultz, B. A. (2006), Revealing classroom complexity: A portrait of a justice-oriented, democratic curriculum serving a disadvantaged neighborhood. *Annual Meeting of the American Educational Research Association*. Available at: https://eric.ed.gov/?id=ED491662 (accessed 15.11.13).

Schultz, A. (2001), John Dewey's conundrum: can democratic schools empower? *Teachers College Record*, 103 (2), 267–302.

Webster, R. S. (2009), Dewey's democracy as the Kingdom of God on Earth. *Journal of Philosophy Education*, 43 (4), 615–632.

White, J. (2010), *The Coalition and the Curriculum* [online]. Available at: http://eprints.ioe.ac.uk/6298/ (accessed 6.12.13).

Winch, C. (2006), Georg Kerschensteiner – Founding of the dual system in Germany. *Oxford Review of Education*, 32 (3), 381–396.

Winch, C. and Hyland, T. (2007), *A Guide to Vocational Education and Training*. London: Continuum.

Chapter 8

Dewey Anticipates Habermas's Paradigm of Communication: The Critique of Individualism and the Basis for Moral Authority in *Democracy and Education* ☆

Brian Dotts

Abstract

The chapter presents a novel account of a key concept in John Dewey's reconstructionist theory specifically related to the nucleus underlying his idea of democracy: intersubjective communication, what Dewey called the 'democratic criterion'. Many theorists relate democracy to a form of rule. Consequently, discussions of democracy tend to be limited to functionalist theories. Dewey's idea of democracy establishes an important distinction from conventional theories by developing its radical, critical, evolutionary, and intersubjective potential. I argue that Dewey anticipated Jürgen Habermas's Paradigm of Communication in his reconstructionist social theory with potential to de-reify institutions and to empower human beings democratically.

Keywords: Dewey; Intersubjectivity; communication; democracy; normative legitimacy

---

☆ This essay originally appeared in Brian W. Dotts, Dewey Anticipates Habermas's Paradigm of Communication: The Critique of Individualism and the Basis for Moral Authority in Democratic Education, *Education and Culture*, 32.1, Article 9, pp. 111–129. This material appears courtesy of Purdue University Press. All rights reserved. http://docs.lib.purdue.edu/eandc/vol32/iss1/art9

Introduction

Of unparalleled importance in John Dewey's democratic philosophy is his focus on the process of change, or the 'continuous reconstruction of experience' (Dewey, 1944, p. 80). But how is change to take place and under what circumstances does it best occur? What are the ramifications of Dewey's theory of change and reconstruction on representative government and political rule? Is change expected to occur pragmatically as a planned process, or is change understood as inchoate phenomena occurring sporadically in Dewey's philosophy? Who determines change and the degree to which it shall take place? Why does Dewey prioritize democratic communication over other forms of communication?

Dewey clearly connects his philosophy of change and reconstruction to governance, but he develops an ontological basis for change that subsumes more than mere political rule. For Dewey, change and reconstruction are such fundamental parts of human experience that he represents them as part of a biological and evolutionary process of human adaptation to social and natural environments. Change and reconstruction encompass all forms of life, not just politics, and because he perceives change in this way, he links the process of change with a deeply moral attribute of human existence, namely, democracy and communication. Since we all experience change naturally, Dewey develops a democratic moral theory of how social change should take place. Therefore, Dewey ruptures traditional political theories that view democracy purely as a form of governance, 'as a system of command and obedience,' as Markell asserts, which 'risk[s] sacrificing the spirit of insubordination that animates ... change, interruption, openness, and novelty' (Markell, 2005, p. 2). Dewey's philosophy elevates democratic change and social reconstruction, making them the background against which politics (and other spheres of social existence) are measured. In other words, the substance of social practices, economic activities, and political rule are assessed by the extent to which they adhere to the moral expectations of democratic experience.

The other key component in Dewey's philosophy of change and reconstruction is communication, also an experience that must adhere to democratic principles in reaching consensus in a social order. Furthermore, the moral value of democratic communication is that it changes the participants involved in interaction. Again, Dewey conceives of this democratic process as an evolutionary means of social adaptation and transformation. For example, in *Democracy and*

Education he asserts that the experience of communication 'requires' the participants 'to formulate' perspectives that are 'not their own,' to understand something 'as another would see it'. This is a process, he asserts, wherein participants 'assimilate, imaginatively, something of another's experience'. Moreover, it is virtuous because it contributes to actualizing 'what one is capable of becoming through association with others in all the offices of life' (Dewey, 1944, p. 358). Growth requires penetrating the confines of custom and habit. The fundamental importance of communication and change or reconstruction are summarized by Dewey in terms of his 'democratic ideal:'

> The two elements in our criterion both point to democracy. The first signifies not only more numerous and more varied points of shared common interest, but greater reliance upon the recognition of mutual interests as a factor in social control. The second means not only freer interaction between social groups ... but change in social habit— its continuous readjustment through meeting the new situations produced by varied intercourse. And these two traits are precisely what characterize the democratically constituted society (Dewey, 1944, pp. 86–87).

Dewey's focus on change, democracy, and communication anticipates Jürgen Habermas's communication paradigm. In what follows, I analyze and compare Dewey's and Habermas's analysis of the moral and democratic (qua Dewey) dimensions of communication, and the intersubjective normative basis (qua Habermas) that both theorists develop. Dewey offers a distinctive philosophy of democratic communication that appears to have informed Habermas and contributed to the latter's construction of an equally elaborate moral basis for social order. I attempt to explicate Dewey's theory of democratic communication and how it anticipates the moral basis of Habermas's contemporary communicative action theory, which is grounded in intersubjectivity. Both Dewey and Habermas emphasize the following elements in their underlying theories, which are listed in Figure 1. Change or reconstruction serves as a necessary expectation of any critical theory intended to advance or emancipate individuals from systems of power. Democratic experience contributes to growth or actualization through communication, the latter of which is a fundamentally natural means of experiencing the other elements.

Table 8.1. Understanding the Cultural Requirements for Change and Reconstruction.

	Dewey	**Habermas**
Change	Social reconstruction for progressive adaptation	Social change for human emancipation
Democracy	Mode of associated living through communication	Deliberative social action based on processes of opinion—and will—formation
Communication	Interdependent learning experiences that contribute to growth	Reaching intersubjective understanding provides a normative public basis for holding the political system accountable

Indeed, the degree of change permitted during any specified time, epoch, or place, whether social, political, economic or religious, remains circumscribed by existing cultural parameters and the extent to which these parameters are penetrable. Cultural limitations, for example, delimit the framework for acceptable debate and discourse, which include defining the participants who can enter into communication, the extent to which cultural and mystical traditions may be critiqued, and the presence or absence of expert, authoritative, or privileged 'validity claims'. Additional considerations include the extent to which institutional structures either facilitate or obstruct participation, and the degree to which existing cultural knowledge is capable of distinguishing between what Habermas refers to as 'the objective, social, and subjective worlds,' and the extent to which rationalities are differentiated as 'propositional truth, normative rightness, [and] subjective truthfulness,' according to Habermas. In addition, 'cultural tradition must permit a reflective relation to itself' to allow for critique, and 'action-oriented ... success ... freed from the imperatives of an understanding that is to be communicatively renewed' (Habermas, 1984, pp. 71–72, 100).

Likewise, Dewey asserts that readjustments to our understanding depend upon the extent to which education can 'modify mental and moral attitudes' that have become static. What is necessary, according to Dewey, is 'an educational reformation' that stimulates 'thoroughgoing change in social life' (Dewey, 1944, pp. 328–329, 331). The process of education, which includes recurring intersubjective critiques of the status quo in order to actualize desired change, is as instinctive, Dewey believed, as one's adaptation to an altering natural environment. Habituation is also a natural human inclination. We settle into new surroundings through a process of readjustment and adaptation, and what was once new becomes familiar and commonplace. 'This enduring adjustment,' according to Dewey, 'supplies the background upon which are made specific adjustments, as occasion arises' (Dewey, 1944, p. 47). Likewise, in criticizing Talcott Parson's social theory, Habermas addresses the fundamental importance of this background knowledge in developing his own communication theory. According to Habermas, it is 'the interpretive accomplishments of participants in interaction, which make consensus possible [and] central to the concept of social order'. It is through the 'language-dependent processes of reaching understanding, he argues, [that] take place against the background of an intersubjectively shared tradition, especially of values accepted in common' (Habermas, 1987, p. 214).

Long before Habermas published his magnum opus on communicative action, Dewey concluded that humanity had yet to understand the significance of, and the potential benefits that could be generated by, socializing and systematizing democratic communication. More recent scholarship focusing on Dewey's communication theory, often referred to as the 'neopragmatic interpretation of Dewey ...' or 'the pragmatic renaissance,' views Dewey 'as an advocate of education as communication,' according to Englund. From this perspective, one that I share, 'education is just one aspect of a democratic form of social life that is communicative' (Englund, 2000, 308). Education, like democracy, is overwhelmingly part of complex human experiences and therefore cannot be reduced solely to formal schooling, although it is the latter that rightfully takes center stage in Dewey's philosophical agenda.

Too often, Dewey asserted, 'Men ... want the crutch of dogma, of beliefs fixed by authority, to relieve them of the trouble of thinking and the responsibility of directing their activity by thought'. Paraphrasing John Stuart Mill, Dewey concluded that traditional schooling, for example, was 'better adapted ... to mak[ing] disciples than inquirers' (Dewey, 1944, p. 338). Dewey refers to 'the ideal of a continuous reconstruction ... of experience,' which derives its 'meaning or social content' by augmenting 'the capacity of individuals to act as directive guardians of this reorganization,' otherwise known as his 'democratic criterion' (ibid., p. 322). Acknowledging the 'risks' that are often present during inquiry, only by increasing the number of individuals who take part in communicatively reconstructing society, 'a widening of the area of vision through a growth of social sympathies,' Dewey argued, 'does thinking develop to include what lies beyond our direct interests: a fact of great significance for education' (Dewey, ibid., p. 148). Adhering to custom is a rational human response, according to Dewey, for it provides a settled and fixed foundation upon which to subsist, but he viewed parochialism and conventionality as 'rigid' and too mechanical, thus inhibiting mankind's potential for progressive change. 'By its very nature, a state is ever something to be scrutinized, investigated, searched for' (Dewey, 1988, p. 31), according to Dewey, but we too often reify social institutions by our 'passive acquiescence ... and a minimum of active control' (Dewey, 1944, p. 47). Habermas refers to this as a process of system integration that has been decoupled from the lifeworld (Habermas, 1987, pp. 150–53).

Inquiry and critique of the status quo, the fundamentals of scientific investigations, are bold endeavours that Dewey sought to socialize in order to 'dissolve' outdated, routinized, or prohibitive 'custom[s]'. Dewey's 'democratic ideal' requires 'the recognition of mutual interests,' which can only take place through intersubjective communication, and it must always be amenable to change or 'continuous readjustment' (Dewey, 1944, p. 86). In *Democracy and Education*, for example, Dewey recognizes the value, in fact the necessity, of intersubjective (democratic) discourse when he claims that 'competing philosophies' must come together for the practical purpose of reaching agreement. Diverse social, economic, and political groups often view their environments differently and sometimes in conflicting ways, and it is necessary, he argues, to make possible the dialectical and democratic deliberations that can respond to emerging conflicts, broaden cultural horizons, and renew thinking (Dewey, 1944, pp. 326–327). Recognizing the state as a fallible human construction, Dewey concluded that, 'Almost as soon as its form is stabilized, it needs to be re-made' (Dewey, 1988, pp. 31–33). History provides proof of this, according to Dewey, in that as much as we try to achieve a utopia, it is impossible to construct a perfect state once and for all. There will always be unforeseen problems, even in a state that has been studiously predetermined by its founders. The ideal preconceived polity will always fall short of its conception, which is why 'the formation of states must be' viewed as 'an experimental process' and dependent upon continuous reconstruction through shared communication. Put differently, 'The State must always be rediscovered,' he declared (Dewey, 1988, pp. 33–34).

Dewey disliked institutional inertness, and, like Habermas, he believed the state should not determine social relationships, but that social relationships should be organized in ways that facilitate intersubjective communication and potentials for progressive change. 'The belief in political fixity,' he declared, 'of the sanctity of some form of state consecrated by the efforts of our fathers and hallowed by tradition, is one of the stumbling blocks in the way of orderly and directed change,' and 'it is an invitation to revolt and revolution' (ibid., p. 34). Likewise, Habermas viewed systems as 'forming one system or discourse, which steer[s] communications ... described in a language that objectivistically disregards actors' self-understanding' (Habermas, 1999, p. 48). The State forms an important aspect of our environment, political and otherwise, and Dewey sought means to ensure the constant social adaptation to changing conditions and to enable citizens to hold systems accountable to a public will formed by intersubjective communication. States are merely reconstructions of what used to be considered new or novel. The seeds of change may be dormant for a time, but they eventually germinate into a new form. Political revolutions inform change, but the institutions that emerge after the dust has settled should be prevented from concretizing social relationships that simply regenerate a new 'objective reason manifested in the [new] state' Dewey, 1944, pp. 94–95). Building upon Immanuel Kant's *Pedagogics*, 'creative effort' is facilitated when 'men consciously strive ... to educate their successors not for the existing state of affairs but so as to make possible a future better humanity'. Otherwise, systems of education become mere conduits used to functionally reinforce the existing state of affairs, similar to the goals of 'social efficiency' (ibid., pp. 94–95).

Dewey's concern about the problem of freezing social institutions after the establishment of a state is shared by Sheldon Wolin. For example, Wolin asks what might be considered a Deweyan question: 'If democracy is rooted in revolution, what of democracy is suppressed by a constitution?' In other words, according to Wolin, 'When a democratic revolution leads to a constitution, does that mark the fulfilment of democracy, or the beginning of its attenuation' (Wolin, 1994, p. 29)? Of course, the answer to this question depends on the constitution and the extent to which it facilitates democratic participation and communication. Dewey was critical of contemporary politics because, as he put it, 'the Public seems to be lost;' that 'popular imagination can conceive of no other way by which ... governmental affairs [may be] carried on than by the façade of representative government,' which often serves as a veneer to perpetuate the interests of a few (Dewey,

1988, pp. 116 & 119). 'A society which makes provision for participation in its good of all its members on equal terms,' according to Dewey, 'and which secures flexible readjustment of its institutions through interaction of the different forms of associated life is in so far democratic' (Dewey, 1944, p. 99). Bynum appears to agree, contending that 'Dewey's antiessentialist assertion that society exists 'in transmission, in communication,' develops from an account of 'life' that opens *Democracy and Education* and forms the philosophical basis for Dewey's conception of society and education' (Bynum, 2005, p. 369). The lingering problem, which Dewey acknowledges, is that the American founding was not an attempt at democracy. Rather, the founding resulted in a constitution that separated, through a number of checks and balances, democratic accountability while contributing to a system, in Habermasian terms, which mostly took on a life of its own distinct from popular control. The problem of reifying political and social institutions can best be understood through Dewey's view of the American and French Revolutions.

Looking Back to the American and French Revolutions: Understanding Dewey's Criticisms of the Enlightenment

During the American and French Revolutions, emotional claims and diatribes were devoted to the subject of regime change and the transformation of older systems or systems that had gone astray. The more radical perspective was expounded by individuals like Thomas Paine, who believed that the revolutions symbolized legitimate breaks from the dead weight of tradition once reflective conditions cultivated the possibility to reconstruct inherited practices. New powerful critiques of Britain's and France's monarchical regimes, founded on 'Superstition' and 'Power,' according to Paine, justified their overthrow and the substitution of new institutions based on enlightened reason to promote the common good. Believing the British government to be rotten to the core, Paine argued for supplanting it root and branch. 'All hereditary government is in its nature tyranny,' Paine demurred (Paine, 1984, pp. 69 & 172). The more conservative Edmond Burke, on the other hand, who believed that many of Britain's and France's cultural traditions were worth saving, believed that generational change must be gradual, pragmatic, respectful of existing institutions, and lawful. In his *Reflections on the Revolution in France*, Burke quotes from Euripides's *Telephus*, '*Spartam nactus es; hanc exorna*' (Your lot is cast in Sparta, be a credit to it). Burke's point was that a citizen must 'make the most of the existing materials of his country' by balancing his 'disposition to preserve' that which is beneficial with 'an ability to improve' upon existing defects (Burke, 1987, p. 161).

Burke and Paine helped define the parameters of debate and possibilities for change during the late eighteenth century, with Burke viewing the body politic as a naturally evolving organism that is historically conditioned and relatively stable, and Paine shifting the emphasis from a pragmatic position to radically questioning the very premises upon which British representative government stood regardless of its duration. Both men saw value in change, but Burke admired tradition and prudence as much as Paine sought extrication from history by seeking revolutionary change and rebirth (Vannatta, 2012). While Burke may have been too deferential to traditional authority and Paine too bombastic in developing a predetermined state of affairs, neither focused on the value of political arrangements that could enable an intersubjective and normatively based process of frequent renewal. Dewey recognized this shortcoming.

Dewey was critical of many Enlightenment thinkers beyond Paine and Burke, including Hobbes, Locke, Marx, and Adam Smith, all of whom were overly committed to establishing predetermined blueprints for ideal political arrangements. Dewey criticized Locke's foundationalism, for example, in the latter's development of 'a rigid doctrine of natural rights inherent in individuals independent of social organization', as well as Locke's privileging 'natural law' (metaphysically devised) over 'positive law' (socially devised) (Dewey, 2008, p. 7). In other words, Dewey criticized Locke and others because their theories hinged on ethereal and abstract principles, such as natural law, which had no social or worldly basis. In addition, Dewey found fault in their developing hyper-individualistic theories that not only privileged economic interests, but also resulted in what Habermas referred to later as 'an anonymous system independent of the intentions of unconsciously sociated individuals, a system that followed its own logic and subjected society as a whole to the economically decoded imperatives of its self-stabilization'. Of utmost importance is the fact that, as a 'mechanism of social integration,' the 'political economy' emerged as 'a non-normative one' (Habermas, 1999, p. 45).

Habermas is reemphasizing the same scathing criticism that Dewey made half a century earlier with regard to the eclipse of the public. 'Till the Great Society,' by which Dewey meant individualistic, impersonal, economic society, 'is converted into a Great Community' that gives priority to collective action, 'the Public will remain in eclipse,' he demurred. Antonio and Kellner similarly explain one of Habermas's criticisms of the western Enlightenment project as 'seeking an Archimedean point' that is historically and culturally indefatigable, or in Habermas's own words, a theory that 'start[s] with 'concrete ideals immanent in traditional forms of life.'' On the contrary, Habermas concludes, 'the theory of communicative action ... must proceed 'reconstructively'' and democratically as a function of 'social critique' (Antonio and Kellner, 1992, pp. 280–82).

Furthermore, Dewey voiced concern over the fact that 'mass production' was not merely 'confined to the factory,' but that it had invaded the intimate and social spaces that should otherwise exist as venues for collective action. The 'Public' was 'lost,' he complained, and the only way to restore the Public was to democratize communication. It 'alone,' he asserted, 'can ... create a great community' (Dewey, 1988, pp. 96, 98, 116, 142). Similarly, in Democracy and Education Dewey writes about the significance of intersubjective communication:

> Impulses of communication and habits of intercourse have to be adapted to maintaining successful connections with others; a large fund of social knowledge accrues. As a part of this intercommunication one learns much from others. They tell of their experiences and of the experiences which, in turn, have been told them. In so far as one is interested or concerned in these communications, their matter becomes a part of one's own experience. Active connections with others are such an intimate and vital part of our own concerns that it is impossible to draw sharp lines, such as would enable us to say, 'Here my experience ends; there yours begins'. In so far as we are partners in common undertakings, the things which others communicate to us as the consequences of their particular share in the enterprise blend at once into the experience resulting from our own special doings (Dewey, 1944, pp. 185–86).

According to Sheldon Wolin, Dewey disparaged the Enlightenment philosophers whose economic theories undermined their simultaneous support for the liberalization of politics. In other words, their support for a free market cultivated 'a business culture that thwarted the democratic potential of' republican institutions. They fused the act of seeking self-interest in the economic realm with the political and civic realm. This 'reduction of politics to interest,' according to Wolin, 'has cast a powerful shadow on modern politics' (Wolin, 2004, pp. 251, 512—13), and Dewey was cognizant of this fact during his day. Government was conceived as an arbiter of conflicting individual interests rather than as a political means of facilitating democratic communication. Of course, the American Revolution was not intended to secure a democratic government, which is why Dewey finds fault with it. 'Mobocracy' was conflated with democracy, and the founders structured the new constitution to delimit democratic possibilities. Political liberty was tempered while freedom in the economic realm was left virtually unfettered.

In 1971, John Rawls similarly reflected upon the rationalities that distinguished a liberal market with liberal democracy by asserting, 'The theory of competitive markets [is] not moved by the desire to act justly' and to realize 'just ... arrangements'. Rather, these 'normally require ... the use of sanctions' in order to 'stabilize' conflict resulting from 'persons who oppose one another as indifferent if not hostile powers'. The atomistic and self-interested nature of 'private society,' including the competitive market that is intended to channel and give life to these principles, reminds us that 'private society is not held together by a public conviction that its basic arrangements are just and good in themselves, but by the calculations of everyone ... pursu[ing] their personal ends' (Rawls, 1971, pp. 512—22). The traditional emphasis on negative liberty and individualism has resulted in modern political institutions that focus primarily on managing the indifferent and competing interests of private individuals and groups. And because political institutions have been infected by powerful groups lobbying for private interests, in the same way that increased capital can offer advantages in the economic sphere, the public realm has been eclipsed by a market mentality. In this sense, political institutions become mere mechanisms for pursuing private benefits, and those persons or corporate bodies that possess the greatest capital too often enjoy not just market share, but political influence and political benefits (Citizens United v. Federal Election Commission 588 U.S. 310). Communication has been removed from the great mass of citizens, which Dewey describes as the loss of the Public. The 'machinelike ... relationships' that have emerged from a market ethos and spilled over into the social and political spheres have resulted in the objectification of individuals as means to achieve self-interested and competitive ends, according to Dewey. These relationships, what Habermas subsequently refers to as instrumentally oriented, are not 'social' ones, but rather embody attempts to control. 'Genuine social life,' according to Dewey, 'is ... identical with communication,' and when communication is reserved for select members of a community or group, it is neither 'social,' in Dewey's terms, nor 'educative'. Agreement 'demands communication, and communication must be democratic for agreement to achieve legitimacy' (Dewey, 1944, p. 5).

Interest group politics results in too many policies that fail to meet Dewey's democratic expectations; namely, the notion that public policies should be the result of democratic processes that privilege equal and comprehensive communication so that the normative agreements generated by this process gain the broadest possible legitimacy among those who must live under their results. In Habermasian terms, 'A communicatively achieved agreement has a rational basis' in that 'it cannot be imposed by' any of the parties 'whether instrumentally through intervention in the situation directly or strategically through influencing the decisions of opponents'. Furthermore, 'agreement can ... be objectively obtained by force, but what comes to pass manifestly through outside influence or the use of violence cannot count subjectively as agreement' (Habermas, 1984, p. 287).

Rather than extensive political oversight of the economy, the market has subverted representative government's potential normative legitimacy. However, unlike Dewey, who viewed democracy as an existential activity, Rawls's liberalism prioritizes 'the role of administration,' according to Wolin, over participatory democracy. Conceptualizing the state as an arbiter of competing interests not only results in the encapsulation of politics within a market ideology, but it also reduces the citizen and civic virtue to instrumental—and goal-oriented—rationalities. Wolin concludes, for example, that 'The demos has been hammered into resignation, into fearful acceptance of the economy as the basic reality of its existence, so huge, so sensitive, so ramifying in its consequences that no group, party, or political actors dare alter its fundamental structure' (Wolin, 2004, p. 578).

Hannah Arendt likewise concluded that the constitution's structure not only diminished possibilities for democratic governance, but it also circumvented this ideal in favor of a labyrinth-esque framework that largely protected the power of external economic and aristocratic interests (Arendt, 1990, 253). This is why most democratic gains that have been achieved by women, the disabled, African Americans, Hispanics, and others have largely occurred through the use of extra-constitutional or unconventional political means. Without the communicative democracy Dewey strove to justify, individuals 'are given up to the service of ends external to themselves' (Dewey, 1944, p. 252). They are treated as objects that 'lose ... identity as ... living thing[s]' (ibid., p. 1). They are acted upon rather than acting together for agreed upon ends. The key for achieving progress, Dewey believed, lies in social 'intercourse and communication of experience'. In *Democracy and Education*, for example, he concludes that

> A society which makes provision for participation in its good of all its members on equal terms and which secures flexible readjustment of its institutions through interaction of the different forms of associated life is in so far democratic. Such a society must have a type of education which gives individuals a personal interest in social relationships and control, and the habits of mind which secure social changes without introducing disorder (ibid., p. 99).

Likewise, Habermas asserts that, 'To the extent that the hypothetical discussion of normative validity claims is institutionalized, the critical potential of speech can be brought to bear on existing institutions'. However, instrumentally oriented action manifested in the economic sphere has permeated the public sphere to such an extent that it has narrowed opportunities to institutionalize civic spaces that could otherwise democratically empower intersubjectively determined agreements. 'With the legal institutionalization of the monetary medium,' according to Habermas, success-oriented action steered by egocentric calculations of utility,' action typical within market systems, 'loses its connection to action oriented by mutual understanding' Habermas, 1987, p. 196). Furthermore, according to Habermas,

> This strategic action, which is disengaged from the mechanism of reaching understanding and calls for an objectivating attitude even in regard to interpersonal relations, is promoted to the model for methodically dealing with a scientifically objectivated nature. In the instrumental sphere, purposive activity gets free of normative restrictions to the extent that it becomes linked to flows of information from the scientific system (ibid.).

In addition to the instrumentally oriented action prevalent in the economic sphere, the social sphere, according to Habermas, has undergone what Weber referred to earlier as 'total administration'. Social relationships have become ever more regulated by bureaucratic systems and institutionalized legal processes that are void of democratic communication. In other words, these relationships, whether or not identified by recipients receiving public assistance, are 'embedded in the context of a life history and of a concrete form of life' that often gets reduced 'to a violent abstraction, not merely because it has to be subsumed under the law, but so that it can be dealt with administratively' (ibid., pp. 362–63). The administrative and legal processes take priority over understanding the multifarious complexities of each client, and the latter become objectified in the same way that an inanimate object is acted upon as described by Dewey in *Democracy and Education* (Dewey, 1944, pp. 1–5). Similarly, Habermas's criticism of the welfare state is that its administrative and legal functions take on the same kind of instrumental, goal-oriented action embodied in the economic sphere, but for different purposes: "The process of providing social services takes on a reality of its own, nurtured above all by the professional competence of public officials, the framework of administrative action, biographical and current 'findings', the readiness and ability to cooperate of the person seeking the service or being subjected to it" (Habermas, 1987, p. 363).

Dewey criticized this social phenomenon, witnessing its growth following the Gilded Age and during the early twentieth century. In the midst of the Great Depression, for example, Dewey wrote in *The Social Frontier* and criticized the implementation of 'compulsory patriotic rites,' required Bible reading in schools, and teaching a doctrinaire knowledge of the constitution. 'Three [American] states' he disparaged made it 'a crime' to teach 'evolution,' and several more required 'loyalty oaths' among 'students as a condition of graduation'. He was appalled by the fact that teachers unions and tenure were under attack, all of which represented an atmosphere that he described as 'militant' and formulaic (Dewey, 2011, pp. 27, 29). These were reactionary attempts to impose doctrinaire and self-interested curricula onto the public schools in order to reproduce the status quo and allegiance to an imposing dominant culture. In *Democracy and Education*, Dewey clarified this by asserting that an individual's 'seeming attention, his docility, his memorizings and reproductions ... will partake of intellectual servility'. Moreover, 'such a condition of intellectual subjection is needed for fitting the masses into a society where the many are not expected to have aims or ideas of their own, but to take orders from the few set in authority' (Dewey, 1944, p. 314).

What Dewey was defining in the early twentieth century was antisocial, and therefore, anti-communicative forms of existence and control. Such conditions are 'not adapted to a society which intends to be democratic,' he concluded (ibid., p. 305). The permeation of the market's influence in areas that were once considered to be public responsibilities, including schooling, has been so extensive as to relegate civil society to a pliable condition that allows it to be moulded to serve the former's demands and interests. Contributing to the eclipse of the public and civic realm is the fact that the language of economics, which has been so prevalent in our contemporary national discourse, appears neutral in the same way that positivism positioned the social sciences during the twentieth century. In other words, the laws of supply and demand, inflation and interest rates, changes in employment and unemployment are often invoked as natural phenomena (i.e., laws) and, therefore, void of ideology. Of course, this is inaccurate, but the contemporary ideologies of neoliberalism and libertarianism tend to be portrayed as naturally apolitical and amoral market mechanisms that are simply the result of uninhibited interest-seeking individuals. These ideologies are portrayed as innocuous and free from racist, classist, and sexist intentions or effects because their outcomes are depicted as merely the natural outgrowth of an invisible hand, which represents nothing more than the sum of society's properly functioning organic parts. According to Habermas,

> To the degree that the economic system subjects the life-forms of private households and the life conduct of consumers and employees to its imperatives, consumerism and possessive individualism, motives of performance, and competition gain the force to shape behavior. The communicative practice of everyday life is one-sidedly rationalized into a utilitarian lifestyle; this ... induced shift to purposive-rational action orientations calls forth the reaction of a hedonism freed from the pressures of rationality. As the private sphere is undermined and eroded by the economic system, so too is the public sphere by the administrative system. The bureaucratic disempowering and desiccation of spontaneous processes of opinion- and will-formation expands the scope for engineering mass loyalty and makes it easier to uncouple political decision-making from concrete, identity forming contexts of life. Insofar as such tendencies establish themselves, we get Weber's (stylized) picture of a legal domination that redefines practical questions as technical ones and dismisses demands for substantive justice with a legalistic reference to legitimation through procedure (Habermas, 1987, p. 325).

Preceding Habermas, Dewey once concluded that 'the state,' the political sphere that embodies the entire realm of public activity, 'was a sum of [all its] units' (Dewey, 1988, p. 111), and Honohan more recently declared 'civil society' a larger public unit that comprises all of its parts including 'associations' that 'are hierarchical, non-deliberative and [that] operate out of the public eye' (Honohan, 2002, p. 234). Dewey (and Habermas after him) developed theories that strive for genuine democratic governance. A genuine democracy results in policies that are normatively and legitimately authoritative because, as opposed to the decisions produced by authoritarian regimes, the decisions and actions of its subunits, such as the market, are held accountable to a higher archetype.

Today, the economy continues to expand its reach into new areas of life—privatization of military defence, prison services, and public education, to name just a few—and this is inverting what should be the predominant authority exercised by a genuine democratic government over its subunits. A government whose policies embody the confluence of democratically developed norms of consensus has, on the other hand, very different implications than a government whose policies are implemented as a result of oblique or unscrupulous schemes. Political and public decision making should not 'be organized like corporate bodies,' according to Habermas (Habermas, 1999, p. 171), but Dewey goes farther by arguing that democratic decision making should filter into other subunits including, but not limited to, the economy. Democracy is prioritized by Dewey in its relation to the market. In fact, Harbermas asserts that Dewey, more than any other philosopher, wrote about "the essential need' to advance 'the methods and conditions of debate, discussion and persuasion." It was Dewey's neopragmatism, and his emphasis on communication, that resulted in Habermas drawing the following conclusion about his own discourse theory: 'the democratic procedure is institutionalized in discourses and bargaining processes by employing forms of communication that promise that all outcomes reached in conformity with the procedure are reasonable'. Deliberative democracy 'is especially meant to be educative, by providing the "methods and conditions' of political will-formation that Dewey ... considered '*the* problem of the public" (Habermas, 1999, pp. 304, 316).

In response to the overwhelming influence of the market and industrialization during his day, Dewey offered a newly developed reconstructionist approach that shifted the focus to fostering a pervasively democratic system of communication that could continually renew normatively constructed agreements among citizens who were themselves subjected to these agreements. Too many associations in society, Dewey argued, 'lack ... [a] reciprocity of interest,' such as is the case when 'a gang or clique brings its antisocial spirit into relief,' a spirit that embodies 'interests 'of its own" and 'which shut it out from full interaction with other groups, so that its prevailing purpose is the protection of what it has got, instead of reorganization and progress through wider relationships' (Dewey, 1944, p. 86). According to Dewey, his 'Democratic Ideal' required that we acknowledge our interdependence, a 'recognition of mutual interests as a factor in social control,' and the desire for 'continuous readjustment' by confronting change with continuous 'intercourse' (Dewey, 1944, p. 87). Democracy served as the archetype in Dewey's sociopolitical theory and his educational philosophy. Hierarchically speaking, democracy, which requires reflective and ongoing communication, is given priority over all other subunits. 'A democracy,' Dewey famously asserted

> ... is more than a form of government; it is primarily a mode of associated living, of conjoint communicated experience. The extension in space of the number of individuals who participate in an interest so that each has to refer his own action to that of others, and to consider the action of others to give point and direction to his own, is equivalent to the breaking down of those barriers of class, race, and national territory which kept men from perceiving the full import of their activity. These more numerous and more varied points of contact denote a greater diversity of stimuli to which an individual has to respond; they consequently put a premium on variation in his action. They secure a liberation of powers which remain suppressed as long as the incitations to action are partial, as they must be in a group which in its exclusiveness shuts out many interests (ibid., p. 887).

Learning is, therefore, not simply the act of inculcating in children a society's traditional values, norms, and customs, as important as this is. It is an attempt to cultivate unknown potentialities in each individual, which cannot be fully known unless the individual is freed from the stultifying institutions that privilege individualistic ontologies. Individuals must be given opportunities to engage in and reconstruct their environment interdependently with fellow social beings, beings who vary in multiple respects and therefore contribute multiple perspectives from which each can engage with, reflect upon, and act collectively to solve problems. Only by experiencing the widest possible range of a person's diverse social environment through communication with others can he or she break the parameters of a limited parochial knowledge and evolve into a higher plane of existence and potential, what Dewey refers to as growth. Aaron Schutz summarizes this goal nicely when he paraphrases from Dewey's Democracy and Education that, 'democratic communities create a tremendous web of conscious interdependence in which there are 'numerous and varied ... points of shared' interest that are interpreted and acted upon differently by different participants. In this way, 'the intellectual variations of the individual in observation, imagination, judgment, and invention ... can become 'the agencies of social progress'" (Schutz, 2001, p. 292).

Dewey's Sociopolitical Philosophy: A Democratic Society

Will Shape Possibilities for Democratic Schools

Despite relevant concerns over the pragmatic problems that would likely emerge in expanding access to deliberations in a multicultural society, as highlighted by Heather Voke, democratic schooling is an essential ingredient in Dewey's philosophy conceived to overcome these difficulties. The rules of speech and communication vary among cultures, but this is justification for supporting a communicative theory rather than an argument opposing it, as with Voke (Voke, 2001, pp. 361–69). Everyone should have their perspectives challenged or critiqued, which is the essence of Dewey's democratic and intersubjective theory. How else can we diffuse conflict and implement public policies that have been considered from multiple perspectives? Differences in perspectives must be brought together, according to Dewey, in order to broaden understanding and intellectual horizons in a diverse society.

Furthermore, Bynum successfully corrects an oversimplified reading of Dewey by Cornell West. According to Bynum, West criticizes Dewey's idealism, arguing that the latter's deliberative democracy is impracticable due to deeply institutionalized forms of oppression in the United States. Despite West's reasonable concern, Bynum responds to this criticism by clarifying Dewey's philosophy: 'It is far from clear that the future way of life Dewey envisions would' be so limited, 'considering his belief that we must constantly modify social life by chopping away the 'dead wood' of newly useless traditions as we reshape conjoint social projects in response to constant, critical reevaluations of our present experiences' significance' (Bynum, 2005, p. 371). In response to West, Bynum clarifies Dewey's definition of 'the social,' which is elaborated in chapter seven of *Democracy and Education*: It is 'not simply anything that goes on within a social group, but rather as a particular kind of nonoppressive, mutually interested relatedness that enables growth in the range and quality of human experience'. Accordingly, 'Dewey prepares a standard for judging societies,' according to Bynum, which adequately addresses West's criticism, in my opinion (ibid., p. 372). Rømer refers to Dewey's idea of growth as 'a kind of endless doubling of intelligence,' which 'can only take place in an open and democratic society'. Contrarily, 'closed groups ... cannot be genuine social groups and, therefore, are unable to offer education in its proper sense (they can only offer instruction),' as Rømer explains (Rømer, 2012, p. 136).

It is not surprising, for example, that Dewey chose schooling and education as parts of his ontological theory, which give priority to the democratic and interdependent elements of human nature and recognize the necessity of bridging multicultural communities through the education of youth. Where better, we might ask, in a society absorbed by institutions that otherwise promote instrumental-, strategic-, and utilitarian-oriented rationalities to develop future citizens than in schools that could, if freed from these rationalities, inculcate democratic and communicative capabilities in future citizens? Democratic schooling, Dewey hoped, would focus on developing the natural or instinctual tendency for humans to engage in social communication and reconstruction in order to cooperatively cohabitate. As a subunit of the state, formal schooling represents the broader culture from which it was conceived and for which it is utilized.

Schooling in modern society is to serve as a conduit for developing in children 'virtue' or the 'means to be fully and adequately what one is capable of becoming through association with others in all the offices of life,' Dewey urged (Dewey, 1944, p. 358). It appears that Dewey viewed formal schooling as the necessary institutional means for countering the otherwise negative impact of a cultural ethos that privileged individualistic culture buttressed by both political and economic institutions. Dewey viewed these institutions as antithetical to the development of human potential, which required meaningful associational practices resulting from free and equal communication. 'All education which develops power to share effectively in social life is moral,' Dewey concluded. 'Learning' has 'a social aim,' and when it effectively encompasses Dewey's idealized sociality, 'the school becomes itself ... a miniature community' (ibid., p. 360).

Dewey was one of the first modern theorists to methodically fuse education and democracy into a sociopolitical philosophy. Educational philosophers since Plato and Aristotle have promoted education as a public good (albeit for different purposes), but today, we are witnessing a paradigmatic attack on the idea of the public itself as it is consumed by market forces. I agree with Alison Kadlec when she concludes that, 'Dewey's notion of experience is intersubjective, communicative, and social,' as well as a living through of 'the consequences of our actions,' which 'taken together ... form the basis of a powerful resource for critical reflection and social transformation' Kadlec, 2006, p. 522, footnote 8). Furthermore, Dewey offered a more radical democratic communication theory than did Habermas because he sought to extend this normative process beyond political institutions to include 'economic, international, educational, scientific ... artistic, [and] religious' (Antonio and Kellner, 1992, p. 291) institutions.

Habermas clearly perceived Dewey's contribution to a pragmatic theory of communication when he offered the following conclusion: 'No one has worked out [an institutionalization of the democratic procedure ... by employing forms of communication ... that promise reasonable outcomes ... more energetically than John Dewey' (Habermas, 1999, p. 304). Anticipating Habermas's communicative action theory, Dewey developed a deeply moral philosophy by ontologically locating social action and change democratically through communication. This, in my opinion, is Dewey's most formidable accomplishment and one that can be seen throughout his works, but, in particular, in *Democracy and Education*.

References

Antonio, R. J. and Kellner, D. (1992), Communication, modernity, and democracy in Habermas and Dewey. *Symbolic Interaction*, 15 (3), 277–297.
Arendt, H. (1990), *On Revolution*. London: Penguin Books.
Burke, E. (1987), *Reflections on the Revolution in France*. Buffalo, NY: Prometheus Books.
Bynum, G. (2005), John Dewey's anti-essentialism and social progress. *Journal of Social Philosophy*, 36(3), 364–381.
Dewey, J. (1944), *Democracy and Education: An Introduction to the Philosophy of Education*. New York, NY: The Free Press.
Dewey, J. (1988), *The Public and Its Problems*. Athens, OH: Swallow Press.

Dewey, J. (2008), *The Later Works of John Dewey*. In Ann Boydston, J. (Ed.), vol. 11. Carbondale, IL: Southern Illinois University, pp. 1935–1937.

Dewey, J. (2011), Can education share in social reconstruction? In Provenzo, E. F. Jr. (Ed.), *The Social Frontier: A Critical Reader*. New York, NY: Peter Lang, pp. 26–30.

Englund, T. (2000), Rethinking democracy and education: towards an education of deliberative citizens. *Journal of Curriculum Studies*, 32(2), 305–313.

Habermas, J. (1984), *The Theory of Communicative Action: Reason and the Rationalization of Society*. Boston, MA: Beacon Press.

Habermas, J. (1987), *The Theory of Communicative Action: Lifeworld and System: A Critique of Functionalist Reason*. Boston, MA: Beacon Press.

Habermas, J. (1999), *Between Facts and Norms: Contributions to a Discourse Theory of Law and Democracy*. Cambridge, MA: MIT Press.

Honohan, I. (2002), *Civic Republicanism*. New York, NY: Routledge.

Kadlec, A. (2006), Reconstructing Dewey: The philosophy of critical pragmatism. *Polity*, 38(4), 519–542.

Markell, P. (2005), The rule of the people: Arendt, arche, and democracy. *American Political Science Review*, 100 (1), 1–14.

Paine, T. (1984), *Rights of Man*. New York, NY: Penguin Books.

Rawls, J. (1971), *A Theory of Justice*. Cambridge, MA: Harvard University Press.

Rømer, T. A. (2012), Imagination and judgment in John Dewey's philosophy: intelligent transactions in a democratic context. *Educational Philosophy and Theory*, 44 (2), 133–150.

Schutz, A. (2001), John Dewey and 'a Paradox of Size': democratic faith at the limits of experience. *American Journal of Education*, 109 (3), 287–319.

Vannatta, S. (2012), Pragmatic conservatism: a defense. *Humanitas*, 25 (1–2), 20–43.

Voke, H. M. (2001), Public deliberation, communication across difference, and issues-based service learning. *Philosophy of Education*, 361–369.

Wolin, S. (1994), Norm and form: the constitutionalizing of democracy. In Euben, J.P., Wallach, J. R. and Ober, J. (Eds.), *Athenian Political Thought and the Reconstruction of American Democracy*. Ithaca, NY: Cornell University Press.

Wolin, S. (2004), *Politics and Vision: Continuity and Innovation in Western Political Thought* (Expanded Ed.). Princeton, NJ: Princeton University Press.

Chapter 9

The Role of the Educators' Disposition and Mental Processes in a Student's Experience of Democracy

Victoria Door and Clare Wilkinson

Abstract

Dewey argues throughout *Democracy and Education* that schooling plays a powerful role in forming how we are disposed towards democracy. Disposition underlies and determines both thinking and activity. A disposition which operates habitually tends to maintain the moral, social and intellectual status quo. A humane democracy demands a disposition which both challenges existing conditions and is concerned to change them for social well-being. A student's experience at school would ideally need to be one which supports the motivation and skills to foster such a democracy. Dewey claims that we dispose ourselves to think in particular ways. If our mental processes are habitual then teaching and pastoral care may be done in a way that might impose rigidity of thought on students. If the intelligent concern for social well-being is missing from our thinking, the educational experience we offer provides neither model nor means for the development of a humane democracy. Using vignettes from our own experience as educators, together with our interpretation of Dewey's thinking in *Democracy and Education* and *How We Think*, we consider how our own mental processes as educators and dispositions which underlie them might impact for good or for ill on students' day-to-day experience. We argue that the main responsibility for conditions of experience falls on policymakers, school leadership, management and teachers, who, we conclude with Dewey, should aim to be aware of their disposition and its manifestation in thinking and activity in order to create conditions which make schooling a truly democratic experience.

Keywords: Democracy; disposition; conduct; awareness; thinking; well-being

> The school ... should contribute through the type of ... disposition which it forms to the improvement of conditions. (Dewey, 1997, p. 136)

> Were all instructors to realize that the quality of mental process, not the production of correct answers, is the measure of educative growth, something hardly less than a(n) (r)evolution in teaching would be worked. (Dewey, 1997, p. 176)[1]

Introduction

How might what students experience in school relate to the practice of democracy, and what relation do both of those have to the nature of the educator's disposition and the quality of her mental process? In the light of Dewey's thinking centrally in *Democracy and Education*, but drawing also on *How We Think*, we consider how our own mental processes as educators and the disposition which underlies them might impact for good or for ill on student day-to-day experience. Our main concerns are with the potential of application of Dewey's thinking to

---

[1]With thanks to Kang Zhao of Zhejiang University, Hangzhou, China, who has translated some of Dewey's lectures in China into English for the first time (Zhao, 2016a). He pointed out that Dewey was not advocating revolution, but gradual change. 'In general, Dewey indeed thinks modification/gradual improvement is more primary than revolution/radical change both in education and social change' (Zhao, 2016b).

on-the-ground school practice as well as the wider thought of 'school as an instrument for forming new society'; specifically one which practises, and looks to develop the practice of something called democracy.

Connections between student experience, quality of thought, disposition and democracy raise larger issues than can possibly be considered here, so we confine ourselves to the following, all of which can be found in *Democracy and Education*. One aspect of 'improvement of conditions' (Dewey, 1997, p. 136) refers to a gradual move towards ways of living together where, among other things, there is mutual understanding and tolerance of a wide range of values, together with 'a constructive interest in the well-being of others' (ibid., p. 45). We try to bring out the importance of 'constructive interest' for the project of democracy in the way Dewey defines it in 1916, by looking at what it might mean in school. Dewey uses the phrase in the context of the prolonged period of dependence of human young upon adults, in terms of 'affectionate and sympathetic watchfulness' (ibid.). In our account, we explore constructive interest in terms of its value as part of the necessary disposition of educators. Dewey is clear that what he calls 'associated living' (ibid., p. 87) is the most fundamental aspect of democracy. A social (as opposed to political) element of democracy is the nature of relations between individuals, and between groups. Relations are determined by the social, moral and intellectual stance the individual takes towards others. Constructive interest in the well-being of others is at once a moral and pragmatic stance towards living in society, requiring an 'intellectual', or intelligently thoughtful attitude to ensure it is put into practice.

Throughout *Democracy and Education* it is made clear that schooling plays a powerful role in forming students' moral, social and intellectual attitudes. Attitudes which prove most constructive are those which encompass openness, a concern for others and an understanding of how we think. Students learn much about morality, social relations and thinking indirectly by interpreting what they experience around them. From our own observations and from the literature (e.g. Taruna, 2016; Gentina et al., 2017), we can add that although other students are a strong influence, the main responsibility for conditions of experience within school falls on policymakers, school leadership, management and teachers (referred in this chapter as 'educators'). We conclude, with Dewey, that those adults should aim, therefore, to be aware of their own moral, social and intellectual attitudes, and how they manifest in activity in the course of creating conditions which give students a truly democratic experience.

As co-authors and educators, we share a concern that students' day-to-day experiences in school may not be conducive to their immediate well-being, nor longer term, to a healthy democratic society, and we are not alone in noticing this matter (e.g. Solomon et al., 1996; Ruus et al., 2007). Clearly there are a range of factors determining student experience, but we agree with Dewey that educator disposition and understanding of 'thinking' are fundamental. To us they seem as important today as they were to Dewey in 1916, with today's pressure on schools to achieve high grades in examinations and discussions on narrowing the curriculum and reducing access to some core subjects for 'low-achieving' students (Bloom, 2016; Henshaw, 2016).

We think that *Democracy and Education*, true to Dewey's spirit of non-dualism, provides both theoretical and practical answers to our questions and we hope we do him justice in teasing them out, using illustrations from current school life to show how they might work. The names of those involved have been changed to provide anonymity.

Long-Term Project

In the spirit of 'evolution' rather than revolution, developing a certain quality in thinking and the disposition to do so are considered long-term projects. Development of both is best thought of in terms of Zhao's 'gradual improvement' rather than sudden change. This is because the quality required involves developing critical understanding of self and action, which takes time, but is part of what teaching and learning as 'education' is about. Looked at in a Deweyan way, it is its very essence.

By 1916, thinking and action are inextricably connected for Dewey. Knowledge and practice are intertwined; thought and knowledge together if used purposefully enrich our lives and, although can be described as 'mental', are unfailingly embodied (Dewey, 1933; Alexander, 1987; Door, 2009). Our 'attitude not to this and that thing, nor even to the aggregate of known things, but to the considerations which govern conduct' (Dewey, 1997, pp. 234–235) will determine our thinking and be revealed in our action. Our attitudes take time to form and in the kind of rapidly changing societies in which we now live, as did Dewey, it is better that they keep forming throughout our lives, rather than crystallizing too early, or merely being hand-me-downs from the previous generation. Attitudes are best formed as part of the process of educative growth, which can and should, according to Dewey, continue no matter what our age.

Education for democracy requires an intelligent, realistic model for living democratically and this can happen in the day-to-day life and conduct of the school. This conception of living democratically is in contrast to a model with rigid hierarchy and unthinking acceptance of a status quo, perhaps disguised beneath the cloak of pupil voice and policy rhetoric, or school as factory, where students and teachers are configured as producers of outcomes. As such, it is likely that the existing culture of education needs to be pulled back from the temptation to go for a quick fix to the problem of 'falling standards' (Apple, 2006). The need seems as great now as it was when Dewey was writing *Democracy and Education*.

Educational culture cannot be created purely from the top-down but rather requires commitment of all involved and evolves in a synergy between those who direct policy, those who lead strategically, those at the operational management level and the practice at the chalk face. Here is where *quality r*esides. Classroom practitioners are not the only ones then who have a responsibility to contribute towards building and acting on a shared and evolving vision (Stoll et al., 2003; Cassell and Door, 2016), which we argue is the vision of a professional learning community where school as a site for democratic growth and development is an intrinsic part of pupil learning.

In Dewey's terms, our account is moral philosophy rather than psychology or politics because it aims to bring to light our assumptions as educators about what student experience *could* and *should* be, and how our dispositions impact upon it. The aim of our philosophical account is to move towards 'wisdom which would influence the conduct of life' (Dewey, 1997, p. 324) by bringing 'to consciousness what men have come to think in virtue of the quality of their current experience about ... themselves and the reality they conceive to include or to govern both' (ibid.). We argue that bringing assumptions to consciousness can result in increased self-awareness, and awareness of others, allowing educators and students alike to live better.

How Does Dewey Relate Democracy to Living Better?

'A democracy is more than a form of government; it is primarily a mode of associated living, of conjoint, communicated experience' (Dewey, 1997, p. 87). In this mode, the wider the range of interests and understanding of those interests the better. Also required is a strong sense of connection between diverse individuals and groups. Individuals need to find and develop capacities for living in a widely understanding and tolerant way, and it makes sense for schooling to be a means for helping them do that. There is more, though. Proper democratic relations do not exist where people or groups regard each other primarily and exclusively as means to their own ends. To do so, to behave instrumentally, is not to be in a proper social relationship. A less-than-proper relationship is one 'on a machine-like plane' where '(i)ndividuals use one another so as to get desired results, without reference to the emotional and intellectual disposition and consent of those used' (ibid., p. 5). Dewey explicitly mentions school, along with family, workplace and government, as a place where such potentially damaging behaviour can occur. 'As far as the relations of parent and child, teacher and pupil, employer and employee, governor and governed, remain upon this level, they form no true social group' (ibid.).

We interpret Dewey's picture of democracy to be one of our getting along together as a group in a way that respects the value of the individual. Within school, this means an appreciation that any of us, educator or student, has only one life and the quality of that life is of vital importance to each and all of us. At the same time, we recognize the significance and connection of how we *think* with how we *live* together in society. In Deweyan terms, we live together in school in a 'social group' (ibid., p. 5) experiencing 'an associated life' (ibid., p. 46). The pull of democracy in and beyond school involves a realization of our interdependency, upon which rides the continued, tolerable survival of humanity. There are also positive advantages to the 'right' kind of social relations: 'the very process of living together, educates. It enlarges and enlightens experience; it stimulates and enriches imagination; it creates responsibility for accuracy and vividness of statement and thought' (ibid., p. 6). This statement opens up the possibility of school as a good place for the individual to be, a site for well-being.

The possibility for well-being is blocked if we forget our interdependency and quest for lifelong educative development. Instead, Dewey argues that schooling takes on a 'short-sighted method which falls back on mechanical repetition and routine to secure external efficiency of habit, motor skill without accompanying thought, mark(ing) a closing in the surroundings upon growth' (ibid., p. 49). Allied to lack of a longer, wider vision is a '[m]echanical rigid woodenness' which Dewey sees as 'an inevitable corollary of any theory which separates mind from activity motivated by a purpose' (ibid., p. 170).

We know from our own experience that developing an integrated theory-practice approach to democratic thinking and action in school is challenging and often neglected. In considering education in and for a democratic society, we might properly consider that shift of world view from theory *or* practice, which recognizes that our personal and cultural assumptions or theories are not separate from how we act on a daily basis. This recognition is a move beyond skills and beyond even Bruner's emphasis on understanding (2007), to 'more original and challenging ways of being human' (Hogan, 2015, p. 143).

For example, Hogan speaks of the teacher's 'ways of relating to people and ideas' (ibid.). If 'the teacher's relations with the students are such, or have become such, that the teacher sees most if not all of them as unworthy of entry into the riches of the world in question' (he means the world of the teacher's subject matter) 'or as incapable of meeting even the rudimentary demands for entry' (ibid.), then that teacher is in effect excluding students from that world. Such an exclusionary approach cannot contribute positively to students' quality of learning experience. For a good democratic life, there can be no scenario where citizens are categorized into 'those capable of a life of reason and hence having their own ends, and those capable only of desire and work, and needing to have their ends provided by others' (Dewey, 1997, pp. 260–261).

In our account, the first step is for the educators to recognize how they are disposed towards students and the next is to explore the possible impact (consequences) of that disposition. The insight we have as educators into the nature of thinking, including our own, has a big role to play here, so we go on to explore disposition and thinking, using three illustrations drawn from our own experiences in secondary schools.

What Kind of Disposition and Why?

To illustrate, here is the first of our real illustrations from everyday secondary school life. In this situation, Helen, a link worker,[2] recalled how she had jumped to immediate assumptions about a boy's challenging behaviour in the corridor. Her first thought was that he was showing

---

[2]The role of the link workers is to act as the advocate for the students they work with on the Special Educational Needs and Disabilities Register (Wilkinson, 2015).

off in front of his peers. Taking the time to find out a bit more, the student revealed that he was experiencing a difficult day and that things were not going well for him either at school or at home. He confided that school was, in comparison with home a haven, and that his relationship with Helen herself was important, because he was able to tell her the truth.

This instance illustrates our contention that for some students, no matter how difficult school is, it can be better than their home life, but for this to happen consistently we need to consider how we are disposed towards students, our ideas about democratic living and how they are actualized. Helen's initial reaction to the student's behaviour would not have allowed him to open up and the situation could have escalated. Her willingness to question her own first assumption (part of her disposition) and to take another tack required self-awareness and an ability to distance herself from her own habitual thought patterns (her mental process). Her intention was that the student should reflect on his behaviour and make a change, which would make his day at school go better. We could say that she was involving him in a reciprocal process, albeit unspoken, whereby she, by acting differently, allowed him to act differently too. Here the relationship between student and educator is a positive grounding for social life and for democracy because the child is not conceived of as an object or lesser being by the adult but as a subject, with his own experience, affected qualitatively by his interaction with others, and in turn, affecting others' experience.

In the chapter 'Philosophy of Education' Dewey explains 'philosophic disposition' in the context of the difference between science and philosophy; the former can 'suggest things to do and not to do, and provide means of execution' (Dewey, 1997, p. 324) but the latter concerns the decision-making involved in how we behave. Disposition as a general term indicates that which underlies and determines our behaviour. It can be routine, mechanical, repeating a 'former habit of action' (ibid., p. 325), or it can be consciously directed on the basis of changing situations and growth in understanding. In the first form, it would tend to maintain the moral, social and intellectual status quo, whereas in the second it might challenge existing conditions, being a general or underlying attitude of willingness to learn and find meaning, even in the extreme difficulties of life, together with the realization that its nature will 'govern conduct' (ibid., pp. 234–235).

If an educator intended to provide students with experiences that fit them morally, socially and intellectually for a democratic life, a consciously philosophical disposition would be needed. The nature of the individual's stance on democracy would be fundamental to the disposition. Our particular stance, which we take to be Dewey's, is that the wider view of living together is in stark contrast to one of 'social efficiency' (ibid., p. 122) where there continues to be an acceptance of 'a deprecatory estimate of the masses characteristic of an aristocratic community' (ibid.). How well that society works 'is measured by product or output' that is in our context, 'the production of correct answers' (ibid., p. 5).

In the second illustration, Peter, as deputy head and language teacher, took over some General Certificate of Secondary Education (GCSE) French teaching. He observed one student who seemed to have potential but who was not being adequately challenged. Peter reflected on the situation, wondering if there was a way forward for this particular student by providing him with a more realistic learning environment. It not being practical to send the student to France, Peter took to inviting the student to walk around the school with him, chatting in French as they progressed. The student not only achieved well at GCSE but also went on to take French in the Sixth Form. They modelled a learning activity to the school based on love of learning, of subject and an equality achieved through dialogue. Modelling the use of language was to show the whole school that using a language in this way is both normal and typical. Learning conversations were thus modelled around school as well as positive behaviours. This was an example of the way disposition and thinking are exposed to the world in physical manifestations, words, movements, gestures, in this case, very much for the good.

The consciously philosophical disposition is wider than we can discuss here, but two of its constitutive aspects are especially relevant to quality of mental processes and democracy: those of open-mindedness and those of the essential element of constructive concern for well-being of others. We interpret Peter's actions here as modelling that particular disposition.

How Does 'Mental Process' Relate to Disposition?

Dewey makes his claim about quality of mental process in a section on 'open-mindedness' in a chapter titled 'The Nature of Method'. The statement comes at the end of his argument for a relationship between educative and intellectual growth. Both aspects of growth require a particular disposition. Implicit throughout the chapter is that this disposition is not simply one desirable for students, but also for those teaching them. 'Openness of mind means accessibility of mind to any and every consideration that will throw light upon the situation that needs to be cleared up, and that will help determine the consequences of acting this way or that' (Dewey, 1997, p. 75).

The disposition to open-mindedness is necessarily an active one; we have to work against the tendency to shut off to new stimuli. Capacity for growth, curiosity, responsiveness and openness are natural, but 'lack of interest ... aversion to progress, and dread of the uncertain and the unknown' (ibid., p. 51) are learnt, not only from mechanical pedagogical methods, but also from the way the classroom teacher is constrained to implement such methods.

We have tried to make it clear from the start that improvement of conditions in school is conjoint effort. Classroom teachers should not be scapegoated by those with the executive power for any shortcomings in the system. Operationally, they are the ones with immediate contact with students, but the climate within a school is powerfully influenced by its leaders and managers (Gewirtz et al., 2009; Cassell and Door, 2016). Dewey's references to the power of dispositions to influence those about them for good or ill can be applied to anyone working within a school, but the teacher does spend more time with students than the headteacher. However, the head's disposition sets the climate (Cassell and Door, 2016; Hargreaves and Fink, 2006). Dewey may be explicit about the influence of the teacher as a stimulus to the student: 'How profoundly the mental habits of others affect the attitude of the one being trained. Example is more potent than precept, and a teacher's best conscious efforts may be more than counteracted by the influence of personal traits that he is unaware of or that he regards as unimportant' (Dewey, 1933, p. 58). But that influence can be ascribed equally to those in climate-setting roles.

When that view is taken, all of us – school leaders, managers, teachers, classroom assistants and teacher educators – have responsibility for teaching by example, adopting conscious efforts to educate well, based on purposeful and intelligent understanding of how to keep on 'growing' open-mindedness for students and for ourselves. Dewey outlines what this involves: 'intellectual growth means constant expansion of horizons and consequent formation of new purposes and new responses ... impossible without an active disposition to welcome points of view hitherto alien; an active desire to entertain considerations which modify existing purposes' (Dewey, 1997, p. 175). There are three elements here: willingness and active effort to expand ideas, allowing our purposes to change and being prepared to use different means for achieving those purposes. A sense of the gracious, unforced nature of maintaining this open attitude is communicated in Dewey's affirmation that '(r)etention of capacity to grow is the reward of such *intellectual hospitality*' (our italics) (ibid., p. 175).

To be disposed to be open-minded is then both the responsibility and the natural capacity of individuals. We cannot force or teach others directly to be open, although it has been argued that it is possible to provide something like the optimum conditions for openness to flourish (Noddings, 2003; Higgins, 2010; Cassell and Door, 2016). A school climate of 'result anxiety' (Edginton, 2016) militates towards a closed-minded attitude for staff and students, and is likely to lead to outcomes which are 'fixed and rigid … not a stimulus to intelligence … rendering the work of both teacher and pupil mechanical and slavish' (Dewey, 1997, p. 110).

Open-mindedness does not mean, in Dewey's words 'come right in; there is no one at home' (ibid., p. 175). Critical thinking is one check on routine or capricious thought. Another is that integrally related aspect of disposition that needs cultivation – our 'constructive interest in the well-being of others' (ibid., p. 122).

Dewey describes this interest as 'intelligent sympathy for others' (p. 120), 'cultivated imagination for what men have in common and a rebellion at whatever unnecessarily divides them' (ibid., p. 121). In our first example, it is seen in Helen's willingness to put her first reaction on hold and to attend sympathetically and imaginatively to the student in front of her rather than her own preconceptions. Her solution is, having allowed the student space to open up, to help him consider the likely consequences of his behaviour on the quality of his experience in the day to come. Her sympathy is directed intelligently, in that she uses her professional knowledge, part of which is 'cultivated imagination', where she tries to see things from his perspective and then guide his understanding to allow him to make sense of her guidance. She draws on a commonality of understanding of daily school life, refusing a 'master–slave' relationship. In order to act empathetically, Helen has to be disposed towards the 'constructive well-being' of the student and his role in a democratic, rather than autocratic relationship with others.

Disposition and Habit

One instance does not fix a disposition, but it is one step towards forming it. As Dewey puts it, 'Mental habitudes are gradually assimilated' (Dewey, 1997, p. 14). It appears from our analysis of *Democracy and Education* that Dewey uses the words 'habitude' and habit' interchangeably,[3] and we turn now to looking at how habit might relate to disposition. Because we are suggesting, in the spirit of Dewey, that constructive (well-being focused) individual development, and therefore change, is fundamental to both education and democracy, the question of whether a disposition can be a habit is an important puzzle. In chapter 4, 'Education as Growth', Dewey is careful to make a distinction between mechanical (unthinking) routine habits and the 'full use of intelligence' and 'persistent care' (Dewey, 1997, p. 49) needed to maintain intellectual and emotional growth. At this point in his writing, Dewey is using the term 'habit' broadly, allowing us to see what Hansen has posited might be Dewey's own ongoing conceptual development where he is actively struggling to find ways of expressing what he means by disposition and habit, and inviting the readers to struggle with him (Hansen, 2007). The role of habit in disposition is not simple; Dewey refers to it as being part of the 'formation of intellectual and emotional disposition as well as an increase in ease, economy and efficiency of action' (Dewey, 1997, p. 48). It is not passive; 'it actively seeks for occasions to pass into full operation' and if 'unduly blocked, shows itself in uneasiness and intense craving' (ibid.). It marks an intellectual disposition, but is not separate in that from action. 'Where there is habit, there is acquaintance with the materials and equipment to which action is applied' (ibid.). Habit is both in those things we might think of as 'mental', that is reasoning and judging, and in practical, physical acts: 'habits of mind involved in habits of the eye and hand supply the latter with their significance' (ibid.). In this section, Dewey is endeavouring to express how intelligent thought stops habit from being mechanistic routine and allows us to free ourselves from it and use it productively. Intelligence in approach to any act (mental or physical) is what saves us from becoming fixed, losing flexibility of thought and action, and applying yesterday's solutions to the problems of this moment. There are inevitable processes of maturation and ageing – the 'hardening of

---

[3]The term 'habituated' does seem to refer to a state, produced by ongoing exposure to a stimulus, or on-going activity (e.g. Dewey, 1997, p. 48).

organic conditions ... which affect the physiological structures ... involved in thinking'. However, Dewey's point is that intelligent, conscious thought can overcome such loss of 'organic plasticity' (ibid., p. 49).

If we conceive of life and education as being developmental, the nature of our conception will have consequences, basically inclining our practice either to fixed rigidity or to ongoing reconstruction and growth. The question is, what disposition is it that can be called habitual, and yet is one reflecting this attitude? What might motivate us to hold ourselves critically, that is intelligently, open to the new? We read this to be that we are motivated by an understanding of the need for it in terms of democracy, not autocracy, that is we adopt this attitude freely, because we see it to be of value in 'associated life'. It makes sense to us in the context of our own well-being and that of others.

Can Disposition Be Learned in School?

School is a place where dispositions of the next generation are formed. Dewey elaborates on this in the second chapter of *Democracy and Education*. Disposition cannot be directly taught, but will be learned gradually from a range of sources within daily life over years of schooling. Students have the 'ability to learn from experience ... power to modify actions on the basis of results of prior experiences, the power to *develop dispositions*' (Dewey, 1997, p. 44, emphasis in the original).

The job of educators is to provide conditions for a democratic disposition to develop, one which is capable of cultivating open-mindedness and a constructive interest in the well-being of others. As we have seen, intelligence, or a critical use of mental processes, is essential for such an interest to be constructive. Being well-disposed towards one's students is a necessary end to have but it alone is not enough. If the question 'what do I need to do to promote the well-being of schools and students?' is taken seriously as an end by leader and class teacher alike, it can be used as the guide for discovering the means to develop the climate in which those in school may flourish: '[t]he problem fixes the end of thought and the end controls the process of thinking' (Dewey, 2007, p. 10).

We also need the means to that end and that means is good pedagogy, which is 'action directed intelligently by ends' (Dewey, 1997, p. 170). 'Nothing has brought pedagogical thought into greater disrepute than the belief that it is identified with handing out to teachers recipes and models to be followed in teaching' (ibid.). Mastery of a general method gives the teacher principles of procedure. As such, these provide an indirect guide to action. Following prescribed rules, or 'recipes and models', or 'conformity to orders externally imposed' (ibid.) should be done with extreme caution, as the highly complex and contingent nature of classrooms means that it is hard to identify identical situations.

Thought and Action Go Together

Thinking and acting, including *manner* of acting, are inseparable for Dewey. Action may include engaging mentally with a body of subject knowledge as after all, we are still embodied during such engagement, that is sitting at tables or computers. As a philosopher of education, Dewey had a unique appreciation of embodiment.[4] Chapter 5, 'Preparation, Unfolding and Formal Discipline' lays out his 1916 view of the evolution of intellect through physical action, and the reward of 'direct growth of experience in richness of meaning' (Dewey, 1997, p. 68).

Separating thought from action in human growth, ignoring the essential connectivity between mental and physical, drains meaning from experience and from the richness conferred on the individual's experience. When we educate for academic outcomes alone, we mistakenly go for the quick fix; the 'chief cause of devotion to rigidity of method is … that it seems to promise speedy, accurately measurable, correct results' (ibid., p. 175). Dewey's contention is that such 'rigidity of method' impoverishes both student and teacher.

'[A]bility to think' (ibid., p. 152) is not thinking in a vacuum, learning thinking skills apart from some subject matter or purposeful content. It is useless to separate the learning of skills from the acquisition of information, and training thinking, because '[t]hinking which is not connected with the increase of efficiency of action, and with learning more about ourselves and the world in which we live, has something the matter with it …' (ibid., p. 152). But rejecting the isolation of thought from action or content does not imply any rejection of rigour in thinking.

Our third illustration aims to show how an understanding of allowing a child to bring his or her world into curricular thinking led to the

---

[4]Dewey had an association with F.M. Alexander and his psycho-physical technique from 1915 till his death in 1951 (Door, 2009). See Chapter 4 of this volume.

possibility of reflective or critical thinking. Gwen's role as a Special Educational Needs Coordinator involved her in working with Edward, a student with particular learning needs which kept him at the periphery of the school curriculum. On one pivotal occasion, Edward was seeking refuge in the Special Needs Department and began to tell Gwen what seemed to be a story about his family and their collection of medals. Gwen, aware of the potential of pre-reflective thought (Dewey, 2007) as a precursor to logical, sequential thinking, was on the lookout for a way to draw Edward into the curriculum and so steered the conversation to a consideration of military campaigns and their resultant medals. This allowed Edward to search the Internet to begin to find out about his own grandfather's military service.

Gwen's aim was to move Edward beyond pre-reflective, imaginative thought, but not to stifle his capacity for it. In the short term, she wanted to get him thinking in a logical, sequential way, observing and following a 'true' phenomenon in the world, but one that had meaning for him. She helped him relate his experience both of what he heard at home to a part of the history curriculum and also to the moment-by-moment of being in school. She wanted him to make a 'backward and forward connection' (Dewey, 1997, p. 140) between those three areas of his experience. There is sequence and consequence in how he considered the areas. She helped him move his thinking about his grandfather in a 'capricious' way (ibid.) where having a medal is 'accidental', unconnected to his grandfather's actions, to seeing the consequences in his grandfather's life. She aimed to help Edward find the medals meaningful in their connection with what happened to his grandfather and to the past lives of others in the wider world. At the same time, Gwen hoped that in engaging in the project of exploring his grandfather's award, Edward was 'having fruitful experiences' (ibid.) and that he noticed not only that school was more interesting when he engaged but also that life went better for him at school in his relations with teachers. In other words, he was able to relate the back and forward connection between his actions and the actions of others in the school, and the resources around him in the school environment. 'Experience itself primarily consists of the active relations between a human being and his natural and social surroundings' (ibid., p. 274).

Reflective thought is, as Dewey says, 'not primarily cognitive' (ibid.). Gwen's example illustrates Dewey's contention *re* purpose, value, understanding, meaning-making and enjoyment of a way of thinking, which is more than intellectual and cognitive, and yet also achieves (and this is important) the intellectual and cognitive aims required by the school system. 'In just the degree in which connections are established between what happens to a person and what he does in response, and between what he does to his environment and what it does in response to him, his acts and the things about him acquire meaning' (ibid.).

Edward (we hope) is having something like the quality of experience which Dewey wanted students to have. If this is so, we suggest it is through the actions of a teacher who understands thought processes in the way Dewey describes and is disposed to use her understanding for the well-being of the student. We need to deliberately adapt conditions to promote 'understanding and formation of effective intellectual dispositions' (ibid.). This requires us to develop criticality of thinking through observation of what exists and is experienced, and to take into account the consequences of our actions for us and others.

Bringing Thought and Action to Critical Consciousness

In his earlier writings cited above, and other later texts (e.g. Dewey, 1933), Dewey urges us to become more conscious of our present state of thinking. We suggest that this is what the individual practitioners did in our three illustrations. On the basis of our professional knowledge and understanding, the instances did appear to be changes for the good. With Dewey then, we hold that for the teacher, self-examination is worth doing as it is a necessary precursor to change habitual ways of thinking. Such a change *by the teacher* can help to improve the quality of students' experience, and enrich the teacher's own experience.

Conclusion

Our questions at the start concerned how students' experience in school might relate to the practice of democracy, and the possible relation of both of those to the quality of mental process. Our provisional answers, based mostly on Dewey's 1916 writing and on our own professional experience, are that educators *can* make a positive contribution to students' democratic experience at school through an ongoing disposition of openness and concern for well-being of those around them. The disposition of openness must involve the safety net of a critical awareness and understanding of mental process. Understanding our own thinking can at least help in understanding that of others, if we bear in mind that this process is more than simple 'cognition' (Dewey, 2007, p. 26). Included in it are our disposition towards ourselves and others, as well as towards the subject matter and the role of the nature of social relations.

To say that the quality of student experience day by day can and should include examination success does not conflict with our account in any way, but an insistence on result-based outcomes alone impoverishes them and society. In rejecting a simple push towards 'correct answers', which is itself a symptom of dualistic thinking, we express hope that schools might provide conditions for the kind of associated life that promotes democratic growth. As Dewey claims, if we reject the role of schooling as development of individuals who are members of a democracy, the outlook for a democratic way of life is bleak (Dewey, 1997).

For schooling to educate, then, we need to keep the big picture in mind – 'the larger features of work' – and 'liberal nurture with training in social serviceableness, with ability to share efficiently and happily in occupations which are productive' (ibid., p. 260). Further, 'In the degree in which men have an active concern in the ends that control their activity, their activity becomes free or voluntary and loses its externally enforced and servile quality ... democratic social organisation makes provision for this direct participation in control ... an education which should unify the disposition of the members of society would do much to unify society itself' (ibid.).

It is through daily interactions in the classroom and around the school that values and beliefs are lived. Educators have a responsibility to contribute towards building and acting on a shared and evolving vision of education.

References

Alexander, F. M. (1987), *The Use of the Self*. London: Victor Gollancz.
Apple, M. (2006), Understanding and interrupting neoliberalism and neoconservatism in education. *Pedagogies: An International Journal*, 1 (1), 21–26.
Bloom, A. (2016), *Ofsted Annual Report: Primary Emphasis on Spelling and Grammar Risks Narrowing the Curriculum*. Available at: https://www.tes.com/news/school-news/breaking-news/ofsted-annual-report-primary-emphasis-spelling-and-grammar-risks/ (accessed 12.04.17).
Bruner, J. (2007), Folk pedagogies. In J. Leach and B. Moon (Eds.), *Learners and Pedagogy*, London: Paul Chapman, pp. 4–9.
Dewey, J. (1933), *How We Think* (2nd Ed.). Boston, MA: Heath & Co.
Dewey, J. (1997[1916]), *Democracy and Education*. New York, NY: Free Press.
Dewey, J. (2007[1910]), *How We Think* (1st Ed.). Stilwell, KS: Digireads.
Cassell, D. and Door, V. (2016), *Save Our Teachers' Souls: Professional and Social Well-Being in a Managerial Environment*. Toronto: Word & Deed Press.

Door, V. (2009), Postural configuration as a missing element in reflective epistemology. Global perspectives on dance pedagogy: Research and practice. *Congress on Research in Dance, Conference Proceedings*, Leicester, De Montfort University, pp. 139–142.

Edginton, T. (2016), *How to Deal with Stress over Exam Results*. Available at: www.timeshighereducation.com/student/advice/how-deal-stress-over-exam-results (accessed 06.04.17).

Gentina, E., Kilick, D. and Dancoine, P.-F. (2017), Distinctive role of opinion leaders in the social networks of school adolescents: an investigation of e-cigarette use. *Public Health*, 144, 109–116.

Gewirtz, S., Mahony, P., Hextall, I. and Cribb, A. (2009), *Changing Teacher Professionalism: International Trends, Challenges and Ways Forward*. London: Routledge.

Hansen, D. (2007), *John Dewey and Our Educational Prospect: A Critical Engagement with Dewey's Democracy and Education*. New York, NY: New York University Press.

Hargreaves, A. and Fink, D. (2006), *Sustainable Leadership*. San Francisco, CA: Jossey-Bass.

Henshaw, P. (2016), *The Ebacc effect: Teachers anger at narrowing curriculum – SecEd*. Available at: http://www.sec-ed.co.uk/news/the-ebacc-effect-teachers-anger-at-narrowing-curriculum/ (accessed 12.14.17).

Higgins, C. (2010), The good life of teaching: an ethics of professional practice. *Journal of the Philosophy of Education*, 44 (2/3), (whole volume).

Hogan, P. (2015), Cultivating human capabilities in venturesome learning environments. In R. Heilbronn and L. Foreman-Peck (Eds.), *Philosophical Perspectives on Teacher Education*. Chichester: Wiley-Blackwell, pp. 132–151.

Noddings, N. (2003), Is teaching a practice? *Journal of Philosophy of Education*, 37(2), 241–251.

Ruus,V., Veisson, M., Leino, M., Ots, L., Pallas, L., Sarv, E. and Veisson, A. (2007), Students' well-being, coping, academic success and school climate. *Social Behavior and Personality: An International Journal*, 35 (7), 919–936.

Solomon, D., Watson, M., Battistich, V., Schaps, E. and Delucchi, K. (1996), Creating classrooms that students experience as communities. *American Journal of Community Psychology*, 24 (7), 719–748.

Stoll, L., Fink, D. and Earl, L. (2003), *It's about learning (and it's about time)*. London: RoutledgeFalmer.

Taruna, Y. (2016), School bullying in relation to peer relation and self-efficacy. *Indian Journal of Health Wellbeing*, 7 (12), 1173–1175.

Wilkinson, C. (2015), *Can a Student-Developed Package of Strategies, Which Includes Choice, Improve Motivation and Desire in Order to Develop Reading and Comprehension for Students with a Specific Learning Disability?* (Unpublished report). Hertfordshire University SENCO Award.

Zhao, K. (2016a), Hu Shi's reception of Dewey's philosophy of education and its influences on education in the early republic of China. *Paper Presented at Conference*, 28 September–1 October 2016, Homerton College, Cambridge, John Dewey's 'Democracy and Education' 100 Years On: Past, Present, and Future Relevance.

Zhao, K. (2016b), Personal communication.

Chapter 10

Dewey's Notion of Interest: Antithetic to or Sympathetic with Educational Development?

Valentine Ngalim

Abstract

This chapter sets out to analyse and explain the pedagogic significance of the Deweyan notion of interest. First, it considers what Dewey refers to as the ordinary use of the term. Interest has been described as an emotional force, which pushes one to conscious action. It is an overwhelming impulse that directs one's actions to the achievement of a goal. From this perspective, Dewey presents the different characteristics of interest as dynamic, objective and subjective. In education, the child's interest in a particular subject matter directs all her efforts and energy to studies in this field. Second, Dewey considers interest as a condition for discipline. The main purpose of this chapter is to investigate whether coercion, external stimulus or extrinsic motivations are necessarily inappropriate means of enhancing one's interest in learning a subject matter, using Deweyan arguments. Is sustaining a learner's interest in a subject matter through punishment and other external pressures antithetic to education? Dewey argues that if the teacher employs teaching strategies that appeal to the intrinsic interests of learners, interest is sympathetic to education. The chapter concludes that children do not have uniform interests in a particular subject matter, taking the example of mathematics. Mathematics is a subject characterized with abstract concepts, thereby rendering many students incapable of proper learning attention and concentration.

From this perspective, one is prompted to question Dewey's categorical denial of extrinsic interest in the teaching–learning transaction. I therefore want to draw inspiration from Dewey's argument that interest is both natural and cultural, to analyse and clarify the context in which interest is sympathetic with and antithetic to democratic educational development, that is democratic ways of engaging students in their own learning, rather than imposing top-down pedagogies.

Keywords: Interest; educational development; philosophy of John Dewey

Introduction

Dewey's concept of interest is predominant in his educational philosophy. He conceived the importance of education as a means for individuals to grow, to understand and to control their environment and contribute socially. Dewey insisted on the role of experience in education as a basis on which to build curricula. For example, in a Cameroonian school context where agriculture and farming is predominant, the activity of mapping out plots in a school farm can serve as an occasion to teach mathematics, an opportunity for the children to learn about angles, distances and so on (Leke, 2003). Following Dewey's analysis of interest, is interest antithetic to or sympathetic with education? Interest is a familiar concept in teaching. Does Dewey use this term as understood in the ordinary sense?

Dewey lays great emphasis on the importance of the interest of the child for teaching to be successful. He insists on the child's interest but refuses any attempt to sugarcoat the subject matter in order to make the lesson interesting (Dewey, 1966). Does Dewey's insistence on the child's interest in learning render it sympathetic with education? Does the pedagogy of interest contradict the processes and procedures of teaching in Dewey's *Democracy and Education*? An analytical approach to the term *interest* will enhance our comparison between *interest* in the ordinary sense and Dewey's conception of the term.

As a noun, the term *interest* refers to the feeling you have when you want to know more or learn about somebody or something. It is also the quality that something has when it attracts a person's attention or makes her want to know more about something (Hornby, 2000, p. 625).

When interest refers to connection, it has to do with something that affects your attitude to it, especially because you may benefit from it in some way. Used as a verb, *to be interested* in something or in doing something means to give attention to an activity because you enjoy finding out about it, or doing it: showing interest in something and finding it exciting. For instance, a student can be interested in history (ibid., p. 625). Owing to the ordinary usage of the term *interest*, what does it mean when the child says she likes or dislikes a particular subject matter? Is it possible to set up techniques to cultivate interests? Would this interest be cultural or natural? Within this framework of thought, the chapter sets out to determine the extent to which the concept of interest can be applied in Deweyan education. The chapter analyses the Deweyan conception of interest, bringing out the different forms and characteristics of the concept and then goes on to investigate whether interest is antithetical to a democratic education or sympathetic with it.

The Deweyan Definition of Interest

The concept of interest is a major feature in Deweyan philosophy of education (see e.g. his 1914 essay, 'Interest and Effort in Education').[1] Much of the discussion in this chapter is drawn on Dewey's discussion of *interest* in chapter 10 of *Democracy and Education*, titled 'Interest and Discipline'. The focus of this first part of the chapter is to examine the various characteristics and meanings of the term as used by Dewey. In an attempt to define, clarify and limit the usage of the term 'interest', Dewey presents some of its characteristics. What are the discernible types of interests? How does Dewey apply the term in the context of education? Is this application distinct from the ordinary understanding of interest?

Dewey explains the meaning of interest by underlining the various aspects of its ordinary usage. Dewey applies three different definitions to the concept of interest. First, he contends that the term interest means 'the whole state of active development, the objective results that are foreseen and wanted, and the personal emotional inclination' (Dewey, 1966, p. 126). Second, this ordinary characterization of interest refers to one's attachment to an occupation, an employment, a pursuit or a business. In this regard, Dewey argues that when we talk of

---

[1] The discussion by Mark Jonas (2011) is interesting in this regard.

interest, we refer to a man's interest in politics, journalism, philanthropy and archaeology. In other words, *interest* refers to a point in which something touches or engages someone, and influences him or her.

Third, Dewey contends that *interest* can also mean someone's personal attitude towards something. To be interested is '... to be absorbed in, wrapped up in, carried away by some object' (ibid., p. 102). To take interest therefore means to be on the alert, to care about or to be attentive. When one is interested in something, one is overwhelmed, losing oneself in some affair and at the same time finding oneself in it. From the preceding analysis, we perceive the various aspects of interest in the ordinary sense. What is interesting to note is the emotive and intentional character of interest. When one has interest in an object, one voluntarily searches for it based on some foreseen consequences. At the same time, a person consciously engages into action and is particularly sensitive to it. The point here is the approach Dewey uses to elaborate this concept in his philosophy of education. Interest refers to a force that spurs one to activity. In the later book, *Human Nature and Conduct*, a further definition Dewey gives to *interest* is that of an impulse or force that functions as a means to realize an ideal. The person identifies herself with this means in order to attain her goal, thus making it authentic interest (Dewey, 1922, pp. 57–62). When a person has interest in a particular thing, she employs all her energy to achieve it. In the case of education, *interest* directs the child's attention to a given subject matter giving her reason to apply all efforts and energy to her studies.

Characterization of Interest

In an attempt to define interest as expressed in ordinary usage, Dewey presents three characteristics, namely, the dynamic, the objective and the subjective character of interests. He employs both positive and negative means to explain the meaning of interest. In the first place, Dewey contends that interest has an active character. It is like a dynamic engine, which presents the spontaneous tendencies, impulses and needs of a living organism. This already highlights the fact that interest is a natural feature in an individual. In this case, it is like an impulse that does not need an external stimulus for action. Within this framework, Dewey characterizes interest as a natural impulse that spurs one to action (ibid., p. 53).

Second, interest also has an objective character. Here, it directs a person towards an object. One's interest in a particular occupation or activity aims at the achievement of a certain goal. Interest has an end or serves as a means to an end. An example in this case is a child who develops interest in mathematics because it is a requirement for his specialization in mechanical engineering. Why is the student studying mathematics? It is because he wants to be a mechanical engineer in the near future. This extrinsic aim refers to the practical value of the study of mathematics. A child who studies biology in order to be a medical practitioner also refers to the purpose of studying biology. The intrinsic value of the subjects, such as an understanding of mathematical concepts and human physiognomy, is secondary. The question is, do we learn for a practical outcome or simply for the sake of knowledge itself? Can interest be an end in itself?

Last, there is the subjective character of interest. Interest here is a force that appeals to our emotions. This is a situation where a person engages in an action that takes the whole of her because of her intrinsic interest. It is what she desires and it remains a driving need. The action in which the individual engages is a result of free choice, which does not require any extrinsic stimulus for execution. Dewey's argument is that our intimate being always attributes a certain value to an object that is at the level of our emotional inclination. Dewey observes that interest is a propensity towards what is valuable. In this regard, one has interest in something to the extent that it takes the whole of one's personality. It is noteworthy that there is no other end to interest apart from the activity in question. A child who has interest in geography wants to understand the landforms and changes in the environment, in the same way as a student who studies philosophy wants to understand the different schools of thoughts and their methods of argumentation. One student has interest in geography for its own sake and the other in philosophy for its own sake, not because of any practical value the subjects might have.

Having analysed the three aspects of interest in Dewey, the next significant point is the procedure Dewey uses to characterize interest. Dewey recognizes the necessity of saying what a thing is by saying what it is not (Reboul, 1989). The *via negativa* is one of the procedures he uses to clarify the meaning of the term *interest* as it appears in his thought. Dewey says that interest is not a static and inert feeling towards an object. It does not constitute an end in itself, but it is always directed towards an object, a goal or a motive (Dewey, 1922, p. 53). This *via negativa* process of argumentation becomes an interesting feature in Dewey's attempt to explain interest. This definition by negation enables him to portray the dynamic character of interest as an active engine that pushes one to action and expresses one's natural impulses, spontaneous tendencies and needs, in contradistinction to static and cold experiences. Interest is necessarily directed towards an object and it is not to be seen as an end in itself. When someone says she has interest, she is referring to an activity that affects her personally. There is always an object of reference for interest and this constitutes both the efficient and the final causes of interest.

Dialectical Functions of Interest

Dewey distinguishes two functions of interest: mediate and immediate functions. The mediate function of interest is as the intermediary between the learner's point of departure and the object to which she is directed. The immediate function of interest is the actual object of desire, what is loved for its own sake. Dewey describes mediate interest as one with an objective character. When interest is directed towards an object, it plays an intermediary role between the learner and the subject matter that is desired. Interest in the subject matter is not an end in itself but serves as a means to an end. Consider the example of a student who seriously studies mathematics, not because she desires it but because she sees it as a prerequisite for the study of computer science. The subject has a practical value in terms of her future career. A child may have interest in learning Latin because it is a prerequisite for understanding some concepts in some fields of study like biology or law. The child takes interest in Latin because it plays a mediating role, a means that will lead to some effect in personal advantage or success.

Dewey perceives mediate interest as that aspect of pedagogy that fills the gap or vacuum between the aptitude or the learning powers of the child, which is the initial stage, and the aim or objective of the teacher, which represents the remote end of the learning. In other words, there is a lacuna between the initial stage of the learner and the objective of the teacher. This lacuna is taken charge of by mediate interest. Dewey determines this as 'means' which refers to the middle conditions. 'Means' refers to the acts the teacher performs, the difficulties and obstacles she overcomes, and the devices and appliances she uses. It is through the means of intermediate conditions that the learner grows from the initial stage to the foreseen and desired end of the teacher. Dewey therefore concludes that 'to be means for the achieving of present tendencies, to be "between" the agent and his end, to be of interest are different names of the same thing' (Dewey, 1966, p. 157).

The latter type of interest in Deweyan thought is immediate interest, which does not serve as a means to an end. It does not serve as an intermediary to the achievement of a particular end. It is an end in itself, whereby the activity in question is desired for its own sake. In comparison with mediate interest, Dewey argues that immediate interest is superior and important because it does not refer to a desired end in the distant future. The other, mediate interest, is inferior and impure because it is not an end in itself but a means to an end. With immediate interest, for example, a child does not study a particular subject matter simply for its practical value or purpose in the future. The student chooses the subject matter because of her emotional attachment to it and because it enhances her own self-realization. A child likes to learn mathematics for its own sake because of her emotional and subjective attachment to it. Having a mastery of mathematical concepts is the end of her learning. This is different from the case where a child takes interest in mathematics not because she has passion for it, but because she sees its importance or necessity in a field of specialization in the future. In this case, mathematics serves a practical value as mediate interest. Can the child adequately study the subject matter if she only desires it for its practical purpose? Is it possible to reconcile immediate and mediate interests, where a student learns what she likes and at the same time has ambitions for a particular career?

Aims, Desire, Aptitude and Reinforcement

We have examined the distinction between mediate and immediate interests. It is also important to analyse the terms Dewey uses in the same context with *interest* in order to enhance precision in subsequent argumentations. This subsection studies the different perceptions of interest that can be found in Dewey's work and the way in which he uses other terms seemingly in the same sense as 'interest', such as aims, desire, aptitude and reinforcement. This can be seen as a lack of clarity in what Dewey has to say about interest, but I hope to clarify somewhat in relation to his overall argument and relevance in the following analysis.

When Dewey elaborates the theory of educational aims, he investigates if there is an end outside of the educative process to which education is subordinate. Dewey makes a distinction between results and ends. He observes: 'Any exhibition of energy has results. The wind blows about the sands of the desert; the position of the grains is changed. Here is a result an effect, but not an end. ...There is mere spatial redistribution' (ibid., p. 101). This movement of sand as a result of wind is different from the resultant activities of bees. Dewey considers the results of the bees' actions as ends because there are true completions of what has preceded. When bees gather pollen to make wax and build cells, each step prepares the way for the next. This holds the same for the subsequent activities. On the contrary, the results that arise from the sand blown by the wind in the desert are mere chaos. There is no preconceived end in the process of the action. Moreover, Dewey contends that an aim is a foreseen end that gives direction to activity and influences the steps taken to reach an end.

Dewey outlines three ways in which foresight of ends functions. First there needs to be a study of the given conditions that will provide the means available for the attainment of an end, together with the anticipation of the possible obstacles that might prevent one from reaching this end. The second step is the order that one has to follow in employing the means in order to facilitate arrangement and selection. After taking the first two steps, choosing between alternative courses of action becomes possible, as one can anticipate difficulties and obstacles to achieve the ends. It goes without saying that a person who is in a position to predict the outcome of acting in a particular way, having compared the value of the alternative actions, is in a better position to pass judgement on which course of action is desirable at a given time. For example, if a teacher knows that the absence of interactions between boys and girls is the cause of sexism in schools and consequently in the society, she can find ways to prevent this situation. Given this analysis, Dewey thinks that

> acting with an aim is all one with acting intelligently. To foresee a terminus of an act is to have a basis upon which to observe, to select, and to order objects and our own capacities. To do these things is to have a mind .... To have a mind to do a thing is to foresee a future possibility; it is to have a plan for its accomplishment, it is to know the means, which make the plan capable of execution and the obstruction in the way. (Ibid., p. 103)

Highlighting the above, Dewey aims at underlining the importance of conscious and meaningful actions whenever a person acts with an aim, that is, having a particular interest in view. His conclusion is that 'to have an aim is to act with meaning, not like an automatic machine; it is to mean to do something and to perceive the meaning of things in the light of that intent' (ibid., p. 104). When one acts with an aim, one acts freely, consciously and willingly. This freedom leads an individual to self-realization. Consequently, a person only pursues her interest when she is the master of her own choices. When one has an aim, one takes responsibility for a subsequent action in pursuit of that aim. Dewey argues, 'Aims mean acceptance of responsibility for the observations anticipations and arrangements required in carrying on a function whether farming or education' (ibid., p. 107).

This approach has a major significance in education especially in the dialectic between the interests of the child and her parents. Who chooses what the child has to learn or study? In addition, in the conflict of interests between the learner and her society, does the former pursue her own desires without considering the needs of the latter? Does the educator have the right to impose a particular subject matter on the pupil? If so, is this indoctrination or education? Furthermore, children have transient needs and purposes, which remain indefinitely varied, differing with different children, changing as children grow and with the growth of the experiences of their teachers. For Dewey, these aims should be suggestions to educators on how to carry out their work rather than definite goals to attain (ibid., p. 107).

In his examination of the characteristics of good aims, Dewey argues that these must be founded on the intrinsic activities and needs of the individuals to be educated. In addition, Dewey suggests that a good aim must consider an environment that enhances the development of the child's capacities by promoting self-expression and self-determination. Prepared aims and interests for pupils and students are not acceptable because they diminish the child's academic freedom over what is of interest to her. Dewey therefore concludes: 'A true aim is thus opposed at every point to an aim which is imposed upon a process of action from without' (ibid., p. 110).

The second aspect of interest described by Dewey is desire. Desire is a conscious, intellectual and stimulating feeling, distinguished from blind feeling or animal appetite, which is not conscious of its own goal. One who desires, knows or is conscious of the object of his desire. At the initial stage, Dewey contends that desire must be purely intellectual (Dewey, 1922, p. 67). Moreover, Dewey's analysis of desire brings us again to the immediate function of interest, where one is sufficiently interested in a particular ideal and uses the available and necessary steps to achieve this ideal. There is proper utility of the available energy, thus preventing wastage of resources in the attainment of the goal. The ideal or the object of desire is both the means and the end in which the learner expresses herself. There is a balance of desire because the impulses are under control by the condition of discipline (ibid., p. 69).

The third aspect of interest as Dewey conceives it is aptitude. Every child is unique and must be educated according to her specific nature. Dewey therefore argues that the importance of interest lies in the fact that it enhances our understanding of human differences. Not all minds function uniformly just because the same teacher teaches them or because they use the same textbook. Natural aptitude, past experiences and plans of life make people's response to the same material to vary. In this case, interest serves as a guide to the activities of the teacher. She has to present the subject matter in a way that is agreeable to the students' or pupils' capacities. The child learns more in activity than in listening and their cognitive skills differ according to their different heritage and experiences (ibid., p. 184). According to Dewey, the child thinks in action and not in abstraction.

Finally, Dewey also refers to interest in education as 'soft pedagogy', or 'soup kitchen theory of education' (Dewey, 1966, p. 127). He is aware of the fact that this term is easily misunderstood and used in a depreciatory manner. Dewey holds that to attach importance to interest in education is to subscribe to some feature of seductiveness. In order to sustain the attention and effort of the child in the study of a particular subject matter, the educator has to offer a bribe of pleasure or pain. This is common in situations where the pedagogic method and the subject matter fail to appeal to the needs, concerns, experiences and capacities of the learners. In such situations, it is likely for the teacher to look for objects and appeal to modes of actions, which connect the present powers of the pupils with the subject matter. Dewey contends that these are artificial and external inducements used by the educator to sustain the child's interest. This discernible Deweyan perspective undermines the place of reinforcers in the teaching−learning transaction. Are reinforcements like verbal praise, good grades still important in encouraging the child to work hard? Skinner holds that practices in education should take the form of stimulus−response frames in order to expose the learner to the subject matter in gradual steps. Skinner insists that good performance, which refers to the awaited response, should receive an immediate feedback in terms of secondary reinforcers like praise and good grades (Skinner, 1992). Are external stimuli necessarily inappropriate for learning? Can we say that the behaviourists' approach is detrimental to education because it relies on external reinforcements? The literature in psychology on extrinsic and intrinsic motivation for achievement suggests this is the case (e.g. Ryan and Deci, 2000). However, there is evidently some role for rewards and external motivating approaches and for the reinforcement of practice in exercises, for example in playing a musical instrument or doing sports.

Interest and Discipline in Democratic Education

Dewey conceives discipline from the perspective of the will. It is a strong will, which is neither indecisive nor half-hearted in achieving its chosen ends. This section of the chapter presents the various characteristics of discipline, which include stability of will, intelligent endurance in the chosen course of action, punishment as one means of discipline and, last punishment that degenerates into indoctrination and conditioning.

Dewey contends that people with strong will deploy untiring efforts to carry out their aims but someone with a weak will is unstable, and lacks discipline and purpose. Dewey makes a clear-cut distinction between discipline and obstinacy or stubbornness. The latter implies persistence and not strength of will. There is animal insensitivity in this case because the person in question persists in a particular activity just because she has started it and not for any clearly thought-out purpose. This is pure stubbornness, since there is reluctance to criticize ends that present themselves. With this distinction, Dewey then holds that a disciplined person is one who is trained to consider his actions, to undertake them deliberately and intelligently.

Moreover, discipline is the power to endure an intelligently chosen course in the face of distraction, confusion and difficulty. It is also power at command and the mastery of the resources available for carrying through an undertaken action. To know what one is to do and to do it promptly using the required means is to be a disciplined person. This is applicable to any given situation or persons. Discipline in this sense is positive and helps an individual towards an end. The connection between discipline and interest comes from the fact that any deliberation without an interest is superficial. Dewey gives an example of parents and teachers who complain that children are not getting on in a particular subject, because they fail to see that the subject matter in question does not enter into the concerns and needs of the children. It is not part of their interest or preference. Dewey repeats a joke of an unnamed 'American humourist': 'It makes no difference what you teach a boy so long as he doesn't like it' (Dewey, 1966, p. 134). He summons parents and teachers to look for reasonable remedies to such situations. For example, punishing a child for inattention is one way of trying to make her understand that the subject matter is not a thing of complete unconcern. Punishment serves as a means of arousing interest or bringing about a sense of connection between the needs of the learner and the objective of the lesson (ibid., p. 129). This is applicable in the context of classroom management, because one teacher could have difficulties putting order in a class with many students. However, punishment is only worthwhile when it leads the child to 'think', or reflect upon her acts and giving them meaning in the light of her own ambition. The learner must consciously engage in his activity and perceive the purpose of any particular activity.

On the other hand, if the understanding of discipline is mistaken to be mere physical excitation to compel the young to act in a way desired by an adult, the process of learning will degenerate into indoctrination and conditioning. Dewey conceives the major problem of 'discipline' in schools when the teacher is more preoccupied with the suppression of the child's bodily activities, which distract her from the lesson. In such situations, most teachers insist on physical quietude, silence and rigid uniformity of posture and movement. These exigencies are tantamount to a machine-like imitation of the attitudes of intelligent interests (Archambault, 1964). The child carries out his work by obligation and not by initiative. Creativity is minimized since the learner is conditioned to action rather than acting with intrinsic interest. Accordingly, if this is the situation, the child is not stubborn in not attending to the discipline imposed, but rather it is likely that the material set before her is abstract and does not appeal to her interests. Consider the example of teaching numbers and figures in mathematics. These are abstract concepts that have no meaning in themselves. Critical teaching in this case presupposes that the teacher establishes a liaison between these concepts and the needs and concerns of the child:

> Study is effectual in the degree in which the pupil realizes the place of the numerical truth he is dealing with in carrying to fruition activities in which he is concerned. The connection of an object and a topic with the promotion of an activity having a purpose is the first and the last word of genuine theory of interest in education. (Dewey, 1966, p. 135)

In teaching, it is not enough for a teacher to recount the subject matter to learners. The teacher has the task of letting the pupils know the usefulness of a particular subject matter in their lives. This is simply providing a rationale for learning rather than the reductionist tendency of limiting the value of learning to practical utility.

Interest as Nature and Culture

Where Dewey talks of individual interest, we find an optimistic anthropological perspective. He makes a passionate insistence on the development and perfection of the distinctive temperament and aptitude that the individual has at birth. This section reveals two aspects of interests, its natural and cultural origins. According to Dewey, the child has a natural capacity, a talent that constitutes his interest and serves as the basis of the educational enterprise. He contends:

> Experience knows no division between human concerns and a purely mechanical world. Man's home is nature; his purposes and aims are dependent for execution upon natural conditions. Separated from such conditions they become empty dreams and idle indulgences of fancy.... This philosophy is vouched for by the doctrine of biological development which shows that man is continuous with nature, not an alien entering her processes from without. (ibid., p. 294)

Dewey is writing from the background of materialistic evolutionism. Human nature is the point of departure for education. Apart from human nature, he also acknowledges some native endowments in human beings. He describes them as 'inchoate' and 'scattered impulses', 'native powers and instincts'. These are still at their primitive stage, unlearned, original and uninformed. However, these powers can be directed towards the process of growth. 'The inchoate and scattered impulses' of the infant do not coordinate into serviceable powers except through social dependencies and companionship (Dewey in Forbi, 2004, p. 94). In spite of one's natural endowments that make up the natural interest, it is possible to adapt and improve on this nature for self-realization in the society. In this latter case, the furnished natural aptitude can be subjected under conditions of cultural development. Dewey describes this process as 'transactions' or 'interactions' between an organism and his environment (Zask, 1999, p. 10). The term later maintained is 'transaction' because it rigorously explains his philosophy of experience, where one talks of changes that lead to growth because of one's contacts with the environment (ibid., p. 13). Education therefore serves the goal of releasing the human potential to growth. This understanding portrays the necessity for education to cultivate human character. The innate natural interest enters into dialogue with the cultural interest in the community and Dewey describes the human experience as 'Cultural Naturalism' (ibid., p. 26). The dialectic of the natural and cultural origins of interest reveals the importance of Deweyan synthesis of cultural naturalism as expressed by Zask.

Conclusion

The central interest of this chapter has been to diagnose the pedagogic significance of Deweyan concept of interest. To attain this objective, this chapter preoccupied itself with the analysis of this concept as understood by John Dewey primarily in *Democracy and Education*. Here, we argued that interest refers to aims, aptitude, experiences, needs and desires of the learners. From this understanding, the place of interest in the pedagogic process was examined. This referred to the relationship between interest and classroom discipline and the dialectic of interest as natural or cultural. From the perceptions of interest, the central argument of this chapter constituted the thesis that interest is a cultural naturalism. The significance of this conception in the pedagogic process is that it defines the context in which interest is a natural aptitude. This gives the educator a proper understanding of the type of pedagogic practices to put in place to arouse natural interest. At the same time, this interest can be cultivated. It is cultural in the context of exposing the learner to some experiences in order to enhance learning. This is the activity of the educator because, as an architect of the pedagogic environment, she masters both subject matter and method, thus employing the necessary means to help the learner attain the objectives of her pedagogic activity. Thus, interest is only antithetic to education when it is misconstrued and poorly applied. In Deweyan understanding, interest has an invaluable role to play in education, thereby being sympathetic with educational development.

References

Archambault, R. D. (1964), *John Dewey on Education: Selected Writings*. New York, NY: Greenwood Press.

Dewey, J. (1922), *Human Nature and Conduct: An Introduction to Social Psychology*. New York, NY: Modern Library.

Dewey, J. (1966), *Democracy and Education: An Introduction to Philosophy of Education*. New York, NY: Free Paper Press.

Forbi, K. S. (2004), *Rainbow of Educational Philosophies: Methods and Models*. Bloomington: AuthorHouse.

Hornby, A. S. (2000), *Oxford Advanced Learner's Dictionary*. Oxford: Oxford University Press.

Jonas, M. (2011), Dewey's conception of interest and its significance for teacher education. *Educational Philosophy and Theory*, 43 (2). doi:10.1111/j.1469-5812.2009.00543.x

Leke, T. T. (2003), *Principles and Method in Teaching: Application, in Cameroonian School*. Buea: Anucam, University of Buea.

Reboul, O. (1989), *La Philosophie de l'Education*. Paris: PUF.

Ryan, R. M and Deci, E. I. (2000), Intrinsic and extrinsic motivations: Classic definitions and new directions. *Contemporary Educational Psychology*, 25, 54–67.

Skinner, B. F. (1992), 'Superstition' in the pigeon. *Journal of Experimental Psychology: General*, 121 (3), 273–274. doi:10.1037/0096-3445.121.3.273 (accessed 10.10.17).

Zask, J. (1999), *L'Opinion Publique et Son Double. Livre I: John Dewey. Philosophie du Public*. Paris: L'Harmattan.

Epilogue: The Persistence of Dewey's Pragmatism: On Possibilities and Risks

When John Dewey died in 1952, pragmatism had already largely disappeared from the canon of twentieth-century philosophy, where it was seen as having been superseded by the linguistic turn of analytic philosophy. In education, Dewey had become synonymous with 'progressivism' and educational progressivism was increasingly seen as the root of all evil rather than that it provided the outlook for a meaningful future for education. In philosophy it took until the late 1970s before, mainly through the efforts of Richard Rorty, pragmatism returned on the philosophical map, not as something from the past that would only be of interest to historians of philosophy, but, with Rorty's famous and bold statement from his *Consequences of Pragmatism*, as the philosophy that was 'not only waiting at the end of the dialectical road which analytic philosophy travelled', but that was also waiting 'at the end of the road which, for example, Foucault and Deleuze are currently traveling' (Rorty, 1982, p. xvii).

Although pragmatism didn't become the new philosophical hegemony – analytic philosophy continues to occupy a dominant position in the English-speaking philosophical world, whereas continental philosophy remains strongly influenced by its own indigenous traditions (such as hermeneutics, phenomenology, existentialism and its more recent offspring) – it has become a viable 'position' within the contemporary philosophical landscape, rather than something exotic or outdated. We can see a similar resurgence in the field of education where, since the late 1980s, scholarship on Dewey as an educational thinker has grown exponentially. If the return of pragmatism and more specifically, Dewey's variety within philosophy can largely be explained on intellectual ground – Dewey's work seems to fit almost seamlessly with developments within analytic philosophy such as the work of Quine, Davidson and Putnam – the return of Dewey as an educational thinker has perhaps less to do with the intellectual dynamics of twentieth-century educational thought and more with the politics of education.

'Dewey' – and there is a question to what extent the use of his name coincides with the actual substance of his thought – continues to be invoked in contexts where, either through the impact of policy or through the impact of research, education is steered towards the narrow path of what, in contemporary language, is often referred to as the production of a narrow set of measurable 'learning outcomes'. If those ways of thinking and doing tend to turn education into a matter of control — control of thought, control of action, control of interaction — 'Dewey' stands for an approach to education that values openness, experiment, growth and democracy. 'Dewey', in other words, stands for an approach to education that doesn't seek to reduce schooling to training but seeks to (re)connect the project of schooling to wider, human ambitions. Dewey's work does indeed provide such a different outlook and thus remains a source of inspiration for anyone who seeks to counter the 'closing of the educational mind' — to paraphrase Allan Bloom (1987).

Unlike earlier readings of Dewey's educational thought, Dewey scholars have continued to emphasize the balanced nature of his thinking, showing for example that he was not the extreme child-centred educator his critics took him to be, but that he saw the main task of education as that of the *coordination* of the child and the curriculum or, as he already put it in 1895, as the question of the coordination of 'the psychological and the social factors' (Dewey, 1895, p. 224). Along similar lines, Dewey scholars have continued to highlight Dewey's orientation towards education that is thoroughly democratic, both in its orientation and its forms of 'operation', providing opportunities for all to take part and through this to build democracy from the bottom up, so to speak. These contributions are important if only because they provide a thoughtful antidote against where conservative policy — not always out of bad intentions but often with problematic consequences — seek to steer and keep education. From this angle, the ongoing enthusiasm for Dewey's educational thought, as exemplified by the contributions to this book, is important and heartening.

There are, however, also a number of risks or, more modestly, pitfalls in the return to Dewey and it is important to bear these in mind as well, so that the reference to Dewey remains thoughtful and astute, intellectually and politically. One risk is that the enthusiasm for Dewey's thought transforms into a belief in Dewey's ideas, that is, Dewey's ideas become seen as a 'position' and, even more worryingly, as a set of truths about what apparently is 'the case'. We shouldn't forget, after all, that Dewey's thought is not a set of (ontological) claims or beliefs, but a collection of specific answers to highly contextual questions and problems.

The first question for pragmatism is, after all, not 'What is the case' but 'What is the problem?' There is, therefore, the ongoing need to read pragmatism itself pragmatically, always connecting Dewey's thoughts, observations and insights to the particular problems that motivated his own thinking (see also Biesta, 2009a).

Such an approach to Dewey's work helps to put Dewey's own enthusiasm for the scientific method into perspective. Unlike interpretations that herald Dewey as a proponent of the scientific world view, Dewey's larger intellectual 'project' was actually directly targeted at the hegemony of scientific rationality (for a detailed discussion, see Biesta, 2016). In one of his later publications, Dewey explicitly stated that the idea that science provides us with the ultimate account of what is real has led to the belief

> 'that science exists only in the things which are most remote from any significant human concern, so that as we approach social and moral questions and interests, we must either surrender hope of the guidance of genuine knowledge or else purchase scientific title and authority at the expense of all that is distinctly human' (Dewey, 1991[1939], p. 51).

Dewey's larger 'project' was precisely aimed at the 'crisis in culture' that was the result of the hegemony of modern science. Against this hegemony, Dewey's ambition was to restore rationality to 'all that is distinctly human', or, in a slightly different formulation, to *democratize* rationality.[1]

The third and final pitfall for contemporary scholarship on Dewey has to do with the fact that his educational thought is predominantly rooted in a theory of learning. Whereas his theory of learning is anything but the neo-behaviourism that characterizes the narrowing of contemporary schooling, it is important to bear in mind that a theory of learning is not automatically and not out of itself also a (sound) theory of education. The learning question is, in other words, not the same as the educational question. Whereas some see the shift towards learning as a liberation from top-down forms of educational control, we should be mindful that the shift towards learning — which elsewhere I have

---

[1] In this regard Dewey's 'project' is actually much closer to the ambitions of the Frankfurt School (Adorno and Horkheimer and also Habermas) than is often acknowledged.

referred to as the 'learnification' of education (Biesta, 2009b) – runs the risk that we focus too strongly on processes and pay insufficient attention to what learning processes are supposed to bring about. Whereas Dewey is right that the ends of education can at most be ends in view, we should nonetheless keep an intelligent and politically aware conversation about the ends in view of education going, at least in order not to hand over the question of educational purpose to the market or other forces.

All this suggests that the return to Dewey's educational thought cannot be a matter of repetition but requires thoughtful reconstruction – and Dewey would probably be the first to agree with this.

Gert Biesta
Brunel University, London

References

Biesta, G. J. J. (2009a), How to use pragmatism pragmatically: Suggestions for the 21st century. In A. G. Rud, J. Garrison and L. Stone (Eds.), *John Dewey at 150. Reflections for a New Century*. Lafayette: Purdue University Press, pp. 30–39.

Biesta, G. J. J. (2009b), Good education in an age of measurement: on the need to reconnect with the question of purpose in education. *Educational Assessment, Evaluation and Accountability*, 21(1), 33–46.

Biesta, G. J. J. (2016), Democracy and education revisited: Dewey's democratic deficit. In S. Higgins and F. Coffield (Eds.), *John Dewey's Education and Democracy: A British Tribute*. London: IoE Press, pp. 149–169.

Bloom, A. (1987), *The Closing of the American Mind*. New York, NY: Simon and Schuster.

Dewey, J. (1895), Plan of organization of the university primary school. In J. A. Boydston (Ed.), *The Early Works (1882–1898), Volume 5*. Carbondale and Edwardsville: Southern Illinois University Press, pp. 96–109.

Dewey, J. (1991[1939]), Experience, knowledge, and value: a rejoinder. In J.-A. Boydston (Ed.), *John Dewey: The Later Works (1925–1953)*, vol. 14. Carbondale and Edwardsville: Southern Illinois University Press, pp. 1939–1941.

Rorty, R. (1982), *Consequences of Pragmatism*. Minneapolis, MN: University of Minnesota Press.

Index

Academic/vocational divide, 144–147
Access Space, 50–53
Action, 186, 189, 194
  former habit of, 190
  thinking and, 196–198
Activitymania, 24, 31
Aesthetically consummated experience, 132
Aesthetics, 73, 131, 134, 136
Aidos, 69
Aims, 207–211
Alexander, Matthias F., 87–90
Alexander Technique (AT), 84, 85, 87
  body, mind and thinking, 86–87
  on Dewey's thinking, 84
  embodied learning via, 90–93
  habit and learning, 93–94
  as process of self-development, 96–98
  unreliable sensory appreciation, 94–95
American and French Revolutions, 168–178
American Dream, 102, 107
Analytic philosophy, 217
Analytical somaesthetics, 86, 129
Anti-somatic bias, 86
Antigone, 63
  Dewey and democracy, 67–72

  education experience of creative democracy with, 72–78
  and Nussbaum, 64–67
Attitudes, 185–187, 207–211
Awareness, 187

Between the World and Me (Coates), 102, 106
Black bodies in schools, 101
  American 'Dream' mythology, 107
  using Dewey's transactionalism, 103–106
  Dream, 110
  transactional position, 113
  working towards democracy in education in face of 'plunder', 112–116
Black power, 111
Bodily-led engagement with World, challenge in, 133–134
Body consciousness, 127–129
Bristol Hackspace, 50, 54

Change, 28, 131, 190, 194
  characteristics in location, 121
  communication, 162–163
  degree of, 164
  Dewey's philosophy, 162–164
  generational, 168–169
  parameters of debate and possibilities, 169

political revolutions informing, 167
seasonal, 28
understanding cultural requirements for, 164
Child's interest in learning, 202
Citizen School, 153
Civitas, 77
Clockwork, 25–26
Co-ordination, 218
Collateral learning, 125
Communication, 162–164, 170
  See also Habermas's paradigm of communication
Communicatively achieved agreement, 172
Conduct, 186, 187, 190
Conflict of interests, 209
Consequences of Pragmatism (Rorty), 217
Constructive Conscious Control of the Individual (Alexander), 89
Constructive interest, 185, 193, 195
Contemporary formal educational system, 39
Contradictions, 66
Creative democracy, 23, 62, 73
  Antigone, Dewey and democracy, 67–72
  Antigone and Nussbaum, 64–67
  education experience, 72–78
Creativity, 212
Critical consciousness, 198
Critical thinking, 63, 157, 193, 197
Cultivated imagination, 193
Cultural products, 96
Culture, 110, 179
  crisis in, 219
  interest as, 213–214

Curriculum. *See* Democratic curriculum
Curriculum integration (CI), 154

Degree of change, 164
Deliverology, 23, 24, 27
Democracy, 44, 106, 144, 155, 162, 164, 184, 185
  Dewey relating, 187–189
  education for, 187
  See also Student's experience of democracy
Democracy and Education (Dewey) (D&E), 23, 38, 62, 71, 86, 89, 95, 102, 162–163, 166, 173, 174, 185, 186, 187, 195
Democratic communication
  Dewey's theory of, 163
  moral value of, 162–163
Democratic communities, 38, 178
  case study, 48–53
  conceptualizing makerspaces, 49
  education as experienced naturally and feed into formal setting, 43
  education as experienced naturally in contrast to traditional view, 40
  formally or naturally occurring education, 39–44
  knowledge, 50
  newer forms of space, 44–48
  Quiet Zone at Bristol Hackspace, 54
  signage from Access Space main lab, 51
  20 × 20 Canvas Exhibition at Access Space, 52
Democratic curriculum, 141, 142

democratic education and academic/vocational divide, 144–147
stakeholders and, 152–156
standards and, 147–152
Democratic education, 144–147, 154
Deweyan, 102
interest and discipline in, 211–213
limiting possibilities, 72
reform, 62
Democratic ideal, 102, 105–106, 112, 116, 163, 166, 177
Democratic philosophy, 162
Democratic school, 146, 153
shape possibilities for, 178–180
Democratic society, 145, 146, 151, 153, 178–180, 186, 189
Department for Education, 154–155
Descartian mind/body dualism, 128
Desire, 207–211
Dewey's notion of interest, 202–214
Dewey's philosophy of change and reconstruction, 162–163
Dewey's pragmatism, 62, 63, 217–220
Dewey's theory of democratic communication, 163
Deweyan democratic education, 102
Deweyan democratic ideals. *See* Democratic ideal
Dialectical functions of interest, 206–207
Dictionary of Philosophy and Psychology (Dewey), 69

Digital age, preserving rich experience in, 22
digitally enriched experience in action, 25–26
framework for experience-based, technology-enhanced thinking, 31–32
framing experience, 23–29
framing work in broader contexts, 26–29
lasting impact of experience, 29–31
tool selection and use, 32–34
uses of technology, 34
Digitally enriched experience in action, 25–26
Discipline in democratic education, 211–213
Disposition, 184–185
and habit, 194–195
kind of, 189–191
learning in school, 195–196
mental process relating to, 191–193
Dream, 110
Dynamic character of interests, 204

Early childhood experience, 130
Education, 41, 63, 165
for democracy, 187
Deweyan philosophy of, 203
experience of creative democracy with *Antigone*, 72–78
importance, 202, 209
interest in education as 'soft pedagogy', or 'soup kitchen theory of education', 210
issue of 'standards', 142
learnification of, 219–220

naturalist account of, 104
process, 165
Education in Open, 120
  body, 121
  body consciousness, 127–129
  challenge in bodily-led engagement with World, 133–134
  environment, 125–126
  experience, 123–125
  experiential somaesthetic practice, 130–133
  flexibility in habit and environment, 134–135
  habit, 126–127
  justifying value of activities outdoors, 122–123
  place, 121–122
  somaesthetics, 129–130
Educational development, 201–214
Educational progressivism, 217
Educator's disposition and mental process role
  bringing thought and action to critical consciousness, 198
  Dewey relating democracy, 187–189
  disposition and habit, 194–195
  disposition learning in school, 195–196
  kind of disposition, 189–191
  long-term project, 186–187
  mental process relating to disposition, 191–193
  in student's experience of democracy, 184
  thought and action, 196–198
Embodied inquiry, 116
Embodied learning, 90–93
Empowerment, 155

Enlightenment, Dewey's Criticisms of, 168–178
Environmental Education, 122
"Ethic" of cost-benefit analysis, 147
Existentialism, 217
Experience, 41, 123–125
  aesthetically consummated, 132
  early childhood, 130
  education, 72–78
  Student experience, 185
  See also Digital age, preserving rich experience in; Student's experience of democracy
Experience and Education (Dewey), 24, 95
Experience-based thinking, framework for, 31–32
"Experience-near" methods, 50
Experiential inquiry, 104
Experiential somaesthetic practice, 130–133

Filia, 77
Fire Next Time, The (Baldwin), 102
Flexibility in habit and environment, 134–135
Formal process, 39
Formally or naturally occurring education, 39–44
4D printing, 46
The Fragility of Goodness: Luck and Ethics in Greek Tragedy and Philosophy (Sophocles), 65
From absolutism to experimentalism (Dewey), 70

General Certificate of Secondary Education (GCSE), 147
French teaching, 191
Global Monitoring Reports (GMRs), 148
Good performance, 210
Grand Theft Childhood, 22

Habermas's contemporary communicative action theory, 163
Habermas's paradigm of communication
　American and French Revolutions, 168–178
　on change, democracy, and communication anticipates, 163
　cultural requirements for change and reconstruction, 164
　Dewey anticipating, 163
　Dewey's sociopolitical philosophy, 178–180
　fundamentals of scientific investigations, 166
　problem of freezing social institutions, 167–168
　process of education, 165
Habit(s), 93–94, 105, 126–127
　of amicable cooperation, 74
　disposition and, 194–195
　of intercourse, 170
Habitual disposition, 195
Habituation, 165, 194n3
Hegelian interpretation, 64, 70
Hermeneutics, 217
History of Philosophy (Hegel), 69–70
Human nature, 72, 179, 213

Human Nature and Conduct (Dewey), 89, 90, 204
Humanities, 63

I-R-E model, 29
Imaginative thought, 197
Immaturity, 41
Immediacy, 130–133, 135
Immediate functions, 206
Immediate interest, 207
Improvement of conditions, 185, 192
Individual interest, 68, 171, 213
Informal education, 39, 46, 105
Integrated theory-practice approach, 189
Intellectual growth, 192–193
Intellectual hospitality, 193
Interactions, 213–214
Interest, 202–203
　aims, desire, aptitude and reinforcement, 207–211
　characterization, 204–206
　dialectical functions, 206–207
　and discipline in democratic education, 211–213
　group politics, 172
　individual, 213
　as 'intelligent sympathy for others', 193
　as nature and culture, 213–214
Internet relay chat (IRC), 46
Intersubjectivity, 163

Knowing and the Known, 103
Knowledge, 50, 52, 150
　society, 63

Language of economics, 175
'Learnification' of education, 219–220

Learning, 41, 93–94, 144
Lectures on Aesthetics, 64–65
"Letting-go" process, 53

Makerspace, 38, 44–48, 50, 53, 55–56
  conceptualizing, 49
Man's Supreme Inheritance (Alexander), 89
Mapping Police Violence, 106
'Master–slave' relationship, 193
'Means', 206
Mediate functions, 206
Mediate interest, 207
Mental habitudes, 194
Mental process, 186
  relating to disposition, 191–193
Mind–body unity, 86
Mobocracy, 171
Modern German apprenticeship, 143, 157
Morality, 68, 77, 185

National Literacy and National Numeracy Strategies, 149
Natural aptitude, 210, 213, 214
Natural law, 169
Naturalist account of education, 104
Nature, interest as, 213–214
Nemesis, 69
Neo-liberal educational theory and practice, 149
Neopragmatic interpretation of Dewey, 165
Neuroanthropology, 30
New industrial revolution, 46
No More Robots: Building Kids' Character, Competence, and Sense of Place, 26

Normative legitimacy, 172
Nussbaum, Martha, 62–67, 72

Objective character of interests, 204, 205
Open-mindedness, 191–192, 193
  disposition to, 192
Orçamento Participativo (OP), 153
Outdoor education, 122
Outlines of a Critical Theory of Ethics (Dewey), 68

Participatory Budgeting. *See* Orçamento Participativo (OP)
Personal, Social and Health Education (PSHE), 122
Personal growth, 41
Phenomenology, 113, 114, 217
Philosophic disposition, 190, 191
Philosophy of John Dewey, 203, 204, 214
Photography, 33–34
Platonic utopia, 71
Political liberty, 171
Politics, 171
Potential, 85, 96–97
Practical somaesthetics, 86–87
Pragmatic renaissance, 165
Pragmatic somaesthetics, 86, 129, 134
Pragmatism. *See* Dewey's pragmatism
Pre-reflective thought, 197
Production of narrow set of measurable 'learning outcomes', 218
Programme for International Student Assessment tests (PISA tests), 148

Progressivism, 124, 217
Psuche, 66
Pythagorean theorem, 33

Quality of thought, 185

Race, 105
Racist constructs, 104
Racist ideology, 105
Reconstruction
   Dewey's philosophy, 162–163
   of experience, 124, 126, 162
   understanding cultural requirements for, 164
Reflection cycle, 28
Reflective thought, 197–198
Reinforcement, 207–211
Relations, 185

School, disposition learning in, 195–196
Science, technology, engineering, arts and mathematics activities (STEAM activities), 56
Self-determination, 209
Self-development process, 96–98
Self-expression, 209
Sensory feelings, 94
Seven Against Thebes, 64
Social environment, 41
Social relations, 185
Social relationships, 173
Societies, 112
Sociopolitical philosophy, 178–180
Soft pedagogy, 210
Somaesthetics, 86, 129
Soup kitchen theory of education, 210

Stakeholders and curriculum, 152–156
Standards and curriculum, 147–152
State-devised national curricula, 147
Student-centred CI, 155
Student's experience of democracy, 185
   bringing thought and action to critical consciousness, 198
   Dewey relating democracy, 187–189
   disposition and habit, 194–195
   disposition learning in school, 195–196
   kind of disposition, 189–191
   long-term project, 186–187
   mental process relating to disposition, 191–193
   thought and action, 196–198
The Study of Ethics: A Syllabus (Dewey), 68, 69
Subjective character of interests, 204, 205

Technology-enhanced thinking, framework for, 31–32
Thematic vignettes, 48
Theoretical spectators, 33
Theory of educational aims, 207–208
Theory of learning, 219
Thinking, 185, 186, 189, 191, 195
Third industrial revolution, 46
Thought and action, 196–198
   bringing to critical consciousness, 198
3D printing, 46, 50
Total administration, 173–174
Traditional political theories, 162

Transactional philosophy, 112
Transactional position, 113
Transactionalism, 103–106
Transactionalist 'body-mind' framework, 112
Transactionalist theory, 106

Transactions, 213–214

Unreliable sensory appreciation, 94–95

Via negativa process, 205–206
Volkschule, 146

www.ingramcontent.com/pod-product-compliance
Lightning Source LLC
Chambersburg PA
CBHW051610230426
43668CB00013B/2056